Game Development with Construct 2

From Design to Realization

Lee Stemkoski
Evan Leider

Apress®

Game Development with Construct 2: From Design to Realization

Lee Stemkoski
Garden City, New York
USA

Evan Leider
NY
USA

ISBN-13 (pbk): 978-1-4842-2783-1
DOI 10.1007/978-1-4842-2784-8

ISBN-13 (electronic): 978-1-4842-2784-8

Managing Director: Welmoed Spahr
Editorial Director: Todd Green
Acquisitions Editor: Pramila Balan
Development Editor: Laura Berendson
Technical Reviewer: Julien Kyatric Fantoni
Coordinating Editor: Prachi Mehta
Copy Editor: Kim Wimpsett
Compositor: SPi Global
Indexer: SPi Global
Artist: SPi Global
Cover image designed by Freepik

Distributed to the book trade worldwide by Springer Science+Business Media New York, 233 Spring Street, 6th Floor, New York, NY 10013. Phone 1-800-SPRINGER, fax (201) 348-4505, e-mail orders-ny@springer-sbm.com, or visit www.springeronline.com. Apress Media, LLC is a California LLC and the sole member (owner) is Springer Science + Business Media Finance Inc (SSBM Finance Inc). SSBM Finance Inc is a **Delaware** corporation.

For information on translations, please e-mail rights@apress.com, or visit www.apress.com/rights-permissions.

Apress titles may be purchased in bulk for academic, corporate, or promotional use. eBook versions and licenses are also available for most titles. For more information, reference our Print and eBook Bulk Sales web page at www.apress.com/bulk-sales.

Any source code or other supplementary material referenced by the author in this book is available to readers on GitHub via the book's product page, located at www.apress.com/978-1-4842-2783-1. For more detailed information, please visit www.apress.com/source-code.

Printed on acid-free paper

Contents at a Glance

Contents

About the Authors

Lee Stemkoski is a professor of computer science and mathematics. He earned his Ph.D. in mathematics from Dartmouth College in 2006. He has been teaching at the college level since, with an emphasis on Java programming, computer graphics, and video game development for the past six years. Lee particularly enjoys playing classic games released for the Nintendo and Super Nintendo Entertainment System consoles. He has written another book, *Beginning Game Development with LibGDX*, in addition to many other scholarly articles and game development tutorials.

Evan Leider is currently pursuing a B.S. in computer and management information systems with a specialization in game development, with an expected graduation date of 2018. Since 2012, he has been using Construct 2 to create his own games. Evan has been a teaching assistant in introductory video game programming courses for two years, where he helps college and high-school students learn how to use Construct 2. He enjoys playing video games such as Sonic the Hedgehog and Super Smash Brothers.

About the Technical Reviewer

Julien Kyatric Fantoni is a game maker and Construct expert. Originally learning coding with Visual Basic, PHP, C & C++ with the intent to make games it was only when he found Construct that he was able to release his first completed games.

Julien's an early adopter of Construct and early believer in HTML5. He's been active in Construct 2 community providing tutorials, support and help in the forums and other websites. He's been working and releasing games made during game jams and professional advert-games ordered by various media companies like CanalSat, France 2 or even the music video game "Lazers from my heart" for the band Birdy Nam Nam.

You can find his various works on his website kyatric.com.

Acknowledgments

Thanks to the editorial and support staff at Apress, for without their efforts and support this book you are reading would not exist.

Thanks to Ashley and Thomas Gullen, the creators of the Construct game engine and the founders of Scirra Ltd., whose dedication to bringing game development to the masses has had a profound impact and continues to inspire and empower individuals across the world.

We would particularly like to thank Julien Fantoni, who is an outstanding technical reviewer and made many insightful comments and helpful suggestions on the presentation, style, and content of this book. Julien has been helping countless numbers of aspiring game developers for years (including the authors of this book!) as a moderator on the Scirra online forums. We are honored that he agreed to join us in this endeavor, and we have benefitted greatly from his experience and advice.

Finally, a special thanks to our students and readers, past and present, for their continuous and infectious enthusiasm. Your passion for game development is what inspired us to write this book.

Foreword

At Scirra, we've always believed the future of software is on the Web. Everyone wants to "put a ding in the universe" (as Steve Jobs said), and using HTML5 to power Construct 2's games is our way of trying to do that. While Construct 2 lets you export to a variety of platforms, I've always thought the Web was the most interesting one: it's free, it's open, and there are no gatekeepers who will charge you fees or decline your app. Web technology is also excellent now, having come on in leaps and bounds since we started in 2011. New technologies like WebGL 2 and WebAssembly point to a bright future too.

Another goal of mine is to encourage people to be content producers, not just consumers. It's easy to spend hours clicking or swiping through the Web, just reading and using what other people have made. That can be interesting, but personally I think it's far more exciting to build things. Building software and games has often had a high barrier to entry, and we want to try to make developing and sharing your own games as easy as making a presentation. I hope this book helps get you started on the way.

Construct 2 is designed to let your creativity run free. We specifically wanted to avoid being a "cookie-cutter" game engine, which basically gives you premade templates that you lightly modify. Instead, it provides a series of building blocks to start assembling your own unique game from. This book covers a range of game genres and mechanics to help you learn how to build something of your own, all built from the common building blocks of things such as sprites, behaviors, events, and more.

If you manage to build something and share it with someone else, then we'll be very happy to have helped you be a creator. Persistence can get you a long way too; I started with nothing but a laptop in my bedroom, and now we're a full-fledged business. Who knows where you'll end up if you keep going?

—Ashley Gullen
Founder, Scirra Ltd.
February 2017

Introduction

Welcome to *Game Development with Construct 2*!

In this book, you'll learn how to create video games using the Construct 2 game engine, an ideal program for aspiring game developers who have no prior experience, as well as experienced game developers looking for a tool to rapidly create prototypes of games. The games you will create in this book are inspired by classic arcade games such as Asteroids, Frogger, Breakout, and PacMan; general genres such as car racing or tower defense games; and console games such as Super Mario Bros. and The Legend of Zelda.

Construct 2 is both user-friendly and powerful. The software has been around for more than 5 years, has been downloaded more than 3.5 million times, and has an active user community and responsive development team. Games created with Construct 2 can be exported to run on a variety of platforms and operating systems, such as web browsers (HTML5), Windows, macOS, Linux, Android, and iOS. A free version of Construct 2 is available for download and is sufficient for all the game projects contained in this book.

Much like the software itself, this book does not assume you have any prior programming or game development experience. Over the course of the book, you will be guided in creating a series of 12 different video games of increasing complexity that will teach you both the features of the Construct 2 game engine and the game development topics and logical programming concepts that will serve you well for software development in general.

Thank you for allowing us to be your guides as you begin your journey as a game developer. We hope that you find this book both informative and enjoyable and that it enables and inspires you to create your own video games to share with the world.

CHAPTER 1

■ ■ ■

Getting Started with Construct 2

Welcome to the exciting world of game design and development! In this chapter, you will learn all about Construct 2, the program you will be using to develop games throughout this book.

Designing video games is an enjoyable and rewarding activity. The process of creating video games uses a combination of creative and technical skills, and the end result is a game that can provide entertainment to any audience you choose. Whether you are creating games as a hobby or as a professional, you need to find the best approach that works for you. There are two main approaches to game development: using a traditional programming language (such as Java or Python) or using a *game engine* (a software framework that provides the core functionality needed to create a video game). A game engine automates common tasks such as displaying graphics and animations, playing music and sound effects, and simulating physics. Traditional programming languages usually provide more flexibility and customization options than game engines, but to take advantage of these features, you must first learn how to program. While game engines might have some limitations, this is typically more than compensated for by the benefit of speeding up the development process, which means you can devote more time and energy on game design and content.

For beginners who want to start creating games right away, using a game engine is clearly the better option. As an added bonus, the logical concepts and frameworks you learn will help you to understand advanced game engines or programming languages more quickly, should you decide to use them in the future. However, even experienced programmers will often use game engines for *rapid prototyping*, which means quickly creating a working, preliminary version of a game to test whether the core ideas and gameplay mechanics are enjoyable. Once this is established, if you decide that a game requires more advanced functionality or graphics beyond what the game engine can provide, you could then create the game using the programming language of your choice.

© Lee Stemkoski and Evan Leider 2017
L. Stemkoski and E. Leider, *Game Development with Construct 2*,
DOI 10.1007/978-1-4842-2784-8_1

About the Construct 2 Game Engine

The Construct 2 game engine was developed by Scirra, founded by Ashley and Thomas Gullen, in 2011. Since then, the software has been regularly updated with new tools and capabilities. Of the many game engines available, the following features establish Construct 2 as one of the best:

- *Inexpensive*: There is a free edition available, which contains nearly all[1] the functionality of the full version. The paid personal license is reasonably priced, can be used for commercial purposes (up to $5,000 revenue), and is valid for the lifetime of the software.

- *Easy to learn*: Construct doesn't require any prior programming knowledge. Graphics and sounds are easily added to a game. The software has a drag-and-drop interface, it has a visual editor for designing the layout of your game, and you can program actions by selecting them from lists. There are integrated tools for editing images and viewing animations. It is simple to export completed games so that they can be shared with others. Most important, there is extensive and clearly written help documentation and tutorials on the developer web site.

- *Flexible*: It is possible to implement a great variety of classic and custom game mechanics and actions, which enables you to create games from a variety of genres, such as side-scrolling platformer games, top-down adventure games, slow-paced puzzle games, and fast-paced physics games.

- *Active community*: Construct has a large number of users; the software has been downloaded 3.5 million times. The developers regularly update the software with new features, performance improvements, and maintenance fixes, and they are responsive to the users. There are forums provided for help, discussion, and networking. The developers even maintain the Scirra Arcade, an area where you can upload your games to share them with the world.

Downloading and Installing

To download the Construct 2 game engine, go to the web site www.scirra.com. Figure 1-1 shows the web site as of the date of printing. Click the *Free Download* link and you will be brought to another page, where an installation file should automatically download to your

---

[1]The main limitations of the free version are the amount of customized code that can be written (100 "events"), no access to tools for debugging and inspecting the performance of the game, and limited export options (games can be run in web browsers but not as stand-alone executable files for desktop or mobile platforms).

computer.[2] If the download doesn't start automatically, there will be a link that you can click to manually start the download process. Here, you can also observe that the Construct 2 game engine is updated frequently when new features are added and software bugs or glitches are fixed. These versions are called *releases* and are numbered in sequence; the release number will be indicated near the top of the download page.

Figure 1-1. The Scirra web site, home of the Construct 2 game engine

Once your download is complete, run the installation file. After accepting the license agreement, you can let the installer auto-detect the type of computer you have (a 32-bit or 64-bit system) and create a desktop icon if you desire. When the installation is finished, launch the program!

The User Interface

When you run Construct 2 for the first time, you should see a screen similar to Figure 1-2.

---

[2]Construct will download the latest stable version of the software. If desired, you also have the option of manually downloading the most recent "beta" version of the software, which contains the newest features but has not been as extensively tested as a stable version and may contain errors.

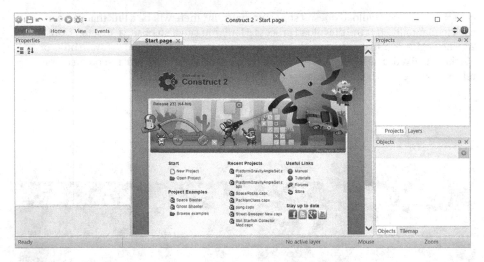

Figure 1-2. *The Construct 2 program after starting for the first time*

In the menu bar near the top of the window, click the *File* menu and select *New* to create a new project. The *Select template or example* window will appear, as shown in Figure 1-3. Template projects have different settings already configured for your convenience for a variety of standard game types and genres. However, in this book, you will always set up your projects manually. Select the option *New empty project* and click the *Open* button. Construct will then create an empty project file for you, and a window will appear, as in Figure 1-4.

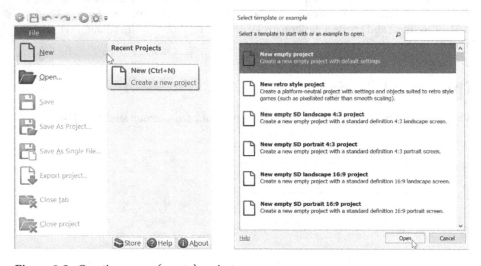

Figure 1-3. *Creating a new (empty) project*

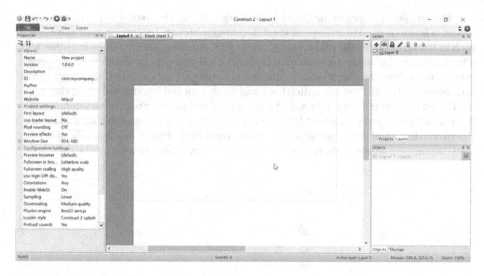

Figure 1-4. *The Construct 2 window when starting a new project*

The number of panels and amount of information displayed can be a bit overwhelming at first, but as you work through the projects in this book, you will quickly become familiar with all the displays and different features that are available. In the following text, we will give you a brief overview of the information that each area contains. After creating your first game, the various areas will contain information specific to your game; for example, Figure 1-5 shows how the Construct window will look after completing the Starfish Collector game in Chapter 2.

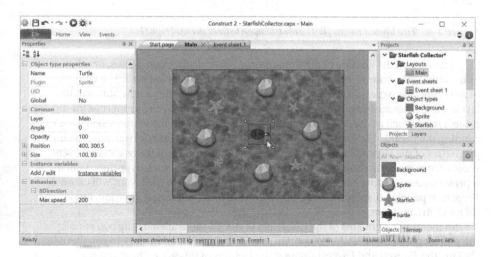

Figure 1-5. *The Construct 2 window after completing a sample game*

The large center area in the Construct 2 window is used to display layouts and event sheets. A *layout* is used to arrange all the different graphics and objects in your game, such as background images and scenery, characters, enemies, items, points and other text information, and so forth. An *event sheet* contains a list of *events*, or instructions, for your game, such as how the player controls the main character, how game entities interact with each other, and so on. You can switch back and forth between layouts and event sheets by clicking the colored tabs at the top of this area. To add items or otherwise interact with these areas, you can right-click to display a mini-menu of actions available for that area. The menu displayed is dependent on where you right-click. Figure 1-6 shows these two mini-menus; the layout menu is on the left, and the event sheet menu is on the right.

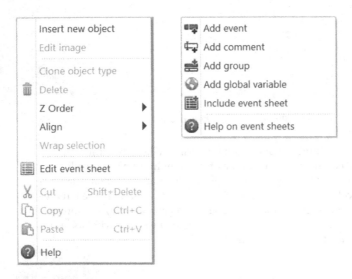

Figure 1-6. *The layout menu (left) and the event sheet menu (right)*

The area on the left side of the Construct window displays *properties*, or related information, of whatever object is currently selected in the layout area. The contents of the *Properties* panel change automatically whenever you click a new object in the layout area. After creating a new project, Construct will display the properties for the project itself (such as the name and author of the project and the window size used when running the game). Clicking the layout area will cause the *Properties* panel to display properties of the layout (such as the layout size and the name of the associated event sheet). Once you learn how to add other objects to the game, such as sprites (which represent your in-game entities), clicking these objects within the layout will cause the *Properties* panel to display related information such as their name, position, angle (of rotation), and size.

In the upper-right area of the Construct window, there are actually two panels: the project panel and the layer panel. You can switch back and forth between them by clicking the *Projects* and *Layers* tabs near the bottom of this area. The *Projects* panel displays a set of folders that contain all the files and objects used in your game, including layouts and event sheets, sprites, the hardware being used for input (keyboard, mouse, gamepad, or touchscreen), audio files, fonts, icons, and so forth. New layouts and event sheets can be created from here, and they can be re-opened from here if they were accidentally closed (by clicking the X in the corresponding tab). The *Layers* panel displays a list of *layers*, which can be created and used to organize the objects in your game (for example, background objects and scenery might be grouped into one layer, characters and items might be grouped into another layer, and user interface information such as points or messages might be grouped into a third layer).

The lower-right area of the Construct window contains the object panel, which displays only the objects that are present in the current layout. If a layout contains more than one instance of a given object, clicking the name of the object in the object panel selects all the instances at the same time, which allows you to change each of their corresponding properties at the same time.

As you can see, there is a lot of information displayed in the Construct window. This information will be reviewed and discussed in more depth in the chapters that follow. With practice, as you create your own games, the user interface will become easier to use, and it will become clear how the Construct window setup organizes the game development workflow for you.

Saving, Previewing, and Exporting Games

While you are creating games in Construct, always remember to save your work regularly. If you click the *File* menu, you will see two related options: *Save As Project* and *Save As Single File*. The option *Save As Project* will create a directory that contains all the components of your project, stored as individual files, organized into a series of directories. One of the files will have the extension .caproj; this file stores the information about the other files needed for your project and can be used to open your project in Construct. However, if you want to transfer your project to another directory, you must also move all the associated files as well. The option *Save As Single File* will create a single file with the extension .capx; all the components of your project will be saved within this file.[3] For simplicity and ease of use, in this book we recommend you save your projects using the .capx file format. In addition, Construct has the ability to automatically save backups of your project at regular intervals. To access this option, click the *File* menu, select the *Preferences* option, and then select the *Autosave* tab; from there, you can configure the settings as you want.

While you are in the process of creating the game, you will no doubt want to test it regularly every time you add a new feature. For instance, you might want to check that the player controls work correctly, that the game objects interact with each other as expected, or that the difficulty level is well balanced. To do so, Construct provides a feature that lets you preview your game, running it in its current state. Along the title bar of the Construct window are a number of small buttons that perform commonly needed tasks: *Save, Undo, Redo,* and *Run layout* (represented with a standard play icon). Clicking the *Run layout* button will run the game, using your default web browser. When you are done playing your game, you can simply close the web browser to stop the game.

---

[3]The .capx file format is actually a "zip file," whose contents can be inspected and extracted with other programs such as 7Zip or WinZip.

Another outstanding feature provided by the Construct game engine is the ability to export your games so that they can be run on many different hardware and software platforms (such as the Internet, desktop computers, and mobile devices). The free version enables you to export your game to HTML5 format, which runs in web browsers (just as the *Run layout* function does). Upgrading to a paid, personal license will give you the ability to export to additional platforms. To export your game, in the *File* menu, select *Export Project*, and choose the desired format. Exporting to an HTML5 web site also creates a directory containing a web page and all the other files needed to run your game; if you have a web site, you can upload the contents of this directory to your site and anyone with the URL will be able to play your game! Alternatively, if you don't have your own web site, Scirra provides hosting for games made with Construct on its web site, at `www.scirra.com/arcade/`. One of the freely available exporting options, Scirra Arcade, will create a file that can then be uploaded; full instructions on how to do so are also provided at this web site.

Summary

In this chapter, you learned about game engines in general and the Construct 2 game engine in particular, including many of its distinguishing features. You also learned how to download and install the software, took a quick tour of the user interface, and got an overview of saving, previewing, and exporting your games. In the next chapter, you will review and revisit many of these topics in practice, as you jump into creating your first game in Construct 2: Starfish Collector.

CHAPTER 2

■ ■ ■

Starfish Collector

In this chapter, you will create your first game with Construct 2, called Starfish Collector, shown in Figure 2-1. The player controls a turtle, whose goal is to swim around the ocean and collect all the starfish she can see. The game features a top-down perspective, and the player moves the turtle using the arrow keys. This chapter assumes no prior knowledge and will introduce the fundamental concepts needed to make a game using the Construct 2 game engine introduced in the previous chapter, such as sprites, events, and behaviors, in the context of creating a game.

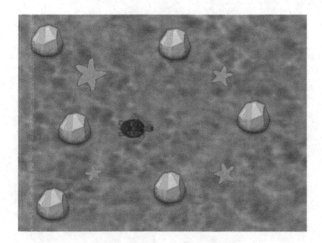

Figure 2-1. *The Starfish Collector game*

Project Setup

To begin, download the zip file containing the graphics for this game from the companion web site for this book. Extract the files to a folder of your choice; there will be images of water, a turtle, a starfish, a rock, and words that say *You Win!* when the player wins. Alternatively, you can use your own images if you desire.

© Lee Stemkoski and Evan Leider 2017
L. Stemkoski and E. Leider, *Game Development with Construct 2*,
DOI 10.1007/978-1-4842-2784-8_2

Next, start the Construct program. In the menu bar, select *New* to create a new project. In the window that appears, select the option *New empty project* and click the *Open* button. Construct will then create an empty project file for you. In the center region you will see the game layout. On the left is the *Properties* panel (which displays information about the currently selected object in the layout), on the upper right is the project panel (which displays the list of files for your project), and on the lower right is the objects panel (which displays a list of object types currently in your layout).

To begin, you will set up the layout. Click anywhere in the layout area, and the *Properties* panel title will change to *Layout properties*; underneath, it will list the different properties of the layout in the left column and their current values or settings in the right column, shown on the left side of Figure 2-2 with the default settings. Click in the area next to *Name*, type Main, and press *Enter*.[1] You should see that the name of the layout has also changed in the project panel. Similarly, click in the properties area next to *Layout Size*, and enter 800, 600. This sets the layout width to 800 pixels and height to 600 pixels, which is a fine size for the game world. When you've completed these changes, the *Properties* panel should look like the right side of Figure 2-2.

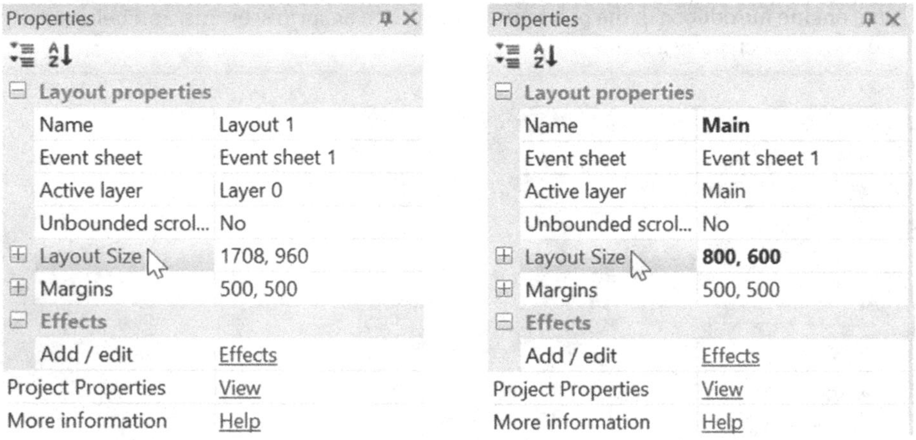

Properties	📌 ×		Properties	📌 ×
⯆ Layout properties			⯆ Layout properties	
Name	Layout 1		Name	**Main**
Event sheet	Event sheet 1		Event sheet	Event sheet 1
Active layer	Layer 0		Active layer	Main
Unbounded scrol...	No		Unbounded scrol...	No
⊞ Layout Size	1708, 960		⊞ Layout Size	**800, 600**
⊞ Margins	500, 500		⊞ Margins	500, 500
⯆ Effects			⯆ Effects	
Add / edit	Effects		Add / edit	Effects
Project Properties	View		Project Properties	View
More information	Help		More information	Help

Figure 2-2. Layout properties

---

[1]Even though this game will have only a single layout, giving objects descriptive names is an important habit to develop right away. The importance of naming layouts will be more obvious in future projects, when you will have different layouts for menus, game levels, and so forth.

Next, you will set up layers on the layout. Layers are used to organize the objects in the layout into groups, such as background images, characters and items, and user interface (UI) or heads-up display (HUD) information. To see the list of layers, underneath the project panel, you will see two tabs: *Projects* and *Layers*. Click the *Layers* tab, and the project panel will be replaced with the layer panel. You will see a list that contains a single layer, named *Layer 0*. Click the add button (indicated with a plus icon) two times to add two layers; they will be given the default names of *Layer 1* and *Layer 2*. To rename a layer, click the layer name in the list to select it and then click the rename button (indicated with a pencil icon). Rename *Layer 0* to Background, *Layer 1* to Main, and *Layer 2* to UI. When you are finished, the layer panel should look like Figure 2-3. The order in which the layer names appear makes a difference; the layer at the bottom of the list will have its contents rendered (drawn on the screen) first. Its objects will appear to be on the bottom, or below the objects from other layers. Similarly, the layer listed directly above the bottom layer will have its objects drawn next, and so on. The layer at the top of the list will have its objects drawn last, so this is the best group for user interface–related information, such as the player's score or time remaining, since this data should be displayed overlaying the game world.

Figure 2-3. *The layer panel*

The last project setup task you will do is to set some of the project properties. This is a place to store information about your game and change settings such as the window size and web browser used to preview your game. Click in the layout area, and underneath the list of layout properties on the left, you will see a *Project Properties* row next to which there will be underlined blue text (similar in style to a link on a web page) that says *View*, as shown on the left side of Figure 2-4. Click *View*, and the *Properties* panel will now change and display project properties, as shown on the right side of Figure 2-4. Here, you might want to fill in the areas next to *Name* (which refers to the name of the project or game) and *Author* (your name). Filling in properties such as *Email* or *Website* is not necessary but can be useful if you plan to share your project file with someone and you want to provide a way for them to contact you. Further down in the *Properties* panel, you should change *Window Size* to 800, 600, just as you did for the *Layout Size* property previously. This is important because the Starfish Collector game world should fill up the program window.

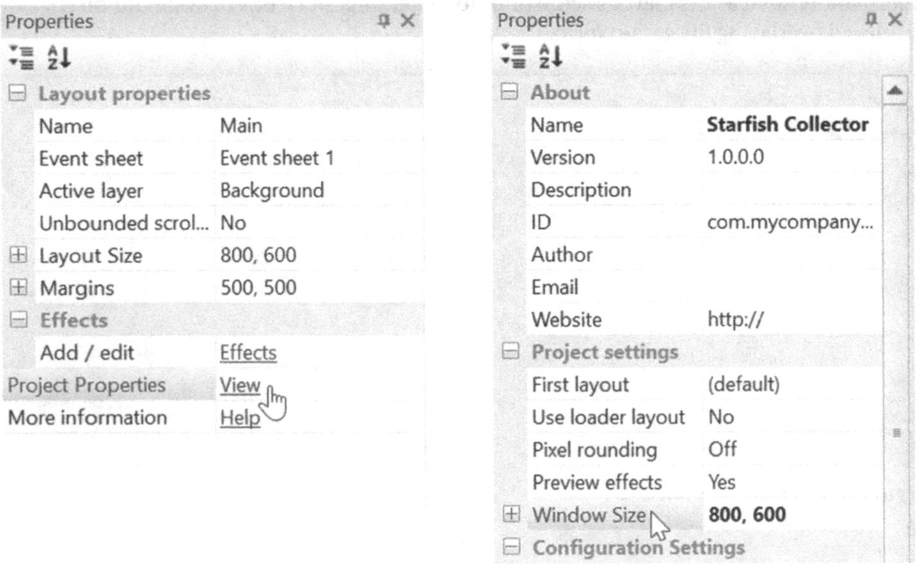

Properties	⏸ ✕
Layout properties	
Name	Main
Event sheet	Event sheet 1
Active layer	Background
Unbounded scrol...	No
⊞ Layout Size	800, 600
⊞ Margins	500, 500
Effects	
Add / edit	Effects
Project Properties	View
More information	Help

Properties	⏸ ✕
About	
Name	**Starfish Collector**
Version	1.0.0.0
Description	
ID	com.mycompany...
Author	
Email	
Website	http://
Project settings	
First layout	(default)
Use loader layout	No
Pixel rounding	Off
Preview effects	Yes
⊞ Window Size	**800, 600**
Configuration Settings	

Figure 2-4. Project properties

Sprites

Next, you will add some Sprite objects to your program. A *sprite* is an image that represents an entity in your game world and has associated properties such as position (specified using x,y coordinates), angle of rotation (measured in degrees), and size (which need not be the same as the size of the original image). To create a sprite, right-click in the layout area, and a menu will appear as pictured on the left side of Figure 2-5. Select *Insert New Object*, and a window will appear, as shown on the right side of Figure 2-5. Click the *Sprite* icon; then in the text box at the bottom of the window next to *Name when inserted*, type Background; and finally click the *Insert* button.

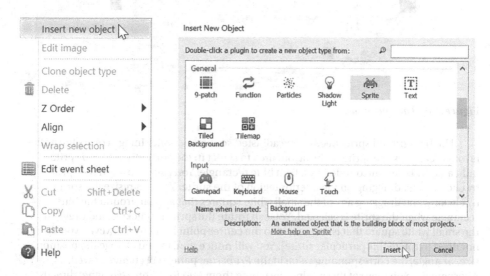

Figure 2-5. *Inserting a new Sprite object*

After clicking the *Insert* button, the mouse pointer icon will change to a crosshair-style icon, which is used to indicate where you would like to place the Sprite object. You can easily change the position of the sprite later, so for now, simply click in the center of the layout area. Next, a set of windows as pictured in Figure 2-6 will appear. These are the image editor windows. With the tools provided, you could draw an image or set up an animation. However, for this project, you will use the graphics provided that you downloaded at the beginning of this project. Click the folder icon along the top of the *Edit Image* window, navigate to the folder where you extracted the images from the zip file, and select the image named water.jpg. The image will appear in the *Edit Image* window. You don't need to modify this image in any way, so close the *Edit Image* window (all the other image editor windows will also close automatically), and the sprite will appear in the layout area.

13

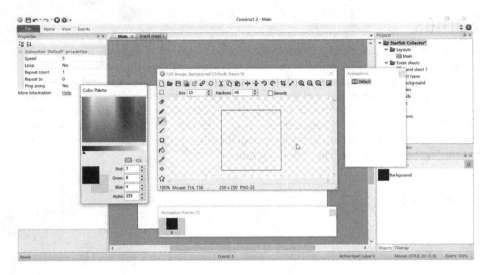

Figure 2-6. *The image editor*

The background sprite needs to be adjusted so that the water image covers the entire layout area. Click the sprite in the layout area to select it; the currently selected sprite is indicated by being surrounded by a light blue rectangle. You can reposition the sprite by clicking and dragging on the interior region of the sprite. You can resize the sprite by clicking and dragging any of the small white squares that appear around the blue rectangle when the sprite is selected. You can rotate the sprite by clicking and dragging the small white square that is connected to the center point by a line (however, you do not need to rotate this particular sprite). You will notice that, as you change the position, size, or angle, the corresponding value in the *Properties* panel will change as well. Alternatively, you may set these values by typing them into the *Properties* panel directly. In addition, change the background sprite's *Layer* property to the Background layer.

Next, you will repeat this process to add a turtle sprite. As before, right-click in the layout area, select *Insert New Object*, click *Sprite*, enter the name Turtle, and click the *Insert* button. When the crosshair cursor appears, click anywhere in the layout to select an initial position, and in the image editor windows that appear next, select the image named turtle.png.[2] Close the image editor windows, resize and reposition your turtle sprite as desired, and change the *Layer* property to Main. Finally, repeat this process one more time to add a starfish sprite, with the name Starfish, using the image starfish. png. When you are complete, the layout should look like Figure 2-7.

---

[2]*The turtle image is stored as a PNG file rather than a JPEG file because the PNG file format supports transparency while the JPEG file format does not; if the image had been stored as a JPEG file, the turtle image would appear on a solid white rectangle.*

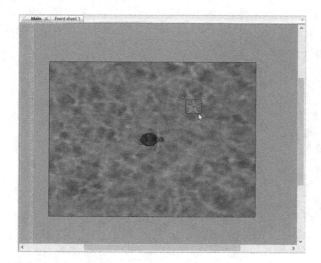

Figure 2-7. The layout window with background, turtle, and starfish sprites added

This game would be quite short if there were only one starfish for the turtle to collect, and thus you will create some copies of the starfish sprite that you previously created. These copies are called *instances* of the starfish sprite. Every instance of an object has its own set of property values that can be adjusted independently of the others. Additional instances can be created in multiple ways. One method is to select the sprite you want to copy on the layout, press *Ctrl+C* to copy it, and press *Ctrl+V* to paste the copy onto the layout; the cursor icon will change to a crosshair-style pointer, allowing you to select the position of the new instance. An alternative (and slightly quicker) method is to select the sprite on the layout, hold down the *Ctrl* key, and click and drag the selected sprite. A new instance of the sprite will be generated on top of the original one, which can then be dragged to its new position on the layout. Using either of these methods, create a few additional instances of the starfish sprite and position them around the screen. Feel free to change their angle and size slightly to add some variation in their appearance. Figure 2-8 shows one possible such layout. Once you are finished, it is a good idea to save your project.[3]

---

[3]In general, you should save your project frequently, such as every few minutes or every time you have finished adding a new feature, whichever comes first.

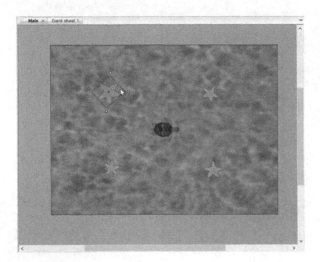

Figure 2-8. *Layout example with multiple starfish sprites*

Events

Next, you will add some instructions, commonly referred to as *code*, to your game to make it interactive. In the Construct game engine, instructions are called *events*. Each event has two parts: a condition and an action. A *condition* is a test that the program can check, which will be either true or false. An *action* is something the program can do. Informally, events can be thought of as "if-then" statements (instructions that say "If this condition is true, then do this action"). Every type of object in Construct has an associated list of conditions and actions that you can select from menus when creating events. This is convenient compared to traditional programming languages, where programmers need to remember and type in the names of each command or function.

The first event you will create will enable the turtle to "collect" the starfish. In many video games, the player's character often collects items by simply coming into contact with them, after which the collected item disappears; the gameplay in Starfish Collector will be the same. Informally, the event could be phrased as "If the turtle comes into contact with the starfish, then remove the starfish from the screen."

To begin entering this event, click the *Event Sheet 1* tab above the layout area, or if the tab is not visible, you can click *Event Sheet 1* in the project panel on the right. The layout will be replaced with an event sheet, which is where all the game events are displayed. Next, click the light gray text that says *Add event* in the event sheet area. A window will appear, which asks you to "double-click an object to create a condition from." The condition is that the turtle makes contact with a starfish, and therefore you should double-click the *Turtle* object, as shown in Figure 2-9. A window will then appear that contains a list of conditions you can select from, as shown in Figure 2-10.

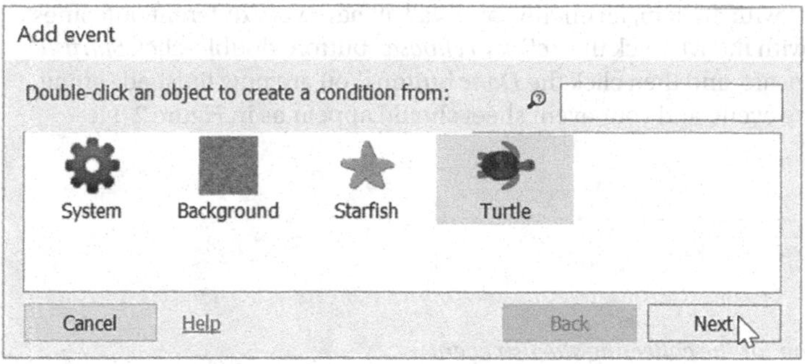

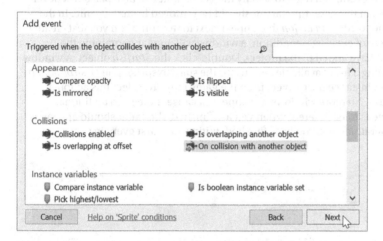

Figure 2-9. *Selecting an object to create a condition from*

Figure 2-10. *A list of available conditions for the turtle sprite*

One of the tricky parts of working with events is determining which of the available conditions (or actions) you need. Sometimes the condition you need is phrased with words other than those you originally thought of in an informal description. For example, there is no condition labeled "comes into contact with," but underneath the *Collisions* group of conditions there is a condition labeled as *on collision with another object*, which has the same meaning. If you are unsure what a particular condition means, you can click it and a short description of the condition will appear at the top of the window. Alternatively, you can click the underlined text *Help on 'Sprite' conditions* at the bottom of the window and you will be brought to the help documentation for Construct. Since you have found the condition you seek, you can double-click this condition (or single-click and then click the *Next* button), and a new window will appear. Such a window will appear whenever there is more information that you need to enter; the additional details that you need to enter are called *parameters*, which is why the word *parameters* appears in the title bar of this new window. For this condition, you must enter which type of object you are checking for collision with, as different types of object collisions may have different results

17

(for example, collisions with an item, an enemy, or a wall all have very different outcomes or actions associated with them). Click the *<click to choose>* button, double-click *Starfish* in the window that appears, and then click the *Done* button. You are now finished setting up the condition for the event, and your event sheet should appear as in Figure 2-11.

Figure 2-11. *Condition for the collecting starfish event*

To complete this event, you need to specify the action that will take place whenever the condition is met; in this case, the starfish should be removed from the game. In the event sheet, click the words *Add action* that appear next to the condition you just created. Similar to the process of creating a condition, a window will appear containing the different sprites you have added to the project. Double-click the *Starfish* object. A window will appear, containing a list of available actions for the starfish sprite. The *Destroy* action is used to remove an instance of an object from the game entirely; select this action and click the *Done* button. No more windows will appear because there is no additional information that needs to be entered. When you are finished, the event should appear as in Figure 2-12. Congratulations; you have finished writing your first event in Construct!

Figure 2-12. *Completed event for collecting starfish*

Behaviors

The next feature to add is movement for the turtle. In this game, pressing any of the arrow keys will move the turtle in that direction: pressing the up arrow key moves the turtle toward the top of the screen, pressing the right arrow key moves the turtle toward the right side of the screen, and so forth. It is clear how to think of these as if-then statements; for example, "If the up arrow key is currently being held down, then move the turtle upward." In terms of events in Construct, the condition is "the up arrow key is being held down," and the action is "move the turtle upward."

Although you could program these events yourself, it is more efficient to use features in the Construct game engine called behaviors. *Behaviors* are like prewritten collections of events that you can attach to a sprite. This saves you, the game developer, the time and effort of creating these events yourself. There are currently approximately 25 different behaviors available for use; they include many commonly used game mechanics such as player controls for movement, visual effects such as fading or flashing, and advanced features such as pathfinding and physics simulation.

Next, you will add a behavior to easily control the movement of the turtle. Return to the layout, select the *Turtle* object, and in the *Properties* panel click the underlined blue text labeled *Behaviors*. The *Turtle: Behaviors* window will appear, containing a row of icons along the top. Click the *Add New* button (represented with a plus symbol icon), and a window of available behaviors will appear, as shown on the left side of Figure 2-13. Underneath the *Movements* group, select the *8 Direction* behavior (either by double-clicking or by clicking once and clicking the *Add* button). This window will close, and the program will return to the *Turtle: Behaviors* window; the *8 Direction* behavior icon should now appear in this window.

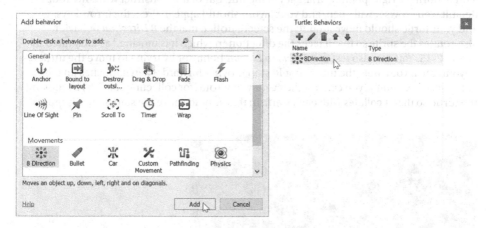

Figure 2-13. *The Add behavior window and Turtle: Behaviors window*

While you are in the process of adding behaviors, there is a second behavior that is helpful for this particular game called *Bound to Layout*, which will keep the associated sprite from moving past the boundaries of the screen. As with all behaviors, you could theoretically add this functionality yourself by creating a set of events; in this case, the events would be "If the left edge of the turtle sprite moves past the left edge of the layout, then move the turtle to the right," and so forth, for all edges of the turtle. However, once again, you will instead add a behavior following the same procedure as before: click the button with a plus symbol icon and select the *Bound to Layout* behavior underneath the *General* group. When you are finished, the *Turtle: Behaviors* window should appear, as in Figure 2-14. Close the *Turtle: Behaviors* window.

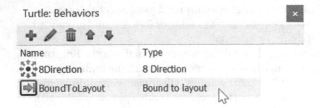

Figure 2-14. *The list of behaviors added to the Turtle sprite*

At this point, you are ready to test your game! Be sure to save your project (as a single file, as usual) and then click the *Run layout* button (represented with the standard play icon featuring a right-pointing triangle) in the title bar of the Construct window. Your default web browser will open, and your layout should appear. Press the arrow keys, and your turtle should move around the screen; notice that the *8 Direction* behavior also rotates the sprite so that it faces the direction in which it is moving,[4] as illustrated in Figure 2-15. You can also test the *Bound to Layout* behavior by trying to move the turtle beyond the layout area (the turtle should stop moving forward when it touches an edge of the screen). Finally, you can test the event you wrote (for collecting starfish) by moving the turtle so that it collides with each starfish; this should cause the starfish to disappear.

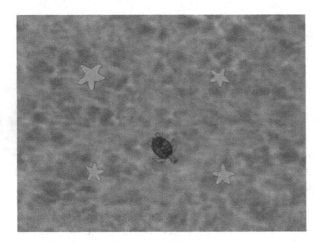

Figure 2-15. *Playing the Starfish Collector game in a web browser*

---

[4]For this feature to work properly, the image used for the sprite must have the character facing to the right because the default angle (0 degrees) points in this direction. If you are using a different image and this is not the case, the image can be rotated using the tools along the top of the image editor window.

Ending the Game

After the initial thrill of seeing your game come to life in a web browser and being able to play it, your experience may be a bit anticlimactic, since after you collect the starfish, nothing happens. The game is presumably finished, but there is no sense of closure. This could lead players to confusion (leaving them to think "Is there something left to do?" or "Did I do something wrong?") or even a sense of frustration. To remedy this situation, you will now add a game-over message that says *You Win!* to the game, which will appear after the turtle has collected all the starfish.

In the layout area, right-click, select *Insert New Object*, and add a sprite named YouWin. Use the image you-win.png and position this sprite so that it is in the middle of the layout. In the *Properties* panel, there are two properties you need to change. First, set the *Layer* property to UI. As mentioned, this helps keep your project organized and also ensures that the sprite will be displayed on top of everything in the layers listed below it: *Background* and *Main*. Second, change the property *Initial Visibility* to Invisible. This makes the sprite invisible to the player at the start of the game (although you will still be able to see it in the layout area); this is important because the player should not see this message until the game is over.

Next, you need to add an event that checks whether all the starfish have been collected, in which case the YouWin sprite should become visible. Informally, the event you will create can be phrased as "If there are zero Starfish sprites left on the layout, then make the YouWin sprite visible." To begin, click the event sheet tab and add a new event. The number of starfish currently on the layout is a property of the Starfish object called *Count*. However, to check this value, you will need to use a condition from the *System* group of conditions. In the *Add event* window, select *System* (represented with a gear icon) and then select the condition named *Compare Two Values* from the *General* group. A parameters window will appear, which allows you to enter the two values to compare and the type of comparison to make (such as equals, less than, or greater than). In the first box, type Starfish.Count (notice in particular that there is a period between the words *Starfish* and *Count*; this tells the program to use the *Count* variable that belongs to the *Starfish* object, rather than the *Count* variable of something else, such as the *Turtle* object). Leave the comparison type set as equal to and leave the second value set to 0. Click the *Done* button, and the condition will appear in the event sheet. Finally, click *Add action* next to the condition, then select the YouWin sprite in the *Add action* window, and finally select the action *Set Visible* from the *Appearance* group. In the parameters window, leave the visibility set to Visible and click the *Done* button. The event is now complete and should appear in the event sheet, as shown in Figure 2-16.

2	⚙ System	Starfish.Count = 0	---YouWin	Set Visible
			Add action	

Figure 2-16. The completed event to display a message at the end of the game

Now is a good time to save and test your project. Maneuver the turtle to collect all the starfish and verify that the *You Win!* message appears after they have all been collected.

Side Quests

Although you have now finished implementing the core game mechanics for the Starfish Collector game, there are still additional optional features you can add to make the game more interesting, challenging, polished, and fun. This section explains how to add these features into your game. While they may not be part of the core gameplay, these features are highly recommended to increase the quality of the gameplay experience for the future players of your game. In particular, you will learn how to add solid obstacles to the game world and how to use motion to animate the starfish.

Solid Objects

Games should have well-defined tasks or goals to accomplish and, at the same time, obstacles to make it challenging to accomplish these goals. In the Starfish Collector game, the turtle encounters no obstacles; she only needs to swim in a straight line from starfish to starfish until they are all collected. To make her journey less straightforward, you will place some obstacles in her way. You will add some rocks (sprites that use a rock image) that behave as solid objects—objects that the turtle cannot move through.

To begin, set the layout property *Active layer* to Main. Right-click in the layout area, select *Insert New Object*, and add a sprite named Rock. Use the image rock.png and position it anywhere on the screen that does not overlap the turtle or any starfish. In the *Properties* panel for the Rock object, click the underlined blue text *Behaviors*, and, similar to the process you used before when adding behaviors to the turtle, add a behavior named Solid. Duplicate the Rock object a few times, as you did when creating additional starfish, and position the new rocks around the layout, with enough space in between them so that the turtle will be able reach each of the starfish. Figure 2-17 shows an example of such an arrangement. Save your project, and click the *Run layout* button in the title bar. Move the turtle around the screen using the arrow keys, and you will notice that you can't move the turtle through the rocks; make sure that the player can win the game.

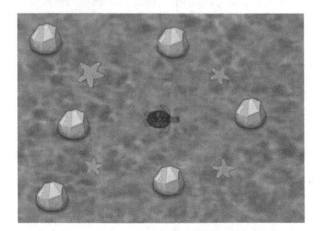

Figure 2-17. Adding rocks to the game

As you navigate the turtle around the rocks, you may have noticed that although image files are rectangular, collision boundaries usually are not. It is typically the case in video games that if two sprites overlap in transparent areas of their images, this typically does not count as a collision. However, checking every pixel of every image for overlap with every pixel of every other image takes a great deal of computation and would cause your game to run more slowly. Therefore, game engines often use an intermediate approach, creating a *collision polygon*: a shape that estimates the boundaries of the object, usually with eight or fewer sides. When you select an image for a sprite, the Construct game engine automatically estimates the boundaries that should be used when checking for a collision between two objects. To inspect or adjust the collision polygon for a sprite, open the image editor (by double-clicking the object), and in the *Edit Image* window, select the icon at the lower left. You will see the collision polygon for the sprite, lightly shaded in blue, with blue edges and red vertex points. Figure 2-18 shows the collision polygons for the rock and turtle sprites. You can adjust the collision polygon if you want by clicking and dragging on any vertex; right-clicking a vertex will bring up a menu where vertices can be added or deleted.

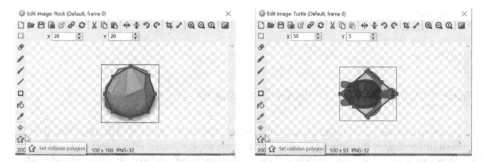

Figure 2-18. *Viewing the collision polygons for the rock and turtle objects*

Value-Based Animations

In game design, it is good practice to draw the player's attention to objects with which they can interact. One way to do so is with animations, which come in two varieties: *image-based*, where a sequence of images are quickly displayed in sequence to simulate a change in appearance, and *value-based*, where a set of numbers are continually adjusted that affect the sprite's position, rotation, size, and so forth. In this section, you will use behaviors to implement value-based animations; image-based animations will be covered in a later chapter.

To begin, select the Starfish object from the object panel in the lower-right area of the Construct window. It is important to use the object panel so that all instances of the starfish are selected so that the changes you are about to make apply to all of them. Add two behaviors to the starfish: *Rotate* and *Sine*. The *Rotate* behavior causes a sprite to spin by continuously changing the angle property of the sprite. In the *Properties* panel, under the heading *Rotate*, change *Speed* to 10; this will cause the angle property to increase by 10 degrees every second, resulting in a nice, slow, spinning effect. The *Sine* behavior causes a property to oscillate between two values. In the *Properties* panel, under the heading *Sine*, change *Movement* to Size (this causes the *Size* property to be the one affected by the *Sine* behavior), change *Period* to 2 (this is how many seconds it will take to cycle through the values), and change *Magnitude* to 10 (this is the amount by which the starting value of the property will be adjusted). The result should be a subtle, rhythmic, pulsing effect as the starfish size increases and decreases by 10 pixels every 2 seconds. Figure 2-19 shows the *Properties* panel with these changes made.

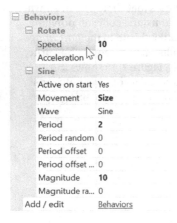

Figure 2-19. *Adjusted values for the Rotate and Sine behavior properties*

As you can see when testing your game, when the turtle collides with a starfish, the starfish immediately disappears. To present a more sophisticated effect, you will add another value-based animation that will cause the starfish to fade out instead of suddenly disappearing. Use the object panel to make sure that all starfish instances are selected and then add the *Fade* behavior. The *Fade* behavior causes a sprite to either fade in or fade out by continuously changing the *Opacity* property, which controls how transparent the sprite image is; *Opacity* values close to 100 are fully visible, while values close to 0 are completely transparent (and thus cannot be seen by the player). In the *Properties* panel, under the *Fade* heading, change *Active at start* to No (*which* means that the sprite does *not* start fading out right away), and change *Fade out time* to 0.2 (which means it will take 0.2 seconds for the opacity to decrease from 100 to 0). Notice that the *Destroy* property is set to After fade out, which means that when the object has completely faded out, the *Destroy* action will automatically be applied to the sprite, removing it from the game.

Next, you need to adjust one of the game events. Go to the event sheet and locate the event with condition *Turtle: On Collision with Starfish* and action *Starfish: Destroy*. Click the action and press the *Delete* key; this will cause the action to be removed from the game. Click *Add action* next to the condition, select the Starfish object, and in the list of actions select *Start Fade* from the *Fade* group. When you are finished, the event should appear, as shown in Figure 2-20. Save and test your game to verify that the fade animation works as expected.

Figure 2-20. Replacing Destroy with Fade in the event sheet

On Your Own

Congratulations on completing the side quests! At this point, you now have a fully functional game with some nice extra features. However, you should feel free to continue developing this game with the skills you have learned in this chapter. Here are some additional ideas of features:

- You could create a maze for the turtle to navigate through, by making the rocks long and thin to create walls and adding more rocks as needed. To give yourself more space to work with in the layout, you could make the turtle and starfish sprites smaller.

- You could make the starfish move back and forth by adding another *Sine* behavior to the Starfish object, with properties configured to adjust the horizontal or vertical position.

- You could create new sprites for scenery, such as seaweed or coral. You may or may not want to add the solid behavior, depending on the type of object they represent.

- You could create a new long and thin sprite with both the *Solid* and *Rotate* behaviors added to it; such a sprite will act like a propeller and will push the turtle if it gets close.

- You could create a new sprite that serves as an "enemy," like a shark, that will destroy the turtle if there is a collision. In that case, you might also want to add another sprite with an image containing the words "game over" that are displayed when that happens.

Summary

In this chapter, you created your first game in Construct and encountered a lot of vocabulary along the way. You learned how to create sprites and adjust their properties, such as position, angle, and size, and how to create multiple instances of a given sprite. You learned that instructions for your game are specified as events, which can be thought of as "if-then" statements. Events consist of conditions and actions; if the conditions are true, then the associated actions are performed. You also learned about behaviors, which are like collections of events, useful for many common types of games. In particular, you worked with the following behaviors: *8 Direction, Bound to Layout, Solid, Rotate, Sine,* and *Fade*.

In the next chapter, you will build upon these fundamental skills and create a space-themed shoot-'em-up game called Space Rocks.

CHAPTER 3

■ ■ ■

Space Rocks

In this chapter, you will create a space-themed shoot-'em-up game called Space Rocks, inspired by the classic arcade game Asteroids, shown in Figure 3-1.

Figure 3-1. *The Space Rocks game*

Introduction

In Space Rocks, the player controls a spaceship, whose goal is to fly around and shoot lasers to destroy asteroids that are floating across the screen. The player must also take care that the spaceship does not get hit by asteroids, as they can damage or destroy the spaceship. The game world space uses *wraparound*, which means that when an object moves past one edge of the screen, it reappears on the other side. The player uses the keyboard to control the spaceship, which may turn left or right, move forward

© Lee Stemkoski and Evan Leider 2017
L. Stemkoski and E. Leider, *Game Development with Construct 2*,
DOI 10.1007/978-1-4842-2784-8_3

in the direction it is currently facing,[1] and fire lasers. The spaceship also has the ability to teleport to a random location on the screen, which can be useful to escape from an imminent collision with an asteroid but also involves a certain amount of risk, as it is possible that the spaceship will appear in the path of another asteroid (or even worse, appear within an asteroid). This game also features animations and visual special effects, such as rocket thruster fire and explosions. As extra optional features, you will learn how to add shields to provide limited protection to the ship and to add UFOs that randomly spawn and present another obstacle for the player to avoid.

This chapter assumes you have mastered the material in the previous chapter. In particular, you should be able to change layout and project properties, add layers to a layout, add sprites and adjust their properties, add behaviors to a sprite, and create events with given conditions and actions. In this chapter, you will learn about some new behaviors, animations, and functions for events.

To begin, download the zip file containing the graphics for this chapter from the book web site. In the layout properties, set the layout *Name* to Main, set *Size* to 800, 600, and set up the three layers named Background, Main, and UI as you did for the Starfish Collector game. In the project properties, change the window *Size* to 800, 600 (and change the *Name* and *Author* properties as you like). In the layout area, create a sprite named OuterSpace, using the image space.jpg, and position and resize the sprite so that it covers the entire layout area. Change the *Layer* property so that the OuterSpace sprite is on the *Background* layer. Your layout should look like Figure 3-2: an image of outer space.

Figure 3-2. *Layout with the outer space background sprite added*

---

[1]This control scheme has a significant difference from the control scheme from the previous game. In Space Rocks, the control scheme is relative to the character's (in this case, the spaceship's) viewpoint. In contrast, the Starfish Collector game featured a control scheme that was relative to the player's viewpoint. For example, pressing the up arrow key moved the turtle toward the top of the screen, regardless of what direction the turtle was facing. Using a control scheme relative to the character can provide a more immersive gameplay experience for the player.

Spaceship Movement

The next step is to add the player's character: the spaceship. To begin, change the active layer in the layer panel to Main. Create a sprite named Spaceship using the image file spaceship.png. Position it near the center of the layout. Your first goal is to set up events for spaceship movement, as described in the introduction of the chapter. However, unlike the situation for the Starfish Collector game, there are no preconfigured behaviors that will create the precise style of movement for this game. Therefore, in this section, you will set up some events for customized movement.

Right-click in the layout area and select *Insert New Object*. In the window that appears, underneath the *Input* heading, select *Keyboard* and press the *Insert* button (you do not need to rename the *Keyboard* object). The *Keyboard* object provides you with the ability to check any keyboard key and determine whether it was just pressed, whether it is currently being held down, and whether it was just released. (You didn't need to add a *Keyboard* object in the previous project because the *8-Direction* behavior automatically checks for keyboard input.)

The first event you will add will be, informally, "If the left arrow key is held down, then turn the spaceship counterclockwise 2 degrees." There are two subtle points to this event that are worth noting before you continue. First, the condition checks whether the key is being held down; this will be true (and the event action will repeat) as long as the player is holding down the key (in contrast to *on key pressed*, which registers as true only at the first instant when a particular key is pressed). Second, the action of rotating by 2 degrees will take place 60 times per second,[2] so the rate of rotation is actually 120 degrees per second; since there are 360 degrees in a full rotation, the spaceship will be able to spin around completely once every 3 seconds.

To add the event, click the *Event Sheet* tab, and click *Add Event*. In the window that appears, select the *Keyboard* object and then select the condition *Key is down*, as shown on the left side of Figure 3-3. A new window will appear containing a button labeled <click to choose>. Click this button, and another window will appear, asking you to press a key. Press the left arrow key on your keyboard, and the name of the key pressed will appear in a text box in this window. When you are finished, click the *OK* button, and you will be returned to the previous window, where you can click the *Done* button. Then, in the event sheet, click *Add Action* next to the condition you just created. Select the *Spaceship* object and then select the action *Rotate Counter-Clockwise* from the Angle group, as shown on the right side of Figure 3-3. A window will appear where you can type the number of degrees to rotate; enter 2 and then click the *Done* button. This completes the event that will enable the player to rotate the spaceship to the left.

---

[2]This assumes your game in running at a rate of 60 frames per second (FPS), which should be the case for nearly all computers running this program. For more complicated games involving large amounts of high-resolution graphics and complicated code, the rate at which the program runs could be slower, and you would need to take the possibility into account when writing the event. This issue will be discussed at length in future chapters.

Figure 3-3. *The lists of conditions and actions for rotating the spaceship*

Next, you will add an event that lets the player turn the ship to the right; informally, this event is "If the right arrow key is held down, then turn the spaceship clockwise 2 degrees." The steps for adding this event are nearly identical to those listed earlier, with only two differences: first, when selecting the key in the condition, you should press the right arrow key, and second, when creating the spaceship action, you should select *Rotate Clockwise* from the list of actions. When completed, these two events should look like Figure 3-4.

Figure 3-4. *Completed events for rotating the spaceship left and right*

Now that your spaceship can turn left and right, the next step is to create events to handle forward motion. While creating actions in the past, you may have noticed some actions in the *Size & Position* group that may be applicable, such as *Move Forward* and *Move at Angle*. However, in this game, the movement is more subtle: when the player presses the key to activate the spaceship's thrusters, this should cause the spaceship to *accelerate* forward, in other words, to slowly increase its speed up to some maximum value. Furthermore, when the player releases this key, the spaceship does not immediately stop; instead, it continues to drift in the same direction, at the same speed. This makes sense in this context because in outerspace there are no opposing forces (such as friction) to slow down the spaceship. The only way for the player to reduce the speed of the spaceship is to rotate the spaceship in the opposite direction and activate the thrusters to counteract the acceleration.

To accomplish this style of movement, you will create the event "If the up arrow key is held down, then accelerate the spaceship at a rate[3] of 100, in the direction that the spaceship is facing." Acceleration is not a property available to sprite objects by default,

---

[3]Since acceleration represents the change in velocity, the units for the rate of acceleration are pixels per second. If the rate of acceleration is 100, this means that during every second the velocity will increase by 100 pixels per second.

so to create this action, you will first add a behavior that provides this functionality. Select the *Spaceship* object in the layout, and add the behavior called *Custom Movement*. Then, in the event sheet, create a new event, selecting the *Keyboard* object and the condition *Key is down*, and select the *Up arrow* key. Next, add an action to this event, selecting the *Spaceship* object and the action *Accelerate toward angle* in the group *Custom Movement: Velocity*. A window will appear where you can enter values for this action. In the *Acceleration* text box, enter 100. In the *Angle* text box, enter Spaceship.Angle. In particular, do not forget the period between the words *Spaceship* and *Angle*; the period indicates that the program should use the value of the *Angle* property that belongs to the Spaceship object (as opposed to the *Angle* property of other game objects). When finished, your event should appear as in Figure 3-5.

| 3 | ⌨Keyboard | **Up arrow** is down | | ⬔ Spaceship | Accelerate ✂ CustomMovement *100* at angle *Spaceship.Angle* |

Figure 3-5. *The completed event for accelerating the spaceship forward*

Another gameplay mechanic that you can easily add at this time is wraparound; when the spaceship moves past one edge of the screen, it should reenter the screen at the opposite edge, as if the edges were connected. To implement this feature, select the *Spaceship* object, and add the *Wrap* behavior.

Now is a good time to save and test your project. After saving (as usual, a single .capx file is the preferred format), click the *Run layout* button in the title bar of the Construct window. Make sure that the left and right arrow keys rotate the spaceship left and right, respectively, and that the up arrow key accelerates the spaceship forward in whatever direction it is currently facing. As you are testing the controls, you might notice that you can continue to accelerate the spaceship to ludicrous speeds, which could cause the spaceship to flicker or move so quickly it appears to be in multiple places at once. We will address this issue by creating an event that forces the spaceship speed to be less than a certain amount.

The next event will cap the spaceship speed at 200 pixels per second and can be phrased as "If the spaceship's speed is greater than 200, then set the spaceship's speed to 200." In the event sheet, add a new event. Select the *Spaceship* object and the condition *Compare Speed* from the group *Custom Movement*; in the parameters window that appears, change *Comparison* to Greater Than, and change the value of *Speed* to 200. Add an action to this event, selecting the *Spaceship* object and the action *Set Speed* from the group *Custom Movement*: Velocity; in the parameters window that appears, change the value of *Speed* to 200, and click the *Done* button. When you are finished, the event should appear as in Figure 3-6. Save and test your project to verify that the event is working as expected.

| 4 | ⬔ Spaceship | ✂ CustomMovement Overall speed > 200 | | ⬔ Spaceship | Set ✂ CustomMovement Overall speed to *200* |

Figure 3-6. *The completed event for capping the spaceship's speed*

Lasers and Rocks

In this section, you will create additional game objects for the Space Rocks game: lasers that the spaceship can fire and asteroids that the player will attempt to shoot with the lasers.

In the layout area, insert a new object: a sprite that you name Laser. Position it above the layout, in the gray margin area (off-screen), and use the image file named laser.png; adjust the size if necessary. As it turns out, most of the functionality of the Laser object can be implemented by behaviors. First, add the behavior named Bullet. The *Bullet* behavior makes objects move in a straight line. After this behavior is added, you will see in the *Properties* panel that the default speed is 400 pixels per second; you may adjust this value later if you want. Also, add the *Wrap* behavior since a laser that moves past one edge of the screen should reappear on the opposite side, as is the case with the spaceship. Next, add the behavior named *Fade*. The *Fade* behavior makes objects fade in or fade out after an optional time delay and can be set to automatically destroy objects after they have faded out. You want to use this behavior, because otherwise the lasers will cycle around the screen forever until they hit something. In the *Properties* panel underneath the *Fade* group, change *Wait Time* to 1, change *Fade Out Time* to 0.5, and leave *Destroy* set to *After Fade Out*.

Next, you will add an event to shoot lasers: "If the spacebar is pressed, then the spaceship creates a laser." To begin, add a new event to the event sheet. For the condition, select the *Keyboard* object and the condition *On Key Pressed*. As with the previous keyboard conditions, you need to specify a key; following the same procedure as before, select the space bar key. This condition will be true only when the key is first pressed; every time the spacebar is pressed, only one laser should be fired.[4] Next, add an action to this event; select the *Spaceship* object, and select the action *Spawn Another Object*. (In game development, creating an object during gameplay is called spawning an object.) In the parameters window that appears, click the button labeled <*click to choose*> and select the *Laser* object; in the *Layer* text box, enter "Main" (including the quotes). Click the *Done* button, and your event is complete; it should appear as shown in Figure 3-7. It is worth noting that you did not need to set the position or angle of the spawned laser because these values are automatically set to match the values of the object that does the spawning (in this case, the spaceship). Now is another good time to save and test your game. In particular, when playing your game, make sure that pressing the spacebar fires one laser, and verify that the laser wraps around the screen and fades out after a short interval. If any of these features aren't working as expected, double-check that the correct behaviors have been added, that any property values discussed have been set correctly, and that the events appear exactly as shown in this section.

Figure 3-7. *The completed event to shoot lasers*

---

[4]If you had instead selected the condition *On Key Down*, the condition would be true for as long as the spacebar is being held down and would result in a continuous stream of laser fire. For the Space Rocks game, using this condition would make the game too easy, but this is a cool effect to keep in mind for other games you might make in the future.

Now that you have lasers to shoot, it is time to add something to shoot at: asteroids. To begin, in the layout area, insert a new object: a sprite that you name `Asteroid`. Position it anywhere on the screen, and use the image file named `rock.png`; adjust the size if necessary. As was the case with the laser, most of the functionality of the rocks can be implemented by behaviors. First, add the *Solid* behavior. Next, add the *Bullet* behavior; in the *Properties* panel, change *Speed* to 100 and change *Bounce Off Solids* to Yes; this will make the asteroids bounce off each other as they move across the screen (later, you will create additional instances of asteroids, after these properties are set). Next, add the *Wrap* behavior to be consistent with the spaceship and lasers. Finally, you want the asteroids to appear as though they are spinning around in space. To this end, add the *Rotate* behavior. You will now also need to change the bullet behavior property *Set Angle* to No. If set to Yes, the bullet behavior moves the object in the direction of the sprite's angle. However, you want the bullet motion to be independent of the sprite angle (the asteroid is traveling in a straight line while the image spins), so you must change the *Set Angle* value to No. After all these behaviors are added and the properties are changed, duplicate the Asteroid object a few times and position the copies around the screen, far away from the spaceship. To add some variety to their appearances, you can make small adjustments to the size or angle for individual instances. When you are finished, your layout should appear similar to Figure 3-8. Save and test your project, and make sure that the rocks move as expected.

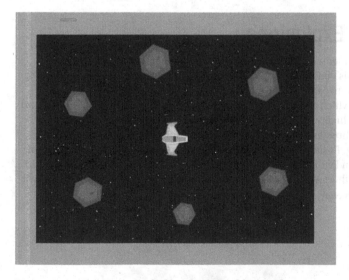

Figure 3-8. The Space Rocks layout after adding rocks

To add interactivity between the game objects, you will now create some additional events. In particular, the spaceship should be destroyed when it is hit by an asteroid, and an asteroid should be destroyed when it is hit by a laser. The first event can be expressed as "If an asteroid collides with the spaceship, destroy the spaceship." To implement this, add a new event. Select the *Asteroid* object and the condition *On Collision with Another Object*; in the parameters window, select the *Spaceship* object. Add an action to this event; select the *Spaceship* object and the action *Destroy*. When completed, your event should appear as shown at the top of Figure 3-9. The second event is "If a laser collides with an asteroid, then destroy the asteroid and destroy the laser." Implementing this is similar to the previous event. One change is that the condition is between a laser and an asteroid. The slightly trickier difference is that there are two actions associated to this event. After adding the first action (to destroy the asteroid), click *Add action* under the previous action. This enables you to add a second action to the event; when the condition is true, both actions will occur. When completed, this event should appear as shown at the bottom of Figure 3-9. As usual (after adding new events), now is a good time to save and test your game. You may find that you need to adjust the position, angle, size, or speed of the rocks to achieve good gameplay balance; ideally, the game should be challenging but winnable.

Figure 3-9. *Collision events*

Thrusters and Explosions

At this point, you have implemented the fundamental game mechanics of the Space Rocks game. This section is dedicated to visual feedback, which is important in providing a quality gameplay experience for the player. The two features you will implement include a thruster effect, which will be visible whenever the spaceship is accelerating, and an animated explosion, which will appear whenever an object is destroyed.

First, you'll add the thruster effect. In the layout area, add a new sprite named Fire using the image fire.png. Position and resize this sprite so it appears to be coming from the spaceship, as shown in Figure 3-10. Add the *Pin* behavior. The *Pin* behavior is used to "attach" one sprite to another; when a sprite moves or rotates, any sprites pinned to it will move or rotate in the same way, as if the sprites were a single unit.

Figure 3-10. *Relative position of the spaceship and fire sprites*

To specify the object to which the fire should be pinned, you need to set up an event. This event needs to take place exactly once, as soon as the game starts, as in "If the layout just started, then the Fire object will pin itself to the spaceship." In the event sheet, add a new event. Select the *System* object and the condition *On Start of Layout* (which was designed to be used for exactly such a situation). Add an action, select the *Fire* object, and select the action *Pin to Object*; in the parameters window that appears, select the *Spaceship* object. The fire should exist only as long as the spaceship exists, so you also need to add an action to the event where an asteroid collides with the spaceship; in this case, the fire also needs to be destroyed. When you are finished, these events should appear as shown in Figure 3-11. Save and test your game; the Fire object and Spaceship object should move around the screen as a single unit. However, the Fire object is currently always visible, while the desired effect is that the fire be visible only when the spaceship is accelerating. This issue will be fixed next.

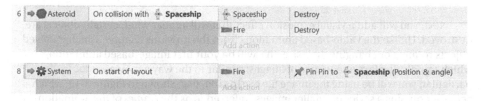

Figure 3-11. The added action Destroy and completed event to activate the pin behavior

The Fire object should not be visible when the game starts, and thus you should select the *Fire* object in the layout and set the property *Initial Visibility* to Invisible. Next, you need to set up a pair of events to control the visibility of the fire: when accelerating, the fire should be visible, and when not accelerating, the fire should be invisible. Recall that acceleration occurs when the up arrow key is being held down, and there is already an event in place with this condition. Therefore, you only need add a new action to this particular preexisting event, so click *Add action* directly underneath the spaceship acceleration action. In the window that appears, select the *Fire* object, and the *Set Visible* action from the *Appearance* group. In the parameters window that appears, leave the visibility set to the default value of Visible, and click the *Done* button. With this addition, the event will now appear as in the top part of Figure 3-12.

To make the fire invisible, the event should be "If it is *not* true that the up arrow key is held down, then the Fire object will set its visibility to invisible." You may have observed that, in general, conditions in Construct are phrased in a positive manner; they each check whether some condition *is* happening rather than if some condition *is not* happening. In cases such as these when the negation of a condition needs to be checked, Construct provides you with the ability to *invert* any given condition. An inverted condition is true exactly when the original condition is not true. Thus, to implement the event described earlier, begin by creating a new event with the *Keyboard* condition *Key is Down*, and via the parameters window, select *Up arrow key*, as you have before. When you are finished and the condition is displayed in the event sheet, right-click the condition and a list of options will appear. From this list, select *Invert*, and a red *X* will appear in the condition, indicating that it has been inverted. Inverting can be thought of as inserting the phrase "It is not the case that..." into the description of the condition.

Then, add an action to this event; select the *Fire* object and the *Set Visible* action, and in the parameters window, change the setting to Invisible. When you are finished, the event will appear as in the bottom part of Figure 3-12. As usual, save and test your game; make sure that the fire is visible only when you are pressing the up arrow.

3	⌨Keyboard	**Up arrow** is down	⦿ Spaceship	Accelerate ✗ CustomMovement *100* at angle *Spaceship.Angle*
			▬Fire	Set Visible
			Add action	

| 9 | ⌨Keyboard | ✗ **Up arrow** is down | ▬Fire | Set Invisible |
| | | | Add action | |

Figure 3-12. *Events for setting the visibility of the Fire object*

Next, you will add a visual explosion effect that will appear when certain objects are destroyed. Unlike the value-based animations from the previous chapter, which involved objects rotating or changing their size, this will be your first image-based animation, which rapidly displays a sequence of images, similar to the way a movie works. In particular, you will be using the image file explosion.png, shown in Figure 3-13, which actually contains a series of smaller images (referred to as the *frames* of the animation) arranged in a rectangular grid. Such an image is referred to as a *sprite sheet* or a *sprite strip*. If these particular images are displayed one after the other, then it will appear as an explosion that starts out bright, changes color from yellow to orange to red, and finally darkens and fades out as smoke.

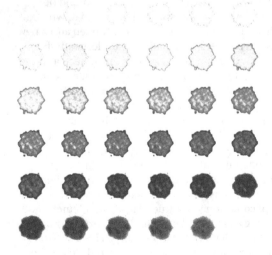

Figure 3-13. *Spritesheet used for an explosion special effect*

To begin, add a new sprite named Explosion to the main layer of the layout. When the set of image editor windows appear, instead of using the large main Edit Image window, you will focus on the window called *Animation frames*. Right-click in this window, and in the menu that appears, hover over the selection *Import Frames* and then click the option *From Sprite Strip*. Select the image explosion.png, and then a window will appear titled *Import Sprite Strip*. This window is used to specify how many subimages are contained in the sprite strip image. In this case, the grid of images contains six images in each row, so enter 6 for the number of horizontal images, and there are six rows total, so enter 6 for the number of vertical images. Also, select the *Replace Entire Existing Animation* check box, as you do not want to save the default blank image provided by the image editor. Click the *OK* button, and when the confirmation dialog appears, click *OK*; you really do want to replace the current animation. After a moment, you should see the individual frames appear in the *Animation frames* window (you may need to use the scroll bar to see them all), as shown in Figure 3-14. Frames can be rearranged by using the mouse to drag and drop, and individual frames can be deleted by right-clicking the frame and selecting Delete; however, you do not need to do either of these at this time. To preview the animation, locate the image editor window titled *Animations*; this contains a list of animations stored for this object and should currently contain only one item, named Default. Right-click the name of the animation and select *Preview*, and a small window will appear and display what will appear to be a very slow and choppy animation. To remedy this, click the name of the animation, and the *Properties* panel should display a short list of animation-related properties. The property Speed represents how many frames are displayed each second; change this value to 20 and then watch the preview again to see a smoother and faster animation. When you are finished, close the image editor windows.

Figure 3-14. *The Animation frames window after importing a sprite strip*

Next, in the layout, position the Explosion sprite so that it is in the gray margin area. This is so that the initial explosion occurs off-screen and is not visible to the player.[5] Next, you will add actions to preexisting events where explosions should occur. In the event

---

[5]You may wonder why you don't simply set the initial visibility of the Explosion object to invisible, as you did for the Fire object. This is because, if you set this explosion instance to be invisible by default, then all the explosions that will be spawned later will also be invisible by default, and you would have to include an extra action to make them visible after they are created. Dragging the initial explosion off-screen is an easy way to avoid this extra code.

sheet, you will add another action to the event involving the spaceship being destroyed. Click *Add Action* directly below this action, select the *Spaceship* object, select the action *Spawn Another Object*, and in the parameters window choose the *Explosion* object and spawn it on the *Main* layer. Similarly, add yet another action to the event involving an asteroid being destroyed: click *Add Action*, select the *Asteroid* object, select the *Spawn* action, choose the *Explosion* object, and set it to appear on the *Main* layer. Finally, you need to add an event that removes the Explosion sprite from the layout after its animation is finished. Otherwise, all the explosions that are spawned will remain in computer memory (even though they are invisible), potentially resulting in a slower frame rate as the game progresses. Add a new event, selecting the *Explosion* object and the condition *On Any Finished* from the *Animation* group. For the corresponding action, select the *Explosion* object and the *Destroy* action. When you are finished, the updated events and the new event should appear as in Figure 3-15. Save and test your game, and watch the explosions appear when the lasers collide with the asteroids (or when an asteroid collides with the spaceship).

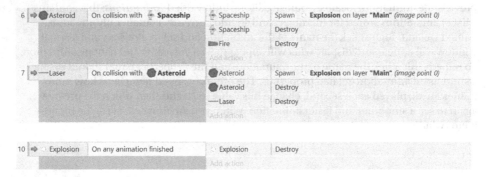

Figure 3-15. *Events related to explosions*

Teleportation

Another game mechanic mentioned at the beginning of this chapter is the ability of the spaceship to teleport to a random location on the screen, a potentially risky method of escape from imminent collision with an asteroid. You will also provide visual feedback in the form of an animated special effect that appears at the original position and the new position of the spaceship, as shown in Figure 3-16.

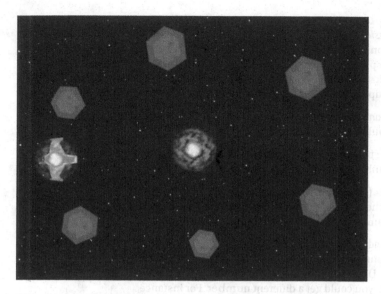

Figure 3-16. Warp effects appearing after ship teleportation

First, you will create an animated sprite representing the special effect. In the layout, create a new sprite named Warp, positioned in the margins of the layout area. Since you are creating an animated sprite, the following process will be similar to the process for creating the explosion animation. When the image editor windows open, right-click in the *Animation frames* window, and select Import from sprite strip. Select the image file warp.png, and in the window that appears, enter 8 for horizontal cells, 4 for vertical cells, and check the box to replace the existing animation. Click *Default* in the window titled *Animation*, and in the *Properties* panel, change *Speed* to 16 and change *Loop* to Yes; this means the animation frames will be displayed in a cycle, returning to the first frame after the last frame is displayed. When completed, also add the *Fade* behavior to the Warp sprite. This will fade out the Warp sprite over the course of one second, and because the *Fade* property *Destroy* is set to *After Fade Out* by default, you don't need to add an event to destroy it as you did with the Explosion sprite.

The event that you will create next is "If the X key is pressed, then the spaceship will spawn a Warp object, the spaceship will move to a random position, and the spaceship will spawn a (second) Warp object." To begin, create a new event with the keyboard condition *On Key Pressed*. In the parameter window, press the *X* key (or any other unused key of your choice). Add an action to this event, selecting the *Spaceship* object, select the action *Spawn Another Object*, and select the *Warp* object. Then add a second action to this event, selecting the *Spaceship* object and the action *Set Position* in the *Size & Position* group. In the parameters window that appears, there are text boxes where you can specify the *x* and *y* coordinates of the spaceship. However, you don't want to enter just a number in these areas because then the spaceship would always move to that particular location and the teleporting would not be random.

Fortunately, the Construct game engine does not limit you to just entering numbers; you can enter *expressions*, which are combinations of values, operations, and functions. In particular, functions are used to transform input values into output values according to a built-in formula or procedure. When entering functions into Construct, the name of the function is written first, followed by parentheses; the input appears between the parentheses, and if there are multiple input values, they are separated by commas. Here's an example:

- The round function transforms the number 3.8 into the number 4; this would be entered as round(3.8).

- The sqrt ("square root") function transforms the number 25 into the number 5; this would be entered as sqrt(25).

- The max ("maximum") function takes two numbers as inputs and yields the larger of the two input values as the output value. For example, max(9, 7) would be equal to 9.

- The random function takes two numbers as inputs and yields as output a randomly generated decimal value between these values. Unlike most other functions, every time this function is used, you could get a different number. For instance, random(10, 20) could yield the output value 14.5337, but the next time it is used, it could yield 19.0042.

For this game, it is the last of these functions mentioned that you will use. Since the layout size is 800 pixels wide, the value of *X* could be anything between 0 and 800. Returning your attention to the parameters window, enter the expression random(0, 800) in the *X* text box. Similarly, since the height of the layout is 600 pixels, enter random(0, 600) in the text box next to *Y*, and click the *Done* button. Finally, add a third action to this event, identical to the first: select the *Spaceship* object, select the *Spawn Another Object* action, and select the *Warp* object. Since actions are activated in sequence, from top to bottom, the second Warp object will be created by the spaceship after it has moved to its new position on the layout. When you are finished, the event will appear as in Figure 3-17. Save your game, play it to test the teleportation mechanic, and verify that it sends the spaceship to random positions and that the Warp objects appear as expected.

Figure 3-17. Event for the teleport game mechanic

Winning or Losing the Game

Finally, you will implement some messages that inform the player that the game is over and whether they have won or lost the game. It is important to provide a sense of closure, as discussed in the previous chapter. The events will also be similar to those in the previous chapter: if there are no asteroids left, then a *Congratulations!* message appears; if there is no spaceship left, then a *Game Over* message appears.

To begin, create a sprite named MessageWin using the image file message-win. png. Position it in the center of the layout, change its *Layer* property to UI, and change its *Initial Visibility* property to Invisible. Repeat this process to create a sprite named MessageLose using the image file message-lose.png. Like before, center it in the layout, set its layer to UI, and make it invisible. Next, add an event with the *System* condition *Compare Two Values*; in the parameters window, enter Asteroid.Count as the first value, Equal to as the comparison, and 0 as the second value. Add an action for this event, selecting the *MessageWin* object and the *Set Visible* action, with the parameter *Visible*. Finally, add one more event with the *System* condition *Compare Two Values*; in the parameters window, enter Spaceship.Count for the first value, Equal to for the comparison, and 0 for the second value. Add an action to this event that sets the *MessageLose* object's visibility to visible. When you are finished, your events should appear as in Figure 3-18. Save and test your game, and verify that you can both win and lose and that the correct message appears in each situation, as shown on the left and right sides of Figure 3-19. If so, congratulations!

12	⚙ System	Asteroid.Count = 0	— MessageWin	Set Visible
			Add action	
13	⚙ System	Spaceship.Count = 0	— MessageLose	Set Visible
			Add action	

Figure 3-18. Events for displaying the win and lose messages

Figure 3-19. Winning the game (left) and losing the game (right)

Side Quests

At this point, you have finished implementing the core mechanics for the Space Rocks game: the controls work as desired; the spaceship, asteroids, and lasers interact with each other; there are some special effects to give visual feedback to the player; the spaceship is able to teleport at random; and there are win and lose conditions for the game. This section will explain how to implement some optional features to improve the gameplay experience. First, in the current version of the game, the spaceship is destroyed after a single collision; to add some balance to the game, you will add protective shields around the spaceship, which enable it to withstand multiple hits. Second, you will create some unpredictability by adding some enemy characters in the form of unidentified flying objects (UFOs), which will appear periodically at random locations and move across the screen in a wave pattern, adding some extra challenge.

Shields

To begin, create a new sprite named Shields, using the image file shields.png. Add the Pin behavior and the Solid behavior. Position the shield sprite so that it is centered on the spaceship. Just as with the Fire object previously, you need to configure the *Pin* behavior, attaching the sprite to another object, using an event. In the event sheet, locate the event you previously created with the *System* condition *On Start of Layout*. Add another action to this event, selecting the *Shields* object and the *Pin* action, and in the parameters window, select the *Spaceship* object. Collision with the shields should also stop the spaceship from moving. To implement this feature, create a new event. Specifically, for the condition, select the *Asteroid* object and the condition *On collision with*. In the parameters window, select the *Shields* object; for the action, select the *Spaceship* object and the action *Stop* from the *Custom Movement: Velocity* group. When you are finished, the modified event and new event should appear as shown in Figure 3-20. Save and run your game, and you should see that as you move the spaceship around, the asteroids bounce right off the shields, and since the shield sprite is larger and completely surrounds the spaceship sprite, this prevents any asteroids from hitting the spaceship at all.

Figure 3-20. *Events involving the shield sprite*

At this point, the shields are overpowered, in the sense that it is impossible for the player to lose (unless they randomly teleport into an asteroid). What the game needs now is a way to "damage" the shields: after a certain number of collisions, the shields should be destroyed, and furthermore, it is desirable for the player to have visual feedback indicating that the shields have been damaged.

One way to accomplish both of these goals simultaneously is to use the opacity of the shields as a measure of the "health" of the shields.[6] The initial value of the opacity is 100; every time there is a collision, this value will decrease by a fixed amount. If the value becomes zero, then the shields will be destroyed, and the ship may be destroyed on collision with an asteroid.

---

[6]In a future chapter, you will learn a more common approach to this problem: how create a customized property, called an *instance variable*, which can be used to store this information.

To set this up, find the event you previously created with the condition that an asteroid collides with the shields. Add an action to this event, selecting the *Shields* object and the *Set Opacity* action; in the parameters window, enter Shields.Opacity - 25. This will set the new value of the shield's opacity to the previous value of the shield's opacity minus 25. Thus, after four collisions, the opacity will be zero. At this time, you must specify that the shield object should be destroyed (otherwise it will continue to cause asteroids to bounce off, even though it can't be seen). To accomplish this, add a new event. For the condition, select the *Shields* object and the *Compare opacity* condition; in the parameters window, change the comparison to less or equal, and the value to 0. For the action, select the *Shields* object and the *Destroy* action. When you are finished, the events should appear as in Figure 3-21. Save and test your game to verify the shields work as expected.

Figure 3-21. *Events for damaging and destroying the shields*

UFOs

In this side quest, you will add a regularly spawning enemy. This enemy will be passive. It won't react to the player in any way; it has no abilities other than moving across the screen. The enemy will spawn at a random location beyond the left side of the layout and move to the right in a wave pattern. This movement style will add an extra challenge to the game because it will be more difficult to avoid and shoot these objects. When adding a new character or object to a game, there are many aspects that you will need to decide on. In addition to movement patterns, you also need to decide whether the character has any abilities, how the character interacts with every other object in the game, how the character could affect the win/lose conditions, and what happens to the character when the game is over. In what follows, each of these issues will be addressed.

First, add a new sprite called UFO with the image ufo.png, and place it in the margin area beyond the right edge of the layout. Add the *Bullet* behavior to the *UFO* sprite, and in the *Properties* panel, change *Speed* to 125. Also add the *Sine* behavior, set *Movement* to Vertical, set *Period to* 1, and set *Magnitude* to 25. This will cause the UFO to move as described earlier, in a wavelike pattern.

Next, you will add functionality for causing UFOs to spawn on the left side of the screen and self-destruct beyond the right side. Add a new sprite named SpawnPoint; this will be placed off-screen and will be used to spawn new instances of the UFO sprite. The image you use for the SpawnPoint sprite is irrelevant since this object will never be seen by the player, so use the image editor tools such as the paintbrush or bucket to draw or fill in the image area with a solid color of your choice. Since you don't really need a 250-by-250-pixel image for this sprite, use the *Resize* tool in the image editor to change the size of the image to 32-by-32 pixels. When you are finished, close the image editor window and position the sprite in the margin area directly to the left of the layout. Your layout (including margins) should appear similar to Figure 3-22.

Figure 3-22. *Layout area with UFO and SpawnPoint placed in margins*

In the event sheet, create a new event. For the condition, select the *System* object, and from the *Time* group, select the *Every X Seconds* condition. In the parameters window, enter 5 for the interval, and click the *Done* button. This condition will be true exactly once every 5 seconds. Next, you will add some actions to randomly reposition the SpawnPoint object and have it spawn a UFO. Click *Add action* next to the condition, select the *SpawnPoint* object, and from the Size & *Position* group select *Set Y*. In the parameters window, enter random(100, 500). This is similar to what you entered previously when creating the teleportation events, except you are changing only the *Y* coordinate (the vertical position) because *SpawnPoint* needs to remain to the left of the layout. Also, the random number will be between 100 and 500 (rather than spanning the full range of the height, between 0 to 600) so that the UFO doesn't spawn too close to the top or bottom edge of the layout. Add another action to this event, once again selecting the *SpawnPoint* object. From the list of actions, select *Spawn another object*, and in the parameters window, select the UFO object. Finally, you need another event that will remove the UFOs from the game once they have passed beyond the right edge of the layout. Add a new event, selecting the *UFO* object, and from the list of conditions, select *Compare X* from the *Size & Position* group. In the parameters window, change *Comparison* to Greater Than, and change *X* to 900. Add an action to this event, select the *UFO* object, and select *Destroy* from the list of actions. When you are finished, these events should appear as in Figure 3-23. Save and test your game, making sure that UFOs spawn as frequently as expected and move across the screen as described earlier.

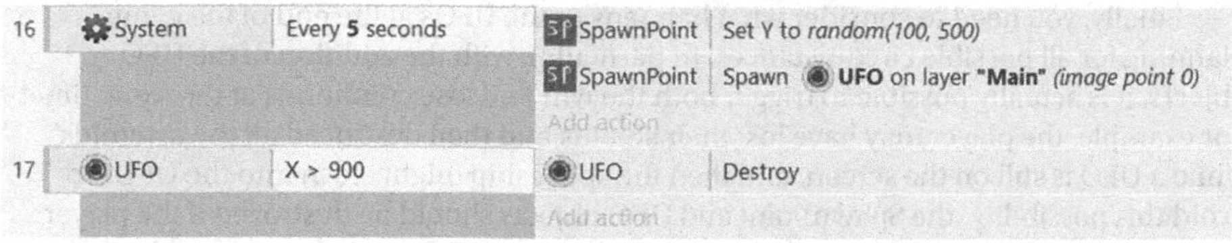
16
System
Every 5 seconds
SpawnPoint
Set Y to random(100, 500)
SpawnPoint
Spawn UFO on layer "Main" (image point 0)
Add action
17
UFO
X > 900
UFO
Destroy
Add action

***Figure 3-23.** Events for spawning and destroying the UFOs*

Next, you have to determine how UFOs will interact with each of the onscreen objects. Here is one possible set of interactions:

- When a UFO collides with an asteroid, the UFO is destroyed.
- When a UFO collides with a laser, both the laser and the UFO are destroyed.
- When a UFO collides with the spaceship, both the spaceship and the UFO are destroyed.
- When a UFO collides with the shields, the UFO is destroyed, and the shield opacity decreases by 25.

In addition, whenever a UFO is destroyed, an explosion effect will be spawned at the location of the UFO. These events are similar to those you have created before. Try to create these events on your own (rereading the process from earlier to refresh your memory, if necessary). When you are finished, the events should appear as in Figure 3-24.

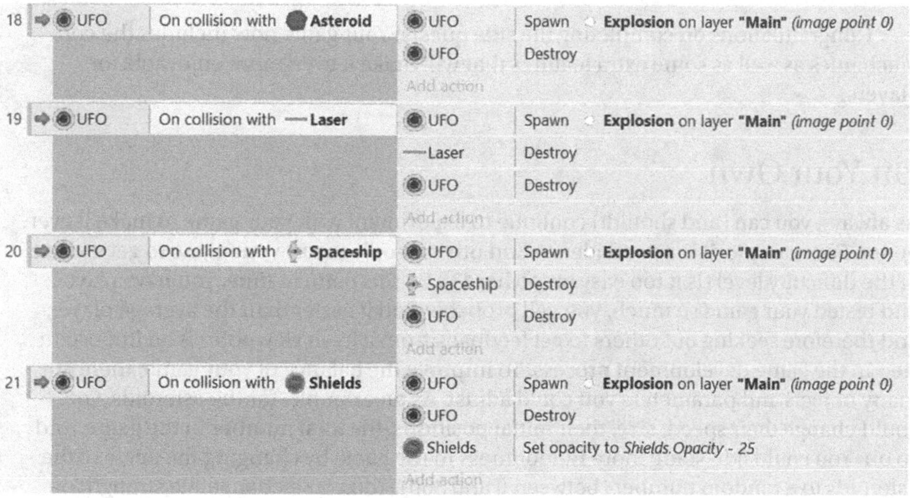
18
UFO
On collision with Asteroid
UFO
Spawn Explosion on layer "Main" (image point 0)
UFO
Destroy
Add action
19
UFO
On collision with Laser
UFO
Spawn Explosion on layer "Main" (image point 0)
Laser
Destroy
UFO
Destroy
Add action
20
UFO
On collision with Spaceship
UFO
Spawn Explosion on layer "Main" (image point 0)
Spaceship
Destroy
UFO
Destroy
Add action
21
UFO
On collision with Shields
UFO
Spawn Explosion on layer "Main" (image point 0)
UFO
Destroy
Shields
Set opacity to Shields.Opacity - 25
Add action

***Figure 3-24.** Events related to UFO collisions*

Finally, you need to consider what happens to the UFOs at the end of the game, planning for all possible circumstances. In particular, with the addition of the UFO objects, it is actually possible to trigger both the win and lose conditions at the same time! For example, the player may have lost their shields and then destroyed all the asteroids while a UFO is still on the screen, and then the spaceship might crash into the UFO. To avoid this possibility, the SpawnPoint and UFO objects should be destroyed if the player wins the game. (This isn't as important if the player loses the game, but you could also set up similar events for that situation as well, if you choose.) In addition, you will have the UFOs spawn warp effects so that they don't just suddenly vanish.

In the event sheet, locate the event that contains the win condition: when the asteroid count is equal to 0. Add a series of actions to this event: the SpawnPoint should be destroyed, UFOs should spawn Warp objects, and UFOs should be destroyed. When you are finished, this modified event should appear as in Figure 3-25. If there are no UFOs on the screen at the end of the game, then this action will simply have no effect. Similarly, after destroying the SpawnPoint object, the previously created event that spawns UFOs every 5 seconds will no longer have any effect.

Figure 3-25. *Modified "you win" event*

Congratulations on completing the side quests! Your game now includes the core mechanics as well as some extra features that will make it even more enjoyable for players.

On Your Own

As always, you can (and should!) continue to experiment with your game to make it even better. For example, it is a good idea to find other people to test your game to get a sense of the difficulty level (is it too easy or too hard?). By this point in time, you have played and tested your game so much, you will probably find it easier than the average player, and therefore seeking out others to get feedback from a fresh viewpoint is an important step in the game development process. To improve the balance of your game, there are many objects and parameters you could adjust. As an example, for the asteroids, you could change their speed, size, their initial positions, the total number in the game, and so on. You could add some more randomness to the game by changing the angle of the asteroids to a random number (between 0 and 360). You could change the strength of the shields by changing the value at which the opacity decreases after a collision; a value of 50 would weaken the shields (they would take only 2 hits), while a value of 10 would strengthen the shields (they could withstand 10 hits). You could increase or decrease the rate at which UFOs are spawned or change their speed or movement pattern. Also, keep in mind that you can change many of these together to maintain the overall balance; for example, you could make the asteroids smaller and faster so that they are more difficult to hit but compensate for the increased difficulty by making the shields stronger.

In addition, you can try experimenting with adding new objects or gameplay mechanics. For example, you could add a sprite that resembles a small moon, add the *Solid* behavior, and place it in the middle of the layout. If you do so, you will have to determine how it interacts with all the other objects. It could provide shelter from the asteroids coming from one direction, but what should happen if the ship crashes into the moon? As another example, you could introduce a new sprite that acts as a powerup (using an image of your choice) that recharges your shields (by increasing their opacity) when the spaceship comes into contact with it. Perhaps these powerups could be spawned when a UFO is destroyed by a laser? These are just a few ideas to get you thinking; the actual possibilities are endless. Have fun!

Summary

In this chapter, you learned about some new behaviors (*Wrap, Custom Movement, Bullet,* and *Pin*). You created image-based animations from spritesheets. It is important to provide visual feedback to the player, and you saw many ways this can be done (in this game, with the *Explosion, Fire,* and *Warp* effects). You also used the random function in events to add a bit of unpredictability to your game.

In the next chapter, you will continue to build upon these skills and create a top-down collection game called Cleanup Challenge.

CHAPTER 4

■ ■ ■

Cleanup Challenge

In this chapter, you will be creating a top-down collection game called Cleanup Challenge, inspired by the classic arcade game Frogger, shown in Figure 4-1.

Figure 4-1. The Cleanup Challenge game

In Cleanup Challenge, the player controls a character (who we will call "the cleaner"), whose goal is to collect pieces of trash scattered around a roadway and return them to a trash can on the opposite side, which ends the game. At the same time, cars are racing across the street, which runs horizontally across the screen. If the person gets hit by a car, the game is over and no points are awarded. The player must strategically decide which pieces of trash they will be able to recover. This is made more challenging by slight variations in the speed of the cars that race past. At the beginning of the game, the trash is

© Lee Stemkoski and Evan Leider 2017
L. Stemkoski and E. Leider, *Game Development with Construct 2*,
DOI 10.1007/978-1-4842-2784-8_4

randomly scattered across the screen, which adds to the replayability value. The cleaner has eight-direction movement, controlled by the arrow keys, and collects trash by coming into contact with it.

This chapter assumes that you have mastered the material from the previous two chapters. In particular, this project requires you to be familiar with using the *8-Direction*, *Bound to Layout*, *Bullet*, and *Fade* behaviors, creating image-based animations, writing events with inverted conditions or multiple actions, and using the `random` function. New topics that will be introduced in this chapter include using the layout grid, creating Tiled Background objects, creating Text objects to display words on the screen, and creating customize variables to store values (such as scores).

Starting in this chapter, we will begin to use a shorter, more efficient description of events. In previous chapters, for example, the process for creating a condition may have been described as follows: "For the condition, select the *System* object, and from the group called *Time*, choose the condition *Every X Seconds*; in the parameters window next to *Interval*, enter the value 5." Since you are now experienced with this process, we will now phrase this more briefly as "Create the condition *System - Time: Every X Seconds*, and set *Interval* to 5." In general, condition descriptions will follow the format "add *Object Name - Group Name: Condition Name*, and set *Parameter Name* to `Value`." Actions will be written in a similar way.

To begin, download the zip file containing the graphics for this chapter from the book web site. In the layout properties, set the layout *Name* to `Main`, and set *Layout Size* to `640, 640`. As you have in previous projects, set up three layers named `Background`, `Main`, and `UI`. In the project properties, change the property *Window Size* to `640, 640` (and change the *Name* and *Author* properties as you like).

Backgrounds

In this section, you will set up a series of background images so that the background of the game appears as in Figure 4-2. In this game, aligning and spacing the graphics are important, so you will use the built-in grid tool to help snap things into place. Click the *View* tab near the top of the Construct window, and click the *Snap to grid* and *Show grid* check boxes. Since the size is set to 32-by-32, every time you move or resize an object, it will automatically round the corresponding value to the nearest multiple of 32. This will be convenient as you will need to position the following objects right next to each other.

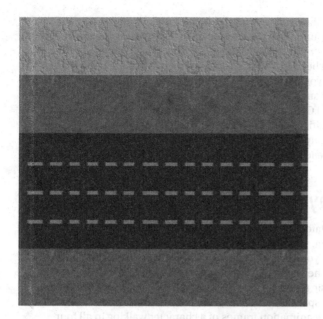

Figure 4-2. *Background images: stone, grass, road, and more grass*

In previous projects, you have used a single sprite object for a background image. You may have noticed that when resizing a sprite, the image stretches or shrinks to fit the dimensions that you choose. For this project, you will use a different object to create backgrounds: a TiledBackground object. The major difference between these two types of objects is that a TiledBackground object will not resize its image. Instead, if the object is larger than the original image, then the image will be repeated until it reaches the size of the object; if the object is smaller than the original image, then the image will be cropped to the dimensions of the object. This is particularly useful when using seamless background images, which are images that line up visually when placed side by side with copies of themselves.

Next, you will add a series of TiledBackground objects to your layout to create the background. In the layout properties, change *Active layer* to Background so that all the objects you are about to add will be placed in the Background layer. In the layout, create a TiledBackground object and name it Grass, using the image grass.jpg. Change the size to 640 by 128, which will be easy to do with the mouse, since you activated the layout grid options earlier; this size corresponds to the width of the layout and a height of four boxes (since 4 times 32 equals 128). Place this object at the bottom of the layout. Create another TiledBackground object named Road, using the image road.jpg, with a size of 640 by 256, and align it next to the Grass object. Create another instance of the Grass object (so it will also be 640 by 128), and position it so that it is aligned with the other side of the Road object. Finally, create another TiledBackground object named Stone, using the image stone.jpg, with a size of 640 by 128, and position it along the top of the layout; this should cover the remaining area in the layout. Also, add the *Solid* behavior to the Stone object; this will stop the player character from walking in this area (because this is where you will place the user interface text later in this chapter).

51

Next, you will set up the dashed yellow lines that mark the separate lanes of the road. Create a new TiledBackground object and name it DashedLines, using the image yellow-dash.png. Using the *Properties* panel, change *Size* to 640, 8. You need to use the *Properties* panel in this case because *Snap to Grid* has been activated, but 8 is not a multiple of 32. (Alternatively, if you prefer to use the mouse, you can hold down the *Alt* key while clicking and dragging an object, which disables the *Snap to Grid* functionality as long as it is being held down.) Change *Opacity* of DashedLines to 50. Make two more instances of this object, and position all three of these *DashedLines* objects so they appear to divide the road into four equally spaced lanes. Once your layout resembles Figure 4-2, save your project, and you are ready to proceed to the next section.

Animating the Player

Previous games have simply rotated the player character to face the direction in which they were moving. In this project, you will use animations instead of a single image for the character, and furthermore, you will set up the project to display a different animation depending on which direction the character is moving (north, south, east, or west), similar to the style used in classic top-down adventure and RPG games like The Legend of Zelda and Final Fantasy. The spritesheet[1] you will use is shown in Figure 4-3. Notice that this spritesheet contains the animation frames of a character walking in all four directions. The first row contains the frames for walking south, the second row contains frames for walking west, and so forth.

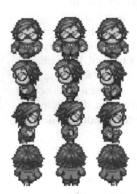

Figure 4-3. *The spritesheet for the main character*

In the layout, set the active layer to Main so that newly added objects are automatically placed on that layer. Create a new sprite, named Cleaner. In the image editor, right-click in the *Animation frames* window, move the mouse to *Import Frames*, select *From Sprite Strip*, and then select the image cleaner.png. This image contains three frames in each row and four images in each column, so in the *Import Sprite Strip*

---

[1]Thanks to Andrew Viola for providing the graphics for this and other player characters in the book.

window, enter 3 next to *Number of horizontal cells* and enter 4 next to *Number of vertical cells*. Check the *Replace entire existing animation* box (to remove the initial blank frame). Twelve frames should appear in the *Animation frames* window, as shown in Figure 4-4.

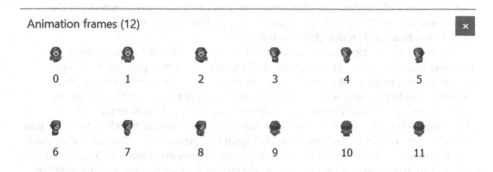

Figure 4-4. Animation frames for the main character, after initial import

However, not all of these frames will be used in each animation. In what follows, you will use this animation as a base to create four animations in total, one corresponding to each direction. First, in the *Animations* window, click *Default* (the name of the current animation), and in the *Properties* panel on the left, change *Speed* to 6, change *Loop* to Yes, and change *Ping-Pong* to Yes. Then, in the *Animations* window, right-click the *Default* animation, and in the context menu that appears, select *Duplicate*. Repeat this two more times so that you have a total of four animations appearing in the list. Then, right-click the first animation, select *Rename*, and enter South as the new name. Repeat this process for the other animations in the list, naming them West, East, and North, respectively. When you are finished, this window should appear, as shown on the left side of Figure 4-5. Next, select the animation named *South* in the list, and in the *Animation frames* window, click each frame that does *not* correspond to the character walking south (those initially numbered 3 through 11), and press the *Delete* key. When you are finished, this window should appear as shown on the right side of Figure 4-5. Right-click the *South* animation from the *Animations* window, and select *Preview* to see how it looks; feel free to adjust the speed if you want. Then repeat this process for the West, East, and North animations, deleting the frames not required within each of the animations. When you're finished, close the image editor windows.

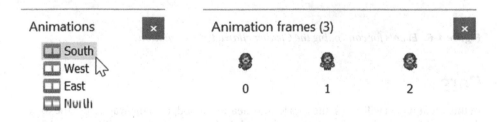

Figure 4-5. Animations list and animation frames for the South animation

In the layout area, change the Cleaner sprite property *Size* to 48,48 and position it in the center of the lower grass area. (Since *Snap to grid* is currently active and the desired size is not a multiple of 32, it is simpler to change these values in the *Properties* panel.) Add the behavior *8-Direction*, and change the properties *Max Speed* to 80 and *Set Angle* to No. (This stops the sprite image from being rotated in the direction it is moving; the animations will handle that effect.) Also add the behavior *Bound to Layout*. Finally, add the behavior *Fade*, and change *Active at start* to No.

Next, you will create some events that will change the Cleaner's animation to one of the four animations you just set up, depending on which key is pressed. First, add a *Keyboard* object to the project. In the event sheet, create a new event with condition *Keyboard - On Key Pressed*, with *Key* set to *Down Arrow*. In this event, add the action *Cleaner - Animations: Set Animation*, and in the parameters window, enter "South" (including the quotation marks; make sure that your capitalization matches the name you entered in the *Animations* window earlier). Repeat this process three times, creating three more events so that pressing the left arrow key corresponds to setting the West animation, pressing the right arrow key corresponds to setting the East animation, and pressing the up arrow key corresponds to setting the North animation. You should also set up your game so that the character's animation stops when the character is not moving. To do so, create a new event with the condition *Cleaner - 8-Direction: Is Moving*, and in the event sheet, right-click and invert the condition. Then add the action *Cleaner - Animation: Stop*. When you are finished with these events, your event sheet should appear as in Figure 4-6. Save and test your project, and verify that when you hold each of the arrow keys, the cleaner moves in the corresponding direction and features the correct animation, and when you let go of the arrow keys and the character comes to a stop, the animation should stop as well.

1	➡ Keyboard	On **Down arrow** pressed	🧹 Cleaner	Set animation to **"South"** (play from beginning)
				Add action
2	➡ Keyboard	On **Left arrow** pressed	🧹 Cleaner	Set animation to **"West"** (play from beginning)
				Add action
3	➡ Keyboard	On **Right arrow** pressed	🧹 Cleaner	Set animation to **"East"** (play from beginning)
				Add action
4	➡ Keyboard	On **Up arrow** pressed	🧹 Cleaner	Set animation to **"North"** (play from beginning)
				Add action
5	🧹 Cleaner	✖ 8Direction is moving	🧹 Cleaner	Stop animation
				Add action

Figure 4-6. Events for controlling the Cleaner character's animation

Cars

In this section, you will add some cars for the cleaner to dodge on the way across the road; the cars will vary in their appearance and speed. To begin, create a new sprite named Car. In the image editor main window, select any one of the car images that you downloaded in the beginning of the chapter. In the *Animations* list window, right-click *Default*, select *Rename*, and enter Car1 as the new name.[2] Right-click in this window again and select *Add animation*. Name this animation Car2, and add an image of a car with a different color. Add two more animations in this way, once again with different images; name them Car3 and Car4. When you are finished, close the image editor windows.

In the layout, add the *Bullet* behavior to the *Car* object, and change *Speed* to 200. Create three more instances of the *Car* object, and place one in each lane of the road area. In the first and third lanes, position the cars on the left side. In the second and fourth lanes, position the cars on the right side, and set their *Angle* to 180 (so that they are facing to the left).

Select the *Car* object in the first lane. In the *Properties* panel, near the bottom of the list (you may need to scroll down), find the property called *Initial animation*. Next to this property, you will see the word *Default*, which means that the sprite will initially display the animation named *Default* (or, if there is no animation with that name, it will display the first animation in the list). Change the text to Car1. Then, for the *Car* in the second lane, change the *Initial animation* property to Car2. Similarly, change the initial animations of the cars in the third and fourth lanes to Car3 and Car4. When you are finished, your layout should appear similar to Figure 4-7 (except the colors of your cars may be different). If you save and test the game, the cars should move in straight lines, eventually moving past the edges of the screen.

Figure 4-7. The layout with cars added

Next, there should appear to be a continuous stream of cars traveling along the road. One way to accomplish this would be to add the *Wrap* behavior to the Car object, but that will in fact be too limiting for our purposes. We want to add some variation to

---

[2]Even if you are using only a single image for a sprite, it is treated as an animation with just one frame (and therefore, properties such as Speed and Loop will have no effect on how it is displayed).

the gameplay by changing the properties of each Car object after it leaves the screen and before it reappears on the other side. Using the *Wrap* behavior and a fixed speed would result in behavior that is too predictable, and once the user sees the pattern in the car movements, it would make the game easier (possibly too easy). It also breaks the sense of immersion, since real car drivers would not act so predictably. Therefore, in this section, you will create some events that produce an effect similar to the *Wrap* behavior and, at the same time, allow you to modify the properties of a car (such as its speed) once it goes past the edges of the screen. To accomplish this, you will next add a new sprite, positioned off-screen, that will serve as a trigger for these actions.

Create a sprite named CarWarp. The image is irrelevant since the object stays off-screen, so you can use the paint tools (like the fill bucket or paintbrush) to color in the provided blank image however you want. When you are done, close the image editor windows, and change the size of *CarWarp* to 32, 32. Create three more copies of this object, and position them in the margins of the layout, one in the path of each car (at the opposite end from where they start), at least one car length beyond the edge. There needs to be enough distance so that the Car objects will not collide with the CarWarp objects until the cars are completely past the edges of the layout. The positioning should be similar to Figure 4-8.

Figure 4-8. *The CarWarp objects and their position relative to the Car objects*

In the event sheet, create a new event with the condition *Car - Collisions: On Collision With Another Object*, and select the *CarWarp* object. The first action will re-create the warplike behavior and place the car past the edge on the opposite side of the screen. Unfortunately, there is no "move backward" action listed, but you can still make it work with the actions available. For this event, add the action *Car - Size & Position: Move forward*, and set *Distance* to -900 (if a distance is negative, then the object will move backward). Then, in the same event, add the action *Car - Bullet: Set Speed*, and set the speed to random(200, 400), which will select a random number in that range for the new speed. When you are finished, the events should appear as in Figure 4-9. Test your game to verify that the cars do in fact continue to reappear on the other side of the screen, traveling at different speeds each time.

Figure 4-9. *An event for a wraplike behavior*

Displaying Messages with Text Objects

Next, you will set up win and lose conditions and display this information on the screen using a new type of object: a Text object. Text objects can display any message you choose and can change their contents while the game is running, so they are more flexible than using sprites that contain images of words (which you have used in the games from the previous two chapters). To begin, right-click in the layout area, select *Insert new object*, and click *Text* once (and not Text box) from the available choices; for the name, enter TextGameOver, and click the *Insert* button. Once on the layout, you will be changing many properties of the TextGameOver object. First, change *Layer* to UI, change *Size* to 640, 64, and position it over the bottom half of the Stone object. To make the displayed text easier to see, in the *Properties* panel, locate the property named Font, and double-click the name of the font next to it. A dialog window will appear, listing the names and variations of all the fonts installed on your computer, as shown in Figure 4-10. Here, keep the default *Font* set to Arial, change *Font* style to Bold, change *Size*[3] to 28, and click the *OK* button. Next, click the *Horizontal alignment* property, and from the drop-down menu that appears on the right, select *Center*. Repeat this process with the *Vertical alignment* property, changing its value to *Center* as well. Now you should see that the text is nicely centered in its box. If you want, you can also click the *Color* property, and in the drop-down menu that appears on the right, you can select from many different colors. If you choose to change the color, be sure to pick a color that can be easily seen against the background color. Finally, set *Initial Visibility* to Invisible. When you are finished, the top part of your layout should appear similar to Figure 4-11.

---

[3]If you change the size to a different value and the text suddenly disappears in the layout area, this is usually because the font size is too large or there is too much text to be displayed in the given area. This problem can be remedied by either choosing a smaller font size or making the Text object larger.

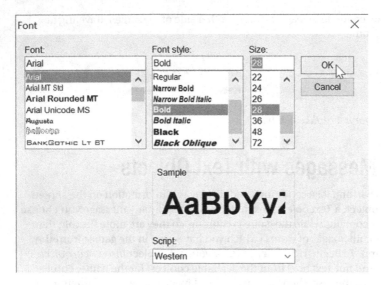

Figure 4-10. *Font selection window for the Text object*

Figure 4-11. *Displaying customized text on the layout*

The lose condition, as you may have guessed, will be when a car collides with the cleaner. The win condition will be when the cleaner reaches a trash can on the other side of the road, which you will now set up. Add a new sprite, named TrashCan, using the image trashcan.png. Set its *Layer* property to Main. Change its size to 38,48, and position it in the center of the topmost Grass background.

Next, you will set up the events for winning and losing the game, each of which will cause a different message to appear in the Text object. When the game is over, you will also make the cleaner fade out and freeze the cleaner in place (it shouldn't move while it is fading) by disabling user input for the cleaner.

In the event sheet, create a new event with the condition *Cleaner - Collisions: On Collision With Another Object*, and select the *TrashCan* object. Then, add the following actions to this event:

- Add *TextGameOver - Appearance: Set Visible*, and set *Visibility* to Visible.

- Add *TextGameOver - Text: Set Text*, and next to *Text*, type "You Win" (including the quotation marks).

- Add *Cleaner - Fade: Start Fade*.

- Add *Cleaner - 8-Direction: Set Enabled*, and set *State* to Disabled.

When you are finished, this event will appear as shown in Figure 4-12. Save and test your project to make sure the *You Win* message appears as expected when the Cleaner touches the trash can.

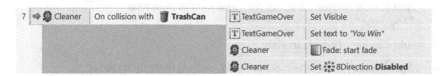

Figure 4-12. Event for the win condition

It is particularly important to understand the use of the quotation marks in the *Set Text* action. Quotation marks are used to specify a literal expression, in a similar way to how they are used in everyday language. For example, if you were asked to write down the name of this book, you would write *Game Development with Construct 2*. However, if you were asked to write down "the name of this book", the quotation marks indicate that you should repeat those words exactly; you would write *the name of this book*. The same situation arises when using the *Set Text* action: using quotation marks will cause that exact text to appear; if no quotation marks are used, the Construct game engine will assume that whatever you entered is an object property or a variable and will try to determine its value. If there is no property or variable, Construct will display a pop-up message that either says *Unknown expression* or *Syntax error*, as shown in Figure 4-13.

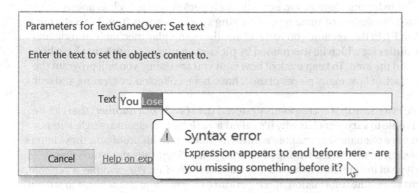

Figure 4-13. What could happen when a parameter is mistyped

Next, you will add the event corresponding to the lose condition for the game. In the event sheet, create a new event with the condition *Car - Collisions: On Collision With Another Object*, and select the *Cleaner* object. Then, add the following actions to this event:

- Add *TextGameOver - Appearance: Set Visible*, and set *Visibility* to `Visible`.

- Add *TextGameOver - Text: Set Text*, and next to *Text*, type `"You Lose"`.

- Add *Cleaner - Fade: Start Fade*.

- Add *Cleaner - 8-Direction: Set Enabled*, and set *State* to `Disabled`.

This event should appear as shown in Figure 4-14. Save and test your project to verify that the *You Lose* message appears as expected.

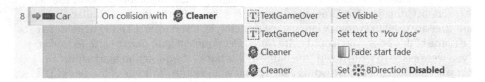

Figure 4-14. *Event for the lose condition*

Keeping Score with Global Variables

Players are used to having some way to evaluate their performance, such as points earned, time to completion, or some type of ranking system (such as from 1 to 3 stars or a grade from A to F). In this section, you will add another gameplay mechanic: the cleaner will fulfill the duties for which he was named by picking up pieces of trash that have been scattered around the area. To keep track of how well you are doing, you will program the game to keep track of how many pieces of trash have been collected by creating and using a new variable.

A variable is a name that corresponds to stored data (such as a number) that can be changed (or is able to vary, which is why it's called a *variable*). In algebra, single letters such as x and y are often used as variable names; in different math problems, these letters may have different values. When writing programs, you will typically use words that describe the type of information being stored to avoid confusion. For example, a variable named t might store time information or temperature information; it is difficult to tell out of context. When creating programs, use *time* or *temp* as the variable name, instead of t, to avoid ambiguity or confusion.

In the previous projects, you already encountered many variables, such as position, angle, size, and so forth. These correspond to values associated with sprites that you are able to change. Because each instance of a sprite object contains its own set of these variables, whose values can be set independently from the variables belonging to other objects, these are called *instance variables*. In this chapter, you are going to create a different type of variable, called a *global variable*, which is not associated to any particular instance. In Construct, a global variable is a variable defined in the event sheet, and it can easily be accessed, modified, and used by all the objects or events in the game.

To begin, in the event sheet, right-click in the margin area and select *Add global variable* from the menu that appears. A window titled *New global variable* will appear, where you can configure its properties. Next to *Name*, type Score. Leave *Type* set to Number, and leave *Initial Value* set to 0. Next to *Description*, type number of pieces of trash collected. Although entering a description of a variable is optional and has no effect on the game itself, it is a good habit to develop and will help you remember what the purpose of the variable is in the future. When you are finished, click the *OK* button.

Next, you will set up a text object that displays the value of the Score variable. In the layout, create a new Text object named TextScore. Change its properties (*Layer, Size, Font, Horizontal Alignment, Vertical Alignment,* and *Color*) to the same values that you used for the TextGameOver object in the previous section. Also, for the *Text* property, enter Trash Collected: 0. Reposition this object so that it is aligned with the top half of the Stone object. When you are finished, this area should appear as shown in Figure 4-15.

Figure 4-15. *The user interface area with more text added*

Next, you will set up objects and events that affect and display the score. In the layout, create a new sprite called Trash, using the image trash.png. Make sure that its *Layer* property is set to Main, and change its size to 38,38. Duplicate this object nine times (for a total of ten trash objects), reposition these objects so that they are appear scattered around the grass and road areas, and rotate each by different amounts so that there is some variation in their appearance.

Since the Trash objects were the most recent additions to the Main layer, they will appear to be above the Car objects. It would look strange in the game if the cars were to drive underneath pieces of trash. To address this issue, you need to change the z-order of the Trash objects, which controls the order in which the graphics are rendered on each layer. Since you want the trash to appear as though it is underneath the cars (and the cleaner), they need to be moved to the bottom of the layer. To accomplish this, click *Trash* in the *Objects* panel in the lower-right region of the Construct window so that all instances of Trash objects are selected at the same time. Next, right-click any of the *Trash* instances in the layout, and from the menu that pops up, select *Z-Order* and then *Send to Bottom of Layer.* Since all instances were selected, this change will be applied to each of them, and in the game they will appear under the cars. Notice that the trash was not moved underneath the Grass or Road objects; that is because the background objects are on a completely separate layer (which illustrates another advantage to keeping game objects organized with layers).

Next, you need to add an event that enables the cleaner to collect the trash objects, updates the Score variable, and displays the updated information in the Text object. In the event sheet, create a new event with the condition *Cleaner - Collision: On Collision With*, and select the *Trash* object. Add the action *Trash - Misc: Destroy*. Also add the action *System - Global and Local Variables: Add to*, and in the parameters window, leave *Variable* set to Score and *Value* set to 1. Finally, add the action *TextScore - Text: Set Text*, and enter the text "Trash Collected: " & Score. Here, the text that is being displayed is a combination of a literal expression (which appears between the quotation marks) and a variable (Score), which appears without quotation marks and therefore will be replaced by its value when the game is running. The ampersand character (&) is used to combine text with variables or other expressions. When you are finished, this event should appear as shown in Figure 4-16. Save and test your project to check that the cleaner can in fact collect the trash and that the score increases and is displayed correctly.

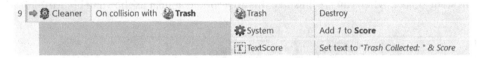

Figure 4-16. *An event for increasing and displaying the player's score*

Congratulations! You have now finished implementing the core mechanics of the Cleanup Challenge game.

Side Quests

In this optional section, you will learn how to add some randomization to your game to improve both the variation of graphics and the gameplay, followed by some suggested additional features for you to ponder.

Randomization

First, you will add some randomization to the initial positions of the Trash objects. For the trash to appear near the road and not too close to the edges of the screen, the *x* coordinate should be somewhere between 40 and 600, and the *y* coordinate should be somewhere between 256 and 512. With this in mind, create a new event with the condition *System - Start & End: On Start of Layout* and the *action Trash - Size & Position: Set Position*. For the *x* value, enter random(40, 600), and for the *y* value, enter random(256, 512). When finished, the event should appear as in the bottom part of Figure 4-17. Save and run your program; click the Refresh button in your web browser to restart the game, and you should see that each time the game loads, the trash pieces appear in different locations.

6	➡️◾Car	On collision with CW **CarWarp**	◾Car	Move forward -900 pixels
			◾Car	Set 🗲 Bullet speed to *random(200, 400)*
			◾Car	Set animation to **"Car"** & **choose(1,2,3,4)** (play from beginning)
10	➡️⚙️System	On start of layout	🗑️Trash	Set position to *(random(40, 600), random(256, 512))*

Figure 4-17. *Events involving randomization*

Next, you will add some randomization to the car graphics. As it stands, the same color car will continue to reappear in each lane. It is possible to randomly select among the graphics stored in the car object, thanks to the naming convention you used when setting up the animations earlier. Remember that the names of the car animations are Car1, Car2, Car3, and Car4. The idea will be to randomly choose one of the numbers, either 1, 2, 3, or 4, and combine that number with the text *Car* to get the name of the animation to set. The random selection will be made with a function named choose, explained next. Locate the event with the condition that a Car object collides with a CarWarp object. Add another action to this event: *Car - Animations: Set Animation*. Set the value of *Animation* to "Car" & choose(1,2,3,4). When finished, the event should appear as in the top part of Figure 4-17. Save and test the game, and verify that the image of each car randomly changes each time it reappears (although it is possible that the same image could be randomly selected multiple times in a row).

The choose function provides a way to randomly select among a given set of values (numbers or text); the inputs of the function represent the different possible choices, one of which will be randomly selected each time the action occurs. Alternatively, instead of "Car" & choose(1, 2, 3, 4), you could instead enter choose("Car1", "Car2", "Car3", "Car4"), which will have the same effect. One of the great things about computer programming is that there are usually many ways to approach and solve a problem!

You may have been surprised that we didn't recommend that you use the function random(1, 4) to create a random number in this case. This is because the random function actually returns a random decimal value, which would then need to be rounded to a whole number in order to correspond to an actual animation name (since there are no animations named Car2.71828, for example). Thus, the expression round(random(1, 4)) produces a result closer to what is actually desired. However, this approach is still not precisely correct because not all numbers will appear equally likely; in this interval, it is more likely that a number will be closer to 2 or 3 than it will be to 1 or 4. (However, this problem can also be fixed. Can you see how?) Because of these unexpected complexities, the choose function is an easier approach for this particular situation.

On Your Own

Now is a good time to find someone to test your game to get a fresh perspective on the difficulty level of your game. If it is too difficult, you could reduce the speed of the cars or increase the speed of the player. You could add even more paper to collect, which will help the game last longer.

You could display the total time the player has been playing the game. Construct has a predefined variable called time that is automatically updated to contain the amount of time that has passed since the game started. You would need to create a new Text object to display this information. If so, you may want to use the condition *Player - Size & Position: Is On Screen* so that the timer appears to stop once the cleaner disappears (which signals the end of the game), and when creating the action for setting the displayed text, use the round function to round the time variable to the nearest second (otherwise, a ludicrous number of decimal places will appear on the screen).

You could add some fading effects by adding the *Fade* behavior to various objects. For example, you could make the paper fade out when it is collected, replacing the *Trash - Destroy* action with a *Trash - Start Fade* action. You could make the TextGameOver object fade in when the game is over.

Summary

In this chapter, you learned about some new object types: *TiledBackground* and *Text*. You created a sprite that contained multiple animations and events that switched between these animations as needed. You also learned how to use variables to keep track of changing values and how to display these values on the screen using the Text object.

In the next chapter, you will learn how to add additional polish to your previous games, in the form of menu screens, audio (sound effects and background music), and alternative sources of input.

CHAPTER 5

■ ■ ■

Adding Polish to Your Game

Whenever you learn new techniques in game development, it is good practice to revisit earlier game projects looking for opportunities to apply your newfound knowledge. Perhaps there are additional gameplay mechanics or features you could implement or improved graphics or effects to add. In this chapter, you will begin by revisiting your first game project, Starfish Collector, and add an image-based animation and text that displays your progress. Then, you will learn some new general techniques and features that can be used in all your past and future game projects: adding buttons to the user interface, adding audio (sound effects and background music), adding menu systems (such as a start menu and an instructions screen), and adding alternative control schemes. Figure 5-1 illustrates some of these additions.

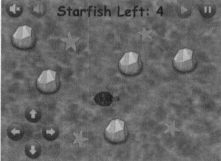

Figure 5-1. Menu for Starfish Collector (left) and improved user interface (right)

To begin, open the .capx file from the Starfish Collector project, and download the zip file containing the additional assets from the book web site for this chapter. Some of these new files include animation frames for the turtle, images of various buttons (some with text and some with graphics), and audio files.

© Lee Stemkoski and Evan Leider 2017
L. Stemkoski and E. Leider, *Game Development with Construct 2*,
DOI 10.1007/978-1-4842-2784-8_5

Adding Animation and Text

First, you will change the single image currently used for the turtle into an image-based animation. As it turns out, the image you used previously for the Turtle sprite is actually the first frame of an animation. Unlike previous animations, however, the images are not contained within a single sprite sheet; they are in separate files. In the object panel, right-click the *Turtle* object and select *Edit animations* to open the image editor windows. In the *Animation frames* window, right-click and select *Import Frames...* and then select *From Files*. From the *Open* window, you can select multiple images at once, as follows: in this window, click the image file turtle-2.png, then hold down the *Ctrl* key, and continue to click the remaining image files in sequence (from turtle-3.png through turtle-6.png). In total, five files should appear selected in this window, and all the file names will appear in the text box at the bottom of this window, as shown in Figure 5-2. Then click the *Open* button, and you should see a total of six images in the *Animation frames* window. Set the *Animation* property *Speed* to 12 and *Loop* to Yes and then close the image editor windows.

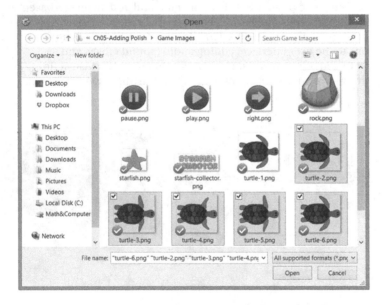

Figure 5-2. *Selecting multiple image files for an animation*

Next, you need to create a pair of events to pause the animation from playing when the turtle stops moving and to resume the animation when the turtle begins moving. Sprites have some animation-related actions that can be used to start and stop animations, but these have the unfortunate effect of changing the current animation frame if not used properly, so instead you will change the animation speed to pause and resume it. Create a new event with the condition *Turtle - 8-Direction: Is moving*, invert the condition, add the action *Turtle - Animation: Set Speed*, and set *Speed* to 0. Add

66

another event with the condition *Turtle - 8-Direction: Is moving*, add the action *Turtle - Animation: Set Speed*, and set *Speed* to 12. When finished, your events should appear as in Figure 5-3. Save your project and run the layout to verify that the turtle's animation appears as described earlier.

Figure 5-3. *Events to pause and resume the Turtle animation*

Next, you will create a Text object for the user interface that displays the number of starfish remaining for the player to collect. Create a new Text object named TextStarfish. Change the *Layer* property to UI, set the alignment properties so that the text is centered, and change *Text* to Starfish Left: N (where you should replace N with however many starfish you have at the beginning of your game). To more closely align with the visual theme of this game, change Font to Comic Sans MS, change the font *Style* to Bold, and change the font *Size* to 36. Increase the size of the Text object so that all the text appears on a single line. Change the font color to a dark blue. Position the Text object in the center near the top of the layout; it should appear as in Figure 5-4.

Figure 5-4. *Adding a text display to the layout*

You don't need to create a variable to keep track of how many starfish are remaining since this information is stored in Starfish.Count. You do, however, need an event to update the text itself; the text needs to be set to "Starfish Left: " & Starfish.Count. However, the placement of this action requires careful consideration. In the past, you would update a Text object immediately after the associated variable was changed; these actions would be part of the same event. In this case, the timing of certain actions can cause unexpected results because the action that destroys a sprite does not actually remove the object from the game until after the event. (This can be useful in certain cases, such as having an asteroid that was just destroyed spawn an explosion in the next action.) In the current situation, this means the value of Starfish.Count does not change until later, so updating the text must take place in a later event. To implement this, create a new event with the condition *System - Every tick*, add the action *TextStarfish - Text: Set Text*, and enter "Starfish Left: " & Starfish.Count. The completed event should appear as in Figure 5-5. Save your project and run the layout to verify that the text display changes as expected.

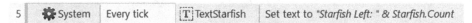

Figure 5-5. *Event for updating the text display*

Mouse Input and Buttons

Next, you will create some buttons that can be used to pause and resume the game. The buttons will be activated by clicking them with the mouse. To provide visual feedback to the player, buttons will appear slightly transparent when pressing a button would have no effect (such as pressing the pause button while the game is already paused). To begin, create a new Sprite[1] object named ButtonPause, using the image pause.png. Create another Sprite object named ButtonResume, using the image play.png, and set its *Opacity* to 50. Place these two buttons in the upper-right corner of the layout, where, ideally, they will not obstruct any of the game objects (starfish or rocks), as shown in Figure 5-6. To get mouse input, a *Mouse* object must be added to the project (similar to the *Keyboard* object). Right-click in the layout area, and in the *Add New Object* window select *Mouse*.

Figure 5-6. *Placement of pause and resume buttons*

Pausing the game can be accomplished by setting one of the system properties called the *time scale*, which controls the rate at which time is processed by the Construct game engine. The default time scale value is 1. Setting it to 2 would cause animations to display twice as quickly, objects to move twice as fast, and so on. Setting the time scale to 0.5 would cause these features to occur at half-speed. Setting it to 0 freezes these features, which effectively pauses the game, as nothing will occur in the game world (although Construct will still respond to input such as key presses and mouse clicks). First, you

---

[1]You may have noticed that there is a Button object you aren't using. The reason is that using sprites gives you more flexibility with images and appearance than the Button object, and it is simple to create the same buttonlike functionality with events.

will set up the pause feature. Create a new event with the condition *Mouse - On object clicked*, and select the *ButtonPause* object. The parameter *Mouse button* lets you select a particular mouse button (left, middle, or right), while *Click type* lets you specify whether the user needs to single-click or double-click; in general, you will leave these values set to their defaults (left mouse button and click). You also have the option to select which mouse button. Add the following three actions:

- Add *System - Set time scale*, and enter 0.

- Add *ButtonPause - Set opacity*, and enter 50.

- Add *ButtonResume - Set opacity*, and enter 100.

Next, you will set up the resume feature; the event is quite similar. Once again, create a new event with the condition *Mouse - On object clicked*, and select the *ButtonResume* object. Add the same three actions as before, but with different parameter values: the time scale should be set to 1, the ButtonPause *Opacity* should be set to 100, and the ButtonResume *Opacity* should be set to 50. When finished, these events should appear as in Figure 5-7. Save your project and run the layout to verify that the pause and resume buttons work as expected (you should see the starfish stop and start moving).

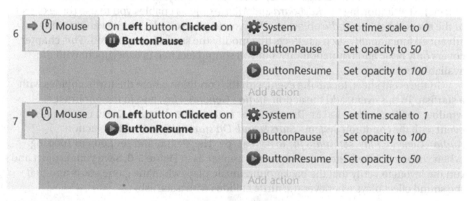

Figure 5-7. Events for pausing and resuming the game

Audio

Audio is an important component that you should add to each game. Background music or ambient sounds (such as rushing water or city traffic) can be effective at setting the tone or mood of the game, while sound effects can provide another form of player feedback; all these aspects work together to increase the sense of immersion and provide a more complete and engaging player experience.

The Construct game engine classifies audio into two categories: sounds and music. Sounds are downloaded completely before playing and typically consist of short audio files used for sound effects, such as laser blasts or explosions. Music is not downloaded before playing; rather, it is *streamed*, or played while being downloaded. Large audio files, such as background music or ambient sounds, typically fall into this category.

Construct supports many different audio file formats, but different web browsers and operating systems require different formats. When sounds are imported into Construct, the software will attempt to convert the files into multiple formats when possible. For cross-platform compatibility, you may want to consider the Waveform audio format (indicated by the .wav extension) for sound files and the Ogg Vorbis audio format (indicated by the .ogg extension) for music files. In particular, the popular MP3 file format may not play correctly in many browsers. However, there are many free programs and online services that can be used to convert audio files to a format of your choice; you can find them easily with an Internet search.

In the game Starfish Collector, you will add two audio elements: some background music and a sound effect of a water drop that will play every time a starfish is collected. To begin, in the *Projects* panel in the upper-right area of the Construct window, right-click the *Sounds* folder, select the option *Import Sounds* from the pop-up menu that appears, and select the file Water_Drop.wav from the assets you downloaded at the beginning of the chapter. Then a window titled *Import audio files* will appear; click the *Import* button, and after the text *Successfully imported* appears, click the *OK* button. Next, right-click the *Music* folder, select the option *Import Music*, and follow the same process as earlier to import the file Master_of_the_Feast.ogg.[2]

Next, in the layout area, right-click, select *Add new object,* and then select the *Audio* object. Just as importing the *Keyboard* and *Mouse* objects enables you to use these objects in the event sheet, the *Audio* object enables you to play sounds, and it even contains advanced functionality such as effects that modify the sound being played. This chapter covers only basic audio functionality, but you should feel free to experiment with the available features.

In the event sheet, locate the event with the condition where the turtle collides with a starfish. To this event, add the action *Audio - General: Play*, and in the parameters window, set *Audio file* to Water_Drop, and set *Loop* to not looping. Next, create a new event with the condition *System - Start & End: On start of layout*, add the action *Audio - General: Play*, set *Audio file* to Master_of_the_Feast, and set *Loop* to looping. When you are finished, these events should appear as in Figure 5-8. Save your project and run the layout to verify that the background music plays when the game starts and that the sound effect plays whenever the turtle collides with a starfish. ˙

Figure 5-8. *Events for playing audio files*

---

[2]The soundtrack *Master of the Feast* was composed by Kevin MacLeod and is licensed under the Creative Commons: By Attribution 3.0 License. This, and many other high-quality soundtracks, can be downloaded from incompetech.com.

Finally, you will add some buttons onto the layout that enable the player to mute or unmute the sounds being played. To begin, create two new sprites: one named ButtonMute with the image audio-off.png and the other named ButtonUnmute with the image audio-on.png and *Opacity* set to 50. Position them in the top-left corner of the layout, symmetrically opposite from the pause and resume buttons you created earlier, as shown in Figure 5-9.

Figure 5-9. Adding audio buttons to the layout (whole set)

In the event sheet, create a new event with the condition *Mouse - On object clicked*, and set *Object clicked* to ButtonMute. Add the following three actions:

- Add *Audio - General: Set silent*, and change *Mode* to silent.
- Add *ButtonMute - Set opacity*, and enter 50.
- Add *ButtonUnmute - Set opacity*, and enter 100.

The process for setting up the unmute button is similar. Once again, create a new event with the condition *Mouse - On object clicked*, and select the *ButtonUnmute* object. Add the same three actions as before, but with different parameter values: the silent mode should be set to not silent, the ButtonMute opacity should be set to 100, and the ButtonUnmute opacity should be set to 50. When finished, these events should appear as in Figure 5-10. Save your project and run the layout to verify that these new buttons work as expected.

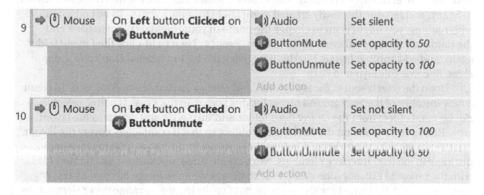

Figure 5-10. Events for muting audio playback

Menus

Menu screens are fundamental in video game development to create a complete user experience. When running game software, there should be a main menu or "splash screen" that gives the player time to prepare before jumping into the game. Additional screens are often used to display the backstory, user controls, in-game items, goals and objects, and credits for the designers, artists, and programmers who developed the game. In this section, you will add a main menu and an instructions screen, as shown in Figure 5-11. This requires the creation of new layouts and event sheets, buttons to navigate between the layouts, and events with actions to switch between layouts when a button is clicked.

Figure 5-11. *Start menu (left) and instructions screen (right)*

To begin, in the *Projects* panel in the upper-right region of the Construct window, right-click the Layouts folder, and select *Add layout* from the menu that appears. A window will appear asking if you want to create a new event sheet for this layout. While not strictly necessary (different layouts can use the same event sheets), it is simpler to organize your code and keep game events and menu events separate. Click *Add event sheet*, and then you will see that a new layout has appeared in the *Layouts* folder; in addition, a new event sheet has appeared in the *Event sheets* folder. Rename the newly created layout to Start, and rename the newly created event sheet to Menu Events. To be consistent with naming, you might want to change the name of your original layout to Game and the name of your original event sheet to Game Events. Then right-click the *Layout* folder again, and add another layout, but this time, click the button labeled *Don't add event sheet*. Rename this layout to Help.

Open the Start layout in the layout area, and change *Layout Size* to 800, 600. To create a new instance of the Background object for this layout, in the *Projects* panel, select the *Background* object from the *Object types* folder and then click and drag it to the layout area. Resize and reposition the Background object so that it completely covers the layout. Also, set its *Opacity* to 50; this will reduce the contrast in the image, making it easier to distinguish the user interface elements. Next, create three new sprites: one named Title with the image title.png, one named ButtonStart with the image button-start.png, and one named ButtonHelp with the image button-help.png. Arrange these elements as shown on the left side of Figure 5-11.

Next, open the Help layout in the layout area, and change the layout size and add the background as you did for the Start layout previously. Click in the margins of the layout area so that the *Properties* panel displays layout properties, and set *Event sheet* to Menu Events. Also, create new instances of the *Title* and *ButtonStart* objects by dragging them onto the layout from the *Projects* panel. Create a new sprite named ButtonBack with the image button-back.png. Next, create a new Text object named TextInstructions, with *Text* set to Use the arrow keys to move the turtle. To keep with the visual theme of the game, change the font to a larger, bold Comic Sans, and set the color to a dark blue. When you are happy with the style, create another instance of the Text object, and change the text of this new object to read Collect all the starfish to win the game. Arrange these elements as shown on the right side of Figure 5-11.

Finally, you need to create events that enable the user to navigate through the menus. Double-click the *Menu Events* event sheet in the project panel to open it in the editor, add a new event with condition *Mouse - On object clicked*, and select the *ButtonStart* object. Add the action *System - General: Go to layout*, and select the layout named *Game*. Repeat this process to create two more events: clicking the ButtonHelp object should go to the layout named Help, and clicking the ButtonBack object should go to the layout named Start. When you are finished, these events should appear as shown in Figure 5-12. In the project properties, set First layout to Start. Then, save your project, and while the *Start* menu is displayed in the layout area,[3] run the layout and test that the buttons work as expected, allowing you to navigate between the different screens.

1	➡ Mouse	On **Left** button **Clicked** on ▬ **ButtonStart**	⚙ System	Go to **Game**
			Add action	
2	➡ Mouse	On **Left** button **Clicked** on ▬ **ButtonHelp**	⚙ System	Go to **Help**
			Add action	
3	➡ Mouse	On **Left** button **Clicked** on ▬ **ButtonBack**	⚙ System	Go to **Start**
			Add action	

Figure 5-12. Events for navigating between menu and game screens

Alternative Controls

Many game enthusiasts have their own preferred way to interact with a game; some prefer keyboard and mouse controls, while others prefer gamepad controllers, and still others enjoy touchscreen-style games. In this section, you will learn how to implement each of these features.

---

[3]Although you set the *First layout* property to be the Start menu, this setting applies only after the game has been exported. When testing your game using the *Run layout* button, Construct will always load the current (or most recently) displayed layout in the layout area.

Changing Default Controls

In the Starfish Collector game, the default controls are the arrow keys. If you want, you can disable the default key setup and use other keys to trigger the *8-Direction* actions. Here, you will configure the W/A/S/D keys[4] to take the place of the up/left/down/right arrow keys, a popular setup with many gamers. To begin, add a Keyboard object to the project. Then select the *Turtle* object, and in the *Properties* panel, underneath the *8-Direction* group, change *Default controls* to No. Next, in the Game Events event sheet, create a new event with the condition *Keyboard - Key is Down*, set *Key* to W, add the action *Turtle - 8-Direction: Simulate Control*, and select *Up* from the list. Create additional similar events for the remaining keys and associated controls. When you are finished, these events should appear as in Figure 5-13. Test your game to make sure that this new control setup works.

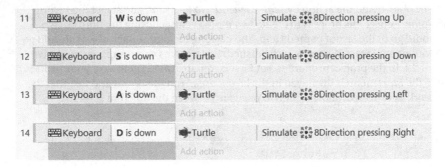

Figure 5-13. *Events for changing the 8-Direction controls*

Gamepad Controllers

Another option for controlling your characters is to use a gamepad controller, such as the Xbox 360 or the Logitech F310 gamepads, as shown in Figure 5-14. Construct 2 uses web browsers to run your game, and many of these (such as Google Chrome and Mozilla Firefox) automatically support gamepad input without any special configuration required. To add gamepad support to your game, right-click in the layout area, select *Insert new object*, and choose the *Gamepad* object. Then, in the event sheet, you will have access to a variety of gamepad-related conditions that can, for example, determine whether gamepads are connected or whether buttons were just pressed or are being held down (similar to the conditions provided by the Keyboard object).

---

[4]While using the W/A/S/D keys for directional movement is a standard practice on QWERTY-style keyboards, it is important to remember that not all keyboards have the same arrangement of keys. For example, the AZERTY-style keyboard positions the W key in a different location, making W/A/S/D controls counterintuitive. When developing for an international audience, this should be taken into consideration; a different key selection (such as E/S/D/F) is more globally accessible.

Figure 5-14. *Xbox (left) and Logitech (right) gamepad controllers*

One possibility is to use the D-pad to control the turtle. The events for this are straightforward: there is a Gamepad object condition named *Is button down*, and in the parameters window, you would leave *Gamepad* set to 0 (this refers to the first gamepad connected) and set *Button* to one of the buttons listed. The associated action would be *Turtle - 8-Direction: Simulate control*, as described in the previous section. However, in this section, you will instead use the analog joysticks on the gamepad to control the turtle. This is often a preferable setup because it gives the player fine-grained control over their character's movement. Any direction can be selected, and the speed of the character can be dependent on how far from the center the joystick is pressed (pressing the joystick all the way to the edge results in full speed).

However, analog joystick controls are slightly more complex to set up than button press controls. Each joystick measures how much the player is pressing in along each of the coordinate directions: the *x*-axis (horizontal) and the *y*-axis (vertical). These inputs are represented as percentages, which can then be used to set the velocity in the X and Y directions (called the *Vector X* and *Vector Y* properties in Construct). To get these values, you use a function belonging to the Gamepad object called Axis. Just as you use the dot notation to access a property belonging to an object (such as Turtle.Angle), you do the same for functions (although this situation occurs far less frequently), so this function is entered as Gamepad.Axis. This function has two inputs. The first input is the ID number of the gamepad (the first gamepad has ID 0, the second gamepad has ID 1, and so forth). The second input is a code for the joystick (left or right) to check on the controller and which axis (*x* or *y*) to check. The codes are as follows:

- 0 for left joystick, *x*-axis

- 1 for left joystick, *y*-axis

- 2 for right joystick, *x*-axis

- 3 for right joystick, *y*-axis

So, for example, if there is only one gamepad (the ID is 0) and the player is using the left joystick, you can determine the percentages to which they are being pressed with the expression Gamepad.Axis(0,0) for the *x*-axis and the expression Gamepad.Axis(0,1) for the *y*-axis. The values returned by these functions are numbers in the range from -100 to 100, so in practice you will divide them by 100 (to convert them to a fraction) and then multiply the result by the maximum possible speed of the object.

To enable gamepad controls for the turtle, create a new event with the condition *Gamepad - Gamepad: Has gamepads*. Add the action *Turtle - 8-Direction: Set vector X*, and enter `Gamepad.Axis(0,0) / 100 * 200`. Add another action similar to the first, which instead sets the *8-Direction* vector Y and replaces `Gamepad.Axis(0,0)` with `Gamepad.Axis(0,1)`. When you are finished, the events should appear as in Figure 5-15. Save your project, connect a gamepad controller to your computer, and run the layout. Once the game starts, you may have to press a button (any button will do) on your gamepad so that the web browser recognizes that a gamepad is connected. Test the joystick controls and verify that the turtle moves as expected.

Figure 5-15. *Events for gamepad controls (if gamepad is connected)*

If you want, you can add events to the Game Events and Menu Events event sheets that allow the player to use the gamepad to interact with the user interface buttons by pressing buttons on the gamepad. Some button associations are standard, such as pressing the gamepad start button to begin or pause the game and pressing the gamepad back button to return to the main menu. For less obvious button associations (for example, determining the gamepad button used to mute the audio), one standard practice is to place small images of gamepad buttons near or slightly overlapping the onscreen buttons, as shown in Figure 5-16. This is an optional feature that you can implement if you want; for your convenience, images of gamepad buttons have been included in the assets provided for this chapter.

Figure 5-16. *Using images to indicate gamepad controls for the user interface*

Touchscreen Input

The final alternative control scheme we will discuss in this chapter is the use of touchscreen controls. From a technical standpoint, implementing touchscreen controls is straightforward. Sprites containing images representing buttons or keyboard keys can be created, there is a Touch object that can be used to detect when objects are touched (similar to the conditions provided by the Mouse object), and you can use actions that simulate eight-direction controls. In addition, if you configure touch controls and run the game on a desktop computer, the mouse input will be used to emulate touch input, which is convenient for testing purposes. From a design standpoint, however, the layout of the touchscreen controls is quite complex. The images used need to be relatively large (64 pixels or greater) so that they are easy to press on devices with small screens. The main problem is the obstruction of the game world since the controls can overlap in-game objects, as shown in Figure 5-17. Making the controls partially transparent does not fully address this problem since the player's fingers will still be covering part of the screen. Solid objects could be placed under the user controls to prohibit game world objects from entering this area, but for games with large worlds that involve scrolling the window, this approach can also be complicated to implement. A thorough discussion of this topic at this time would take us too far afield, so it is left as a design issue for you to ponder in your future game projects.

Figure 5-17. *Game world objects obstructed by onscreen controls*

Summary

In this chapter, you learned many techniques for making your games more polished and professional: adding audio (sound effects and background music), creating additional layouts to serve as menus, and implementing alternative controls for your games. At this point, it would be excellent practice for you to revisit your game projects from earlier chapters (Space Rocks and Cleanup Challenge) and try your hand at implementing the features described in this chapter for those games. In the next chapter, you return to creating new games and creating your first side-scrolling game: Plane Dodger.

CHAPTER 6

■ ■ ■

Plane Dodger

In this chapter, you will create a game called Plane Dodger, an endless side-scrolling game, inspired by the modern smartphone game Flappy Bird, shown in Figure 6-1.

Figure 6-1. *The Plane Dodger game*

In Plane Dodger, the player controls a green plane (which we will simply refer to as "the plane"), whose goal is to collect stars that fly across the sky while dodging the red enemy planes that periodically appear. The stars and enemies appear at random heights in the sky, traveling across the screen from right to left. As time passes, the rate at which the enemies are spawned, as well as the speed of the enemies, will gradually increase, up

© Lee Stemkoski and Evan Leider 2017
L. Stemkoski and E. Leider, *Game Development with Construct 2*,
DOI 10.1007/978-1-4842-2784-8_6

to a certain limit. Since this game is endless, the player's goal is to collect as many stars as possible before crashing into another plane, which ends the game.

The player controls the plane by pressing a single key, which gives the plane a boost of speed upward. However, gravity is constantly pulling the plane downward. While it appears that the plane is flying from left to right, this is actually a visual illusion created by scrolling backgrounds (explained in the next section); in reality, the player's movement is restricted to a single column. The user interface is designed to be simple and minimal, so as to not distract the player from the fast-paced action of the game itself.

As usual, this game relies upon material from the previous chapters. In particular, you should be familiar with using the *Bullet* behavior, creating animations, creating (global) variables, and using *Text* objects. Topics such as creating menus, adding sound effects, and using alternative control systems are also useful for adding polish to your game, but since these features are not part of the core mechanics, they will appear in the "Side Quests" section (but that does not make them any less important). The new material introduced in this chapter includes topics such as adding scrolling backgrounds and parallax, using gravity, and creating difficulty ramps.

To begin, download the zip file containing the graphics for this chapter from the book web site. In the layout properties, set the layout *Name* to Main, and set *Size* to 600, 800. As you have in previous projects, set up three layers named Background, Main, and UI. In the project properties, change the window *Size* to 600, 800 (and change the *Name* and *Author* properties as you like).

Background Effects

In this section, you will set up an "infinite scrolling" effect with background images. Since image files cannot actually have infinite size, there is a technique used to create the illusion of an infinite background. The idea is to use a seamless image for the background so that when two copies of the image are placed side by side, the image appears continuous. Both images will scroll to the left at the same rate, and once one moves off-screen to the left, it will be shifted to the right, on the opposite side of the layout, as illustrated in Figure 6-2.

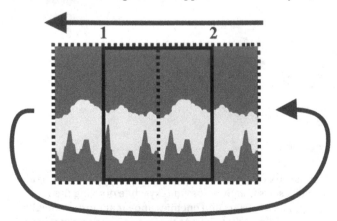

Figure 6-2. *Two copies of a background image (dashed border), moving past layout (solid border)*

First, you will create the background objects. In the layout properties, change *Active layer* to Background. Add a new sprite called Sky, using the image sky.png. Its size should be 600 by 800 pixels, the same size as the layout. This object needs to be precisely centered on the layout, so using the *Properties* panel, set the position to 300,400. Add the *Bullet* behavior, change *Speed* to 50, and change *Set angle* to No (because this object should not be rotated). Unfortunately, the angle of motion for the Bullet behavior cannot be set via the *Properties* panel, so this will be specified by an event instead. In the event sheet, create a new event with the condition *System - Start & End: On Start of Layout*, add the action *Sky - Bullet: Set angle of motion*, and set *Angle* to 180. Create a duplicate of the Sky instance, and in the *Properties* panel, set *Position* to 900,400 so that it is precisely aligned to the right of the previously created Sky object.

Next, you will create the event that causes a Sky object to shift to the right after it moves off-screen to the left. Create another event with the condition *Sky - Size & Position: Is on-screen*. When finished, right-click this condition in the event sheet and select *Invert* from the menu that appears. Right-click the condition again, select *Add another condition*, and create the condition *Sky - Size & Position: Compare X*, changing *Comparison* to less than and the X coordinate to 0. Finally, add the action *Sky - Size & Position: Move at angle*, with *Angle* set to 0 and *Distance* set to 2 * Sky.Width. When you are finished, these events should appear as in Figure 6-3. Save and test your project; the background image should appear to scroll forever, with no noticeable gap between the two images.

Figure 6-3. *Sky initialization and scrolling events*

Once the Sky sprites are configured, the next task is to set up the ground sprites, which follows the same procedure as before. Create a new sprite named Ground, using the image ground.png, which has size 600 by 80 pixels. Position it at 300,760. Add the *Bullet* behavior, change *Speed* to 200, and change *Set angle* to No. Duplicate the Ground object, and position the second one at 900,760. At this point, your layout should appear as in Figure 6-4; in particular, one of the Sky and one of the Ground objects will be positioned in the margin area, directly to the right of the layout, whose boundaries are indicated by a black border.

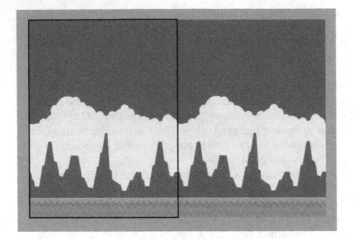

Figure 6-4. *The layout with Sky and Ground objects added*

In the event with the condition *On start of layout*, add a second action to set the Ground object's angle of motion to 180. Finally, create a new event that causes the Ground object to shift after it moves off-screen, just as you did previously for the Sky object. When completed, these events will appear as shown in Figure 6-5. Save and test to verify that the ground scrolls as expected. By setting the distant scenery (the clouds and mountains) to scroll more slowly than the nearby scenery (the ground), it creates an illusion of depth referred to as *parallax.*

Figure 6-5. *Ground initialization and scrolling events*

The Player's Plane

In this section, you will set up the plane that the player controls. In the layout, change *Active layer* to Main so that newly added objects are placed on this layer. Create a new sprite named Player. This object has an animation whose images are stored in separate files, so in the *Animation frames* window, right-click, select *Import Frames*, and then select *From Files*. Use the images planeGreen0.png, planeGreen1.png, and planeGreen2.png, and delete the initial blank animation frame. For the animation properties, set *Speed* to 8, *Loop* to Yes, and *Ping-pong* to Yes. Position the Player object at 100, 300. This plane will only move up and down; a boost of speed upward will be applied when the player taps a key, and the force of gravity will constantly be pulling the plane downward, both of which can be achieved using the Bullet behavior. Add the *Bullet* behavior to the Player object, and set *Speed* to 0, set *Gravity* to 600, and change *Set angle* to No, as the plane should always face to the right, regardless of whether it is moving up or down. Also, add the behavior Bound to Layout; this will stop the plane from moving off-screen.

Next, the plane needs to be stopped from passing through the ground. Your first instinct might be to add the *Solid* behavior to the Ground object, but unfortunately this won't work. By default, objects with the Bullet behavior pass through objects with the *Solid* behavior, unless the property *Bounce off solids* is set to Yes, in which case it bounces, which is also not the desired effect. (Presumably, the *Bullet* behavior was designed this way because in real life, projectiles either bounce or are destroyed upon impact with a wall.) Also, it is not enough to set the plane's speed to zero on collision with the ground because gravity will still apply and will eventually pull the plane through. The simplest solution is to disable the *Bullet* behavior when the plane hits the ground and then re-activate (or enable) the behavior when the player taps a key. When tapping a key, the plane will be moved upward, by setting the angle of motion to 270 degrees with a speed of 300. To begin, add a *Keyboard* object to your project. Then, in the event sheet, create a new event with the condition *Keyboard - Keyboard: On Key Pressed*, and select the *Space* key. Then, add the following three *Player - Bullet* actions to this event: add *Set angle of motion*, and set *Angle* to 270; add *Set speed*, and set *Speed* to 300; and add *Set Enabled*, and set *State* to Enabled. Create another event, with the condition *Player - Collisions: On Collision with another object*, and select *Ground*. To this event, add the action *Player - Bullet: Set Enabled*, and set *State* to Disabled. When finished, these events should appear as in Figure 6-6. Save and test your game; check that pressing the spacebar moves the plane upward and that the plane stops moving at the top of the screen and when it touches the ground.

Figure 6-6. Events for controlling player plane movement

Stars and Score

In this section, you will add stars to the game for the player to collect, a global variable to keep track of the number of stars collected, and a Text object to display this information. To begin, in the event sheet, right-click and add a global variable; set *Name* to Score, Type to Number, *Initial Value* to 0, and *Description* to Number of stars collected.

Next, in the layout, add a new sprite named Star with the image star.png. Add the *Bullet* behavior, with *Speed* set to 200 (to match the Ground speed) and *Set angle* set to No. Also, to draw the player's attention to these objects (so they aren't considered as part of the scenery), you will set up some value-based animations. Add the behavior *Rotate*, with *Speed* set to 30. Also add the *Sine* behavior, with *Movement* set to Size, *Period* set to 1, and *Magnitude* set to 8. While in the layout, add a Text object named TextScore. Set its *Text* property to 0, showing the initial score. Also, set its *Layer* to UI, make the text box large, set the alignment properties so that the text is centered, and change the font size so that it is easy to read (such as Arial, size 48). Optionally, to make the text appear to "pop out" of the screen, there is a simple way to create a drop shadow effect. Make sure that the Text color is set to black and then duplicate the Text object. Change the color of this new text object to white, and position it so that it is a few pixels above and to the left of the black text. Since the black text was created before the white text, it will appear underneath the white text, creating a nice effect, as shown in Figure 6-7.

Figure 6-7. *Drop shadow effect created with a duplicated Text object*

Now you will set up three events related to Star objects: one event to generate the stars, one event for when the player collects a star, and one event for when the player misses a star and it moves off-screen to the left.

First, create a new event with the condition *System - Time: Every X seconds*, and set *Interval* to 2. Add a second condition to this event called *Player - Size & Position: Is on-screen*; the purpose of this second condition is to stop the stars from spawning once the player has lost the game and been destroyed. Next, you will add an action that spawns additional instances of the Star sprite beyond the right edge of the layout. Sprites can be spawned from other sprites, or they can be spawned from the System object; the latter is the approach you will take here. In this event, add the action *System - General: Create Object*. In the parameters window, set *Object to create* to Star, set *Layer* to "Main" (with the quotation marks), set *X* to 700, and set *Y* to random(100,700). Recall that angles of motion need to be set by actions, so add another action called *Star - Bullet: Set angle of motion*, and set *Angle* to 180.

Next, you will create the event that handles what happens when the player collides with a star, which is that the star is destroyed, a point is added to the Score variable, and the Text object displaying the score value is updated. Create a new event with condition *Player - Collisions: On collision with another object*, and select *Star*. Add three actions to this event.

- Add *Star - Misc: Destroy.*

- Add *System - Global & local variables: Add to*, and set *Variable* to Score and *Value* to 1.

- Add *TextScore - Text: Set Text*, and next to *Text*, enter **Score** (without quotation marks so that the value of the variable is displayed, not the word itself).

Finally, you will create the event that destroys a star once it moves off-screen to the left. It is important to specify the side since stars are created off-screen to the right and you don't want them destroyed in that situation. Create a new event with the condition *Star - Size & Position: Is on-screen*, and invert the condition on the event sheet. Also add the condition *Star - Size & Position: Compare X*, change *Comparison* to Less Than, and set the *X* coordinate to 0. Finally, add the action *Star - Misc: Destroy*.

When you have completed these three events, they should appear as in Figure 6-8. Save and test your game to verify that stars do in fact appear onscreen every 2 seconds and travel to the left and that when the player collides with a star, the star disappears and the score display is updated correctly.

Figure 6-8. *Events related to Star objects*

Enemy Planes

In this section, you will add enemy planes to introduce an element of challenge. As an added level of sophistication, you will also create a set of variables that causes the overall difficulty to increase as time passes. The rate at which enemies spawn and their movement speed will both slowly increase. This is known as a *difficulty ramp* and is useful in keeping players challenged and interested in the game; as they play more and their skills increase, they will be able to play the game for longer periods of time and attain higher scores. To begin, in the event sheet, create a global variable; set *Name* to SpawnRate, set *Type* to Number, set *Initial value* to 2, and for *Description* enter Seconds until next enemy spawns. Next, create another global variable; set *Name* to EnemySpeed, set *Type* to Number, set *Initial value* to 300, and for *Description* enter Used when setting speed of newly created enemy planes.

In the layout, create a new sprite named Enemy. Setting up its graphics is completely analogous to the process used for the player plane. In the *Animation frames* window, import the image files for the red, left-facing plane, and set the animation properties Speed to 0, Loop to Yes, and *Ping-pong* to Yes. Position the Enemy plane off-screen, in the margin area above the layout. Add the *Bullet* behavior, and change *Set angle* to No.

Next, you will add a total of five enemy-related events to the event sheet. Three of these events will be quite similar to the star-related events you previously created: an event to spawn new instances, an event to handle collision with the player, and an event to destroy objects that pass beyond the left edge of the screen. Every time a new enemy is spawned, the values of the variables SpawnRate and EnemySpeed will be adjusted; the remaining two events will guarantee that the values of these variables stay within a reasonable range.

In the event sheet, create a new event with the condition *System - Time: Every X seconds*, and set *Interval* to SpawnRate. Add another condition called *Player - Size & Position: Is on-screen*. When the game is over and the player is destroyed, this event will no longer activate. Next, add the following actions:

- Add *System - General: Create object*, and in the parameters window, set *Object to create* to Enemy, set *Layer* to "Main", set *X* to 700, and set *Y* to random(100,700).

- Add *Enemy - Bullet: Set angle of motion*, and set *Angle* to 180.

- Add *Enemy - Bullet: Set speed*, and set *Speed* to EnemySpeed.

Updating the associated variable values requires two more actions to be added to this event.

- Add *System - Global & local variables: Add to*. For *Variable*, select EnemySpeed, and for *Value*, enter 10.

- Add *System - Global & local variables: Subtract from*. For *Variable*, select SpawnRate, and for *Value*, enter 0.05.

Next, you will create two new events even more similar to the previous star-related events. Create a new event with a condition that checks whether the player has collided with an enemy and a corresponding action that destroys the player object. Create another new event with two conditions that check whether the enemy is not onscreen and that compare the *x* value to check whether it is less than zero; also add a corresponding action that destroys the enemy object.

Finally, you need to set reasonable limits on the values of the variables. You previously implemented a similar feature in the Space Rocks game in an event that checked the speed of the player's spaceship; if the speed was greater than 200, the speed was set equal to 200, which effectively became a speed limit for the spaceship. You will create two similar events in your current game. The first of these events will set a bound on how quickly enemy planes can spawn; if the value of SpawnRate gets too close to 0, then there will be a near-continuous stream of enemy planes appearing, which would be impossible to dodge (thus making the game unfair and frustrating for the player). To solve this problem, you will set a lower limit of 0.5 for SpawnRate. To accomplish this, create a new event with the condition *System - Global & local: Compare variable*, changing *Variable* to SpawnRate, *Comparison* to less than and *Value* to 0.5. Then create the action *System: Global and local variables: Set value*, changing *Variable* to SpawnRate and *Value* to 0.5. Once you are finished, create a similar event that checks whether the EnemySpeed variable is greater than 800 and, if it is, then sets the value of *EnemySpeed* to 800.

When you are finished, the enemy-related events should appear as in Figure 6-9. Save and test your game, making sure that the enemies become faster and appear more frequently as time goes on.

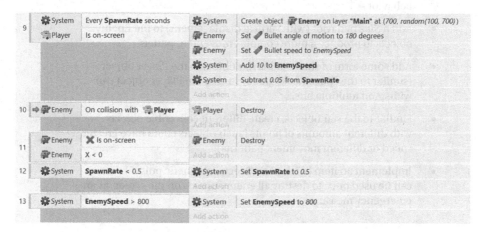

Figure 6-9. Events related to Enemy objects

When you have reached this point, congratulations! You have implemented the core mechanics of the Plane Dodger game.

Side Quests

There are many features you could consider to add polish to this project. For example, you could add the following:

- Animated effects for when stars are collected or the player's plane is destroyed (two spritesheets you could use for this purpose, sparkle.png and explosion.png, are included)

- Background music

- Sound effects that play when a star is collected or when the player's plane explodes

- Alternative controls, allowing the player to use a mouse button click instead of (or in addition to) a keyboard press to control the plane

- Another layout that serves as a start menu

- Objects that appear when the player is destroyed, such as a "game over" message and a button that restarts the layout so that the player can play again

At a more advanced level, you might want to experiment with different gameplay mechanics. The following are some ideas:

- Replace the Player object's *Bullet* behavior with the *8-Direction* behavior.

- Add a *Sine* behavior (with vertical displacement) to the Enemy objects to produce a more complex movement pattern.

- Add some form of shield or barrier object to the Player object (similar to the Space Rocks game) so that the Player object can withstand multiple hits.

- Similar to the star objects, create different collectible objects with different amounts of points (such objects could have greater speed or different movement patterns).

- Implement an item (such as an "electromagnetic pulse") that can be used once to destroy all enemy planes on the screen as an emergency measure.

Summary

In this chapter, you learned how to create an "endless" game, using scrolling backgrounds to create the illusion of continuous movement. Since this was your first game with a side-view perspective, you used the gravity property of the bullet behavior. To keep the gameplay from becoming monotonous, you also implemented a difficulty ramp to make the game more challenging as time progresses. Finally, you were presented with a great variety of aesthetic and gameplay modifications to consider in the "Side Quests" section.

In the next chapter, you will return to a top-down perspective as you create a car-racing game, Racecar 500.

CHAPTER 7

■ ■ ■

Racecar 500

In this chapter, you will create a game called Racecar 500, a top-down racing game, as shown in Figure 7-1.

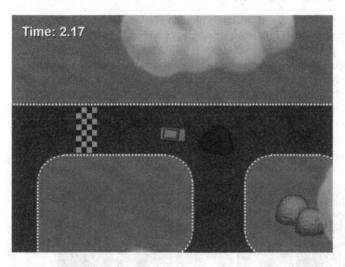

Figure 7-1. The Racecar 500 game

Introduction

In Racecar 500, the player controls a car, whose goal is to drive around a racetrack in the fastest time possible, while maneuvering around obstacles that may slow down or randomly change the direction of the player. The racetrack itself is larger than the game window, so only part of the track is visible at any time; the window remains centered on the car at all times.

The player controls the car using the arrow keys. Specifically, the up arrow key accelerates the car, the left and right arrow keys turn the car in its respective directions, and the down arrow key decelerates the car (and will eventually cause the car to travel in reverse if held down long enough). The user interface displays the total race time (in seconds),

© Lee Stemkoski and Evan Leider 2017
L. Stemkoski and E. Leider, *Game Development with Construct 2*,
DOI 10.1007/978-1-4842-2784-8_7

which begins once the car starts moving, and ends when the car crosses the finish line, displayed as a checkerboard pattern on the racetrack.

For this chapter, you should be familiar with sprites, text objects, and global variables. The *Car* behavior will be introduced as a basis for the movement described earlier. Since the game world (layout size) is larger than the window size, the *Scroll to* behavior will be introduced. To create a customized image for the track, the *Tilemap* object will also be introduced.

To begin, download the zip file containing the graphics for this chapter from the book web site. In the layout properties, set the layout *Name* to Game, and set *Size* to 2048, 1536. As you have in previous projects, set up three layers named Background, Main, and UI. In the project properties, change *Window Size* to 800, 600; the reason for these particular numbers will be explained in the next section.

Tilemaps and Level Design

To create a custom background image, you will use a tilemap. A *tilemap* is an arrangement of rectangular images, called *tiles*, that represent small areas of the game world. This is particularly useful for background images or level designs with lots of similar areas or repeated graphics. Tilemaps can be used for games with a top-down perspective or for side-scrolling platformer-style games, such as the classic Nintendo games The Legend of Zelda and Super Mario Bros. In your current project, the racetrack can be constructed from straight and curved segments of road and grassy areas; Figure 7-2 shows the set of tiles you will be using. Typically, all these images are packed into a single image file called a *tileset*, similar to how a spritesheet contains multiple images corresponding to animation frames for a sprite.

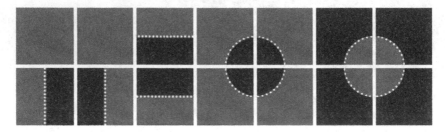

Figure 7-2. *Tiles for creating a racetrack*

These tiles can be arranged in many ways to create all types of road configurations, such as corners and loops, as illustrated in Figure 7-3, where spacing has been added to make the individual tiles more distinguishable.

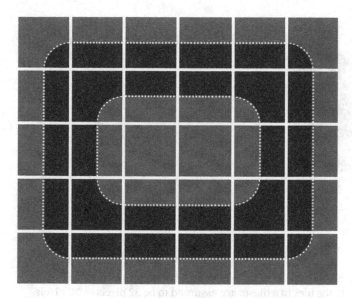

Figure 7-3. *A basic racetrack loop created with the tiles from Figure 7-2*

To begin working with tilemaps in Construct, make sure that the active layer is set to Background, and in the layout, right-click and add a new Tilemap object. A crosshair cursor will appear (similar to when you add sprites); click anywhere in the layout (where you click is irrelevant, as the tilemap will be automatically sized and positioned to cover the entire layout). When the image editor window appears, open the image road-tileset.png, and close the image editor window. A new panel will be added to the Construct window, called the *Tilemap* panel, as shown in Figure 7-4. Depending on your window setup, it may appear as a tab in a preexisting panel (typically alongside the Objects panel). If you are unable to see it, in the *View* tab area, make sure that the *Tilemap Bar* check box is selected. You may want to adjust the panel borders so that there is more room available to see the tileset image, or you may use the scrollbars in the *Tilemap* panel to view the different areas in the image.

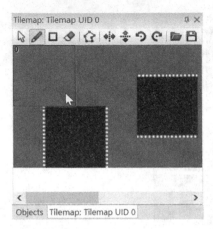

Figure 7-4. The Tilemap panel

Before working with the tilemap, there are a few properties to be changed in the *Properties* panel. By default, the tiles in a tileset are assumed to be 32 pixels by 32 pixels. In this project, however, the tiles are significantly larger (128 pixels by 128 pixels) to accommodate the car sprite that will be added later. With the tilemap object selected, in the *Properties* panel, change *Tile width* to 128 and change *Tile height* to 128. This particular tile size also influences the choice of layout size (2048 by 1536). Since a tilemap adjusts its size to match the size of the layout, it is important that the layout width and height be multiples of the tile width and height; otherwise, there will be an area on the bottom or right borders of the tilemap where tiles cannot be placed because there is not enough space. The layout size in this project was chosen to fit exactly 16 tiles along the width and 12 tiles along the height of the tilemap.

To create your tilemap, click the pencil tool icon in the *Tilemap* panel, which enables you to draw tiles onto the tilemap. Next, click a tile in the panel; your selection will be indicated by a light blue rectangle being drawn over the tile. Hover the mouse over the tilemap in the layout area, and a translucent image of the tile will be displayed in the square above which the mouse is hovering. Click to create a copy of the selected image there. To draw multiple copies of a tile quickly (such as the grass tile, which will be used for large sections of the background), click the rectangle tool icon and then click and drag the tilemap to specify a rectangular region, which will be filled with copies of the selected tile. To remove a tile from the tilemap, you can select the eraser tool icon or simply right-click when the pencil tool is active. Experiment with the placement of tiles and design your own racetrack; make it as simple or as complex as you like. One possible racetrack is shown in Figure 7-5, but yours need not look exactly like this.

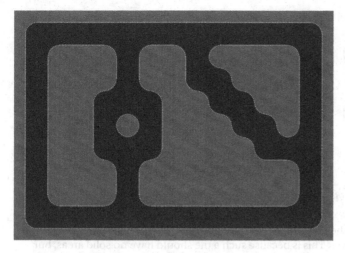

Figure 7-5. A possible racetrack design using the provided tileset

Finally, you want the grassy areas of each tile to act as solid objects or barriers to stop the car from driving off the paved sections of the racetrack. To this end, add the *Solid* behavior to the tilemap object. However, the collision polygon (first discussed in Chapter 2) of each tile is set by default to be a square that completely covers the tile. Therefore, you need to adjust the collision polygons for individual tiles so that the polygon covers only the grassy area in each tile. To begin, in the Tilemap panel, double-click a tile (or single-click a tile and select the polygon tool icon) to open the collision polygon window. The vertices of the polygon will appear as red squares, connected by blue edges. The adjustments to be made are as follows:

- For the solid grass tiles, no adjustments need to be made.

- For the four straight road tiles (half grass and half road), two vertices can be moved so that the rectangle covers only the grass area.

- For the four tiles containing a small quarter-circle of grass, the existing vertices can be rearranged to form a diamond shape that covers the grass fairly well and will be sufficiently accurate during gameplay.

- For the four tiles containing a large arc of grass, two new vertices will need to be added (twice you will need to right-click any vertex and select *Add point*; each newly created vertex will be added at the midpoint of the adjacent edge in the clockwise direction). The six vertices can then be rearranged to cover the grass area.

Figure 7-6 shows sample vertex arrangements for the collision polygons.

Figure 7-6. *Recommended collision polygons for different tile types*

While working with the tileset, you may have noticed that there is no tile containing only pavement and no grass. This is because such a tile should have no solid areas, but it is impossible to remove or disable collisions for individual tiles. Even attempting to shrink a collision polygon to a single point will still result in collisions at that point, which may surprise, confuse, or possibly frustrate a player who is not expecting it. If you decide that your track design absolutely requires collision-free tiles, one workaround is to not place a tile at that position and, in the layout, create a sprite with the image road.jpg and position it so that it exactly covers the missing tile area.

Now that you are done working with the tilemap, select the cursor tool icon from the *Tilemap* panel. This tool lets you reposition the tilemap, although you won't do so here. We recommend making this tool active to avoid accidentally drawing or erasing tiles from the tilemap. To further avoid accidentally selecting or altering the finished tilemap, in the layer panel click the lock icon next to the Background layer. This freezes all objects in that layer; they cannot be selected on the layout again unless the lock icon is clicked again and returned to the unlocked image.

Car Mechanics

In this section, you will set up the Car sprite and configure how it is controlled by the player. Make sure that the active layer is set to *Main*, and add a new Sprite object named Car with the image car-red.png. Position the car on a paved area of the track where you would like the race to begin. Add the behavior *Car*; this adds carlike steering controls to this sprite, as described at the beginning of this chapter. There are many properties that can be changed, such as *Max speed* (which controls how fast the car can move) and *Steer speed* (which controls how quickly the car can turn, in degrees per second). Also, add the behavior *Scroll to* to the car; this keeps the window centered on the car as it moves around the game world. Save and test your game, and feel free to experiment with the values of the *Car* behavior properties.

Just as is the case with driving a real car, the *Car* behavior permits the sprite to be turned only while it is moving; while it is not moving, the left and right arrow keys will have no effect. This may be unexpected or difficult for some players. If you want the car to always be able to turn, add a *Keyboard* object to the project, and implement the following (optional) events. Create an event with the condition *Keyboard - Key is Down*, select the *Left arrow* key, add the action *Car - Angle: Rotate counter-clockwise*, and enter 0.5 degrees. Create a similar event with the condition that the right arrow key is down and the action rotates the car angle clockwise by 0.5 degrees. The events will appear as in Figure 7-7. If you do decide to add these events, then the steering becomes very sensitive; you may want to reduce the *Car* behavior property *Steer speed* to 150 to compensate for this.

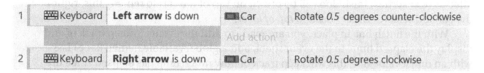

Figure 7-7. *Events for additional car rotation control*

Race Timer

In this section, you will set up a timer that displays how long the player has been racing. This requires some new ideas to not scroll the user interface layer, to start and stop the timer at the appropriate times, and to prevent the player from simply driving backward to trigger the race end condition early.

First, add a new Text object named TextTimer to the project. Place it on the UI layer, and position it in the upper-left corner of the layout. As the car moves around the layout, different parts of the game world become visible; however, the contents of the UI layer should stay fixed in place. To configure this setting, click the *UI* layer in the layer panel, and set the layer property *Parallax* to 0,0. This indicates that the corresponding layer should not scroll at all. Select the TextTimer object again, and change the default text to Time: 0.00. To make the text easier to read, change the font to Arial, bold, size 24. The black font color shows up well on the grass, but it would be hard to read when it appears above the dark-colored pavement. You could try to find a single color that contrasts well with all possible backgrounds, but it is far more effective to use the drop shadow effect discussed in the previous chapter. Create another TextTimer instance, move it a few pixels up and to the left, and then change the font color to white. At this point, the instances should appear as shown in Figure 7-8.

Figure 7-8. *Text object to display race time with drop shadow effect applied*

Next, you will add a finish line, which signals the end of the race when the car reaches it. Change the active layer to *Main* (this will be the active layer for the rest of the chapter). Add a new sprite named FinishLine with the image file checkboard.png. Position this at the "end" of the race track; if the track is a loop, this is typically behind where the car starts. The finish line fits best on a straight, horizontal part of track. Resize it if desired. Change the opacity to 60, and the transparency will make it appear as though it is painted onto the track. Also, since the FinishLine sprite was added to the Main layer after the Car sprite, FinishLine will be drawn on top of the car; to remedy this, right-click the car and select *Z-Order - Send to top of layer*.

With the finish line in place, you are ready to add the events to keep track of and display the elapsed time. In the event sheet, add a global variable named RaceTime with an initial value of 0; this will keep track of how much time has elapsed since the car first moved. However, this variable should be incremented only during the race and not before or after the race. To keep track of which of these three states the game is currently in (before race, during race, and after race), create another global variable named RaceState with an initial value of 0. The value 0 will indicate the race has not yet started, the value 1 will indicate the race is in progress (and the RaceTime variable should be incremented and the text display updated), and the value 2 indicates the race has finished. Add the *Keyboard* object if you have not done so already. Then you will create the following events:

- An event is needed to detect the start of the race. Create a new event with the condition *Keyboard - On key pressed*, and select the *Up arrow* key. Add the condition *System - Compare variable*, checking whether *RaceState* equals 0. The event action to add is *System - Variable: Set value*; set *RaceState* equal to 1.

- An event is needed to update the timer and text display when the race is in progress. Create a new event with the condition *System - Compare variable*, and check whether *RaceState* equals 1. There are two actions for this event. The first action to add is *System - Variable: Add to*. Add to the variable RaceTime the value dt (which stores the amount of time that has passed since the last update/last tick). The second action to add is *TextTimer - Text: Set text*. Set it to "Time: " & round(RaceTime * 100) / 100. This mathematical expression is used to round the value of RaceTime to two decimal places.

- An event is needed to detect the end of the race. Create a new event with the condition *Car - On collision with*, and select *FinishLine*. The corresponding action is *System - Variable: Set value*. Set RaceState equal to 2.

When completed, the events should appear as in Figure 7-9.

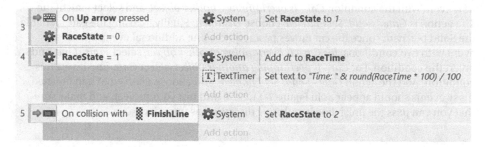

3	⇒▦ On **Up arrow** pressed	⚙ System	Set **RaceState** to *1*
	⚙ **RaceState** = 0	Add action	
4	⚙ **RaceState** = 1	⚙ System	Add *dt* to **RaceTime**
		[T]TextTimer	Set text to *"Time: " & round(RaceTime * 100) / 100*
		Add action	
5	⇒▥ On collision with ▩ **FinishLine**	⚙ System	Set **RaceState** to *2*
		Add action	

Figure 7-9. *Events for determining the state of the race*

Finally, you may have noticed that there is an easy way to "cheat" this game and trigger the end of the race earlier than expected. Instead of going around the track as intended, you can move forward a little bit and then move in reverse directly over the finish line, thus ending the race. To stop players from doing this, you will set up a "one-way gate" mechanic using an extra sprite and two additional events. Create a new sprite named Gate with the image gate.png (although it is the size of the sprite and not the image used that will be important, as you will soon see). Position the Gate sprite directly adjacent to the FinishLine sprite on the side closest to the car, as shown in Figure 7-10, and set the *Initial Visibility* property to Invisible. When making precise adjustments in the layout, it may help to zoom in or zoom out, either via the controls on the *View* tab or by holding down the *Ctrl* key and scrolling the mouse wheel.

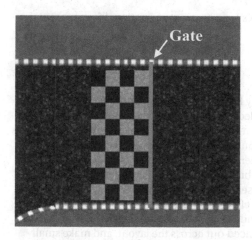

Figure 7-10. *The finish line, gate, and car positions on the race track*

Add the *Solid* behavior to the Gate sprite. The idea is to "open the gate" (disable the *Solid* behavior) when the car is on (overlaps) the finish line. To accomplish this, create a new event with the condition *Car - Is overlapping another object*, and select FinishLine. The action is *Gate - Solid: Set Enabled*; choose *Disabled*. Finally, "closing the gate" (enable the Solid behavior) once the car moves past requires one additional event. Create an event with two conditions: for *Car - Is overlapping another object*, select *FinishLine*, and invert the condition. For *Car - Is overlapping another object*, select *Gate*, and invert this condition. Add the action *Gate - Solid: Set Enabled*, and choose *Enabled*. When finished, these events should appear as in Figure 7-11. Save and test your project, and make sure that you can pass the finish line in only one direction, as intended.

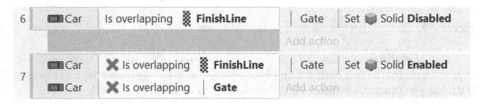

Figure 7-11. Events for a one-way gate mechanic

At this point, you have implemented all the basic mechanics for a racing game. Congratulations!

Side Quests

As usual, after completing the core mechanics for a game, many optional features remain to be added.

Scenery

Although the player's attention will be mostly focused on the road, it would be nice to add some scenery to the grassy areas. Included in the graphics collection for this chapter are some basic images (bushes and trees) that you could use to create sprites for this purpose; for variety, you could create additional instances of these objects and resize them. Alternatively, you could search the Internet for related graphics (more plants, rocks, ponds, etc.) and use them as desired (but for commercial or professional projects, you would need to pay attention to the licenses of the files used).

For a neat cloud/foglike environmental effect, create a sprite named Cloud with the included image cloud.png. Add the *Bullet* and *Wrap* behaviors, change *Opacity* to 80 and *Bullet Speed* to 50, create a few duplicates spaced out across the layout, and make small changes in each instance's *Angle* and *Size* properties for variety. When you start the game, it will appear as though there are clouds or fog drifting over the track.

Figure 7-12 illustrates what a track could look like after these scenic elements have been added.

Figure 7-12. *Racetrack layout with scenery elements added*

Obstacles

To break up the monotony of driving on an empty road, you can add a variety of obstacles. In this section, you will add wooden crates, which reduce your speed (and shatter) when hit, and oil slicks, which randomly change your direction while you are driving over them.

First, add a new sprite named Crate with the image crate.png. Resize the crate so it takes up less than half the width of the road (ideally it should be possible to drive around it). Also, add a sprite named CrateFragments with the image crate-fragments.png; resize it similarly, add the *Fade* behavior, change the fade property *Wait time* to 1, and move it into the layout margins. Add an event with the condition *Car - On collision with another object*, and select *Crate*. Add the following four actions to this event:

- Add *Car - Car: Set speed*, and enter Self.Car.Speed / 2 (this reduces the car's speed by half on impact).

- Add *Crate - Spawn another object*, select *CrateFragments*, and enter layer "Main".

- Add *Crate - Destroy*

- Add *CrateFragments - Z-Order: Move to bottom* (so that the car appears on top of the fragments).

99

The completed events for the Crate obstacle appear in the top part of Figure 7-13.

8	➡️ 🖼️ Car	On collision with 🟫 **Crate**	🖼️Car	Set animation speed to **Self.Car.Speed / 2**
			🟫 Crate	Spawn ✴️ **CrateFragments** on layer **"Main"** *(image point 0)*
			🟫 Crate	Destroy
			✴️ CrateFra...	Move to bottom of layer
			Add action	
9	🖼️Car	Is overlapping 🔴 **OilSlick**	🖼️Car	Simulate 💢 Car pressing Steer left
	⚙️ System	random(0, 100) < 50	*Add action*	
10	🖼️Car	Is overlapping 🔴 **OilSlick**	🖼️Car	Simulate 💢 Car pressing Steer right
	⚙️ System	random(0, 100) < 50	*Add action*	

Figure 7-13. *Complete events for the Crate and OilSlick obstacles*

Finally, add a new sprite named OilSlick with the image oil-slick.png and resize it as you did the crate. Also, since the OilSlick and Crate sprites were added to the Main layer after the Car sprite, right-click these objects in the Objects panel and select *Z-Order - Send to bottom of layer*. Create an event with two conditions; add *Car - Is overlapping another object*, and select *OilSlick*. Then add *System - Compare two values*, checking whether random(0,100) is less than 50. The associated action is *Car - Car: Simulate Control*; select *Steer left*. Create another event identical to this one, but change the simulated control to *Steer right*. When the car drives over an oil slick, these two events will randomly steer the car to the left and right. Sometimes both the random conditions will be true and the motions will cancel each other out, but just as often the car will randomly veer to one side or the other. The completed events for the OilSlick obstacle appear in the bottom part of Figure 7-13.

On Your Own

There are many more features you could add on your own. You could add more complicated obstacles, such as obstacles that move (via the *Sine* behavior). Alternatively, in contrast to the obstacles discussed earlier, you could consider adding items (or *powerups*) that have a positive effect on the player, such as a Boost item that instantly sets the Car's speed to its Max Speed value or a SpeedUp item that permanently increases Max Speed that the car can attain. You could add a variable that serves as a lap counter and end the game only once three (or some fixed number) of laps have been completed. You could display a "Congratulations!" message on the screen once the game is over, or you could display one of a number of messages (such as "Good," "Great," or "Excellent") depending on the total time to complete the race (you will no doubt have to practice repeatedly to determine what qualifies each level of performance). You could add multiple tracks on different layouts, progressing from one to the next after each race is finished. Finally, don't forget about basics such as audio and menus, as these features give your game a polished, professional presentation.

Summary

In this chapter, you created a top-down racing game. You learned how to use the Tilemap object and the *Car* and *Scroll to* behaviors. You learned how to set parallax to fix the UI layer in place when the game world size is larger than the window size. Along the way, you learned tricks and techniques that may be useful in future projects, such as keeping track of gameplay time, using variables to track the current state of the game, rounding a value to a fixed number of decimal places, and creating a one-way gate mechanic. The "Side Quests" section discussed extra features such as scenery, obstacles, and powerups.

In the next chapter, you'll switch gears from racing games to a classic arcade-style brick-breaking game.

■ ■ ■

CHAPTER 8

Rectangle Destroyer

In this chapter, you will create a game called Rectangle Destroyer, a side-perspective physics-based action game shown in Figure 8-1 and inspired by arcade classics such as Breakout and Arkanoid.

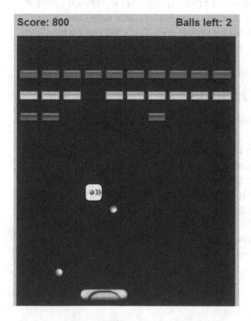

Figure 8-1. *The Rectangle Destroyer game*

Introduction

In Rectangle Destroyer, the player controls a paddle that moves from side to side, which is used to bounce balls into rectangular "bricks" and thereby destroy them. The goal is to destroy all the rectangles on the screen. Occasionally, a destroyed brick will release an item that may either aid or hinder the player by changing parts of the gameplay, such as paddle size, ball speed, and so forth. If the ball falls past the paddle and below the bottom

© Lee Stemkoski and Evan Leider 2017
L. Stemkoski and E. Leider, *Game Development with Construct 2*,
DOI 10.1007/978-1-4842-2784-8_8

edge of the screen, then the ball is lost. The player has multiple balls in reserve; once these run out, the game is over.

The controls and user interface are simple and minimalistic. The paddle is controlled by moving the mouse left and right, and items are collected by "catching" them, which happens when they collide with the paddle. The user interface displays the player's score and the number of balls left in reserve. Some of the powerup items will also cause a change in appearance of the ball or the paddle.

The main material that will be required from earlier chapters includes the Sprite, TiledBackground, and Mouse objects; the *Solid*, *Bullet*, *Fade*, and *Pin* behaviors; the random function; and global variables. You will use animations to store the different images corresponding to the different types of items and for the different appearances of the ball and paddle. You will learn about the choose function, which makes it easy to randomly select a word (or a number) from the given inputs.

To begin, download the zip file containing the graphics for this chapter from the book web site. In the layout properties, set the layout Name to Main, and set Size to 600, 800. As you have in previous projects, set up three layers named Background, Main, and UI. In the project properties, change the window Size to 600, 800. Set the layout's *Active layer* to Background. Add a *TiledBackground* object named Background using the image background.png, and resize it so it covers the entire layout area. Lock the layer when you are finished and then set the layout's *Active layer* to Main.

Paddle, Walls, Bricks, and Balls

In this section, you will create most of the game objects and the events that describe how they interact.

Add a new sprite named Paddle with the image paddle.png, and position it near the bottom of the layout. Add the behaviors *Solid* and *Bound to the layout*. In most breakout games, hitting the ball with the left side of the paddle causes the ball to bounce to the left, and hitting the ball with the right side causes it to bounce to the right; therefore, you need to adjust the collision polygon of the paddle object so that it resembles a dome shape, as shown in Figure 8-2. Next, add a Mouse object to the project (which will be used for controlling the paddle). In the event sheet, create a new event with the condition *System: Every tick*, add the action *Paddle: Set X*, and enter Mouse.X. The event will appear as in Figure 8-3.

Figure 8-2. *The collision polygon for paddle (dome)*

Next, create a TiledBackground object named Wall with the image white-pixels. png. Add the Solid behavior. Create two more instances of the Wall object, and position the three wall instances so that they border the left, right, and top edges of the layout, as shown earlier in Figure 8-1. In particular, you will want to make the top Wall instance thick enough so that there is room to display text on it later.

Add a sprite called Brick using the image brick-red.png (located in the Bricks folder of the assets archive), and in the Animations window, rename the animation to red. Create a new animation named blue, using the image brick-blue.png. Repeat this process as many times as you like to add as many different brick colors as desired (eight different-colored brick images are provided with the downloads for this chapter; additional brick colors can easily be created with graphics editing software). When you are finished, close the image editor windows. Next, add the *Solid* and *Fade* behaviors. In the *Properties* panel, change the fade property *Active at start* to No, and change *Fade out time* to 0.25. You will no doubt want to create many new instances of the Brick object (since a game with only one brick to destroy would be far too short), but before you do, you may want to activate the grid options in Construct, as you did when creating the Cleanup Challenge game in Chapter 4. To do so, in the *View* tab, select the *Snap to grid* and *Show grid* check boxes; you should also change the grid width and height to 8, as this will create a finer grid and allow for more precise adjustment. Finally, create some new instances of the Brick object, and align them in rows near the top of the layout. You can change the colors of the individual bricks by typing in the animation names (that you set up previously) in the *Properties* panel, next to *Initial animation*.

Add a sprite called Ball using the image ball-normal.png. Add the behaviors *Bullet* (changing the properties *Speed* to 300, *Gravity* to 8, and *Bounce off solids* to Yes), *Solid*, and *Destroy outside layout*. Position the ball right above the paddle, and set the property Angle to 280 so that the ball initially moves upward and slightly to the right, toward the bricks. Create a new event with the condition *Ball - On collision with*, and select *Brick*. Then add the actions *Brick - Fade: Start fade* and *Brick - Solid: Set enabled*, and select *Disabled*. This event is shown in Figure 8-3.

Finally, you will add some basic scorekeeping functionality to the project. In the layout, create a new Text object named TextScore with the Text property set to Score: 0 and with a large, easily readable font. Set its *Layer* to UI and position the Text object above the Wall object in the top-left area of the layout. In the event sheet, create a new global variable named Score with an initial value of 0. In the event sheet, create an event with the condition *Brick - On destroyed*; then add the action *System - Variable: Add to*, adding 100 to Score. Locate the event with the condition *System - Every tick*, and add the action *TextScore - Set text*, setting it to "Score: " & Score. These events are also shown in Figure 8-3. When you are finished, be sure to save and test your project, making sure that the paddle moves with the mouse; the ball bounces off the paddle, walls, and bricks; the bricks fade out when hit; and the score increases each time. Now is a good time to save and test your project.

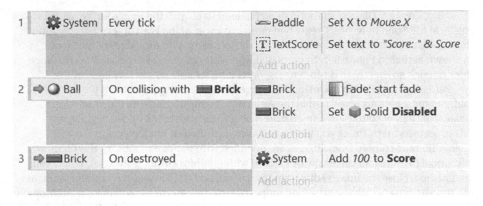

Figure 8-3. Basic events for paddle, ball, and bricks

Game Start and End

Currently, when the game loads, the ball immediately launches into the air and gameplay begins. The next addition to this game will be to add functionality to avoid this sudden start and give the player a chance to aim the ball before it is released. First, add a sprite named MessageStart with the image message-start.png. Set the layer to UI and center it on the layout. Add the behavior Pin to the Ball object. In the event sheet, add a new event with the condition *System - On start of layout,* add the action *Ball - Pin to object,* and select *Paddle* with mode *Position Only.* Also add another action called *Ball - Bullet: Set enabled,* and select *Disabled.* Add another event with two conditions: *Mouse - On any click* and *MessageStart - Is Visible.* Then add these three actions: *Ball - Unpin, Ball - Bullet: Set enabled* (select *Enabled*), and *MessageStart - Set Visible* (select *Invisible*). The events will appear as in Figure 8-4. Save and test your project. When the game starts, the ball should move with the paddle, and when a mouse button is clicked, the ball should be released and launch up toward the bricks.

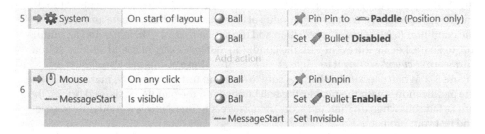

Figure 8-4. Events for launching the ball at the beginning of the game

Now that you've improved the beginning of the game, it's time to pay similar attention to when a ball is lost (when it falls off-screen) and the ending of the game. Add two new sprites: one named MessageEnd with the image message-end.png and the other named MessageWin with the image message-win.png. Position both of these objects in the center of the layout, set their layers to UI, and set Initial Visibility to Invisible. Also, create a new Text object named TextReserve with Text set to Balls left: 2, the same font settings as the TextScore object, and positioned in the top-right area of the layout. In the event sheet, create a new global variable named Reserve with an initial value of 2. Next, locate the event with the condition *Every tick*, and to this event add the action *TextReserve - Text: Set text* to "Balls left: " & Reserve.

Next, you need to create the events that handle what happens when there are no balls on the screen. You will use the condition *Ball.Count = 0* rather than *Ball - On destroyed* in case there are multiple balls on the screen (as may happen with a multiball powerup, discussed later); the following actions should take place only when there are no balls left on the screen. When this occurs, there are two possibilities to handle, each of which has different corresponding actions. Either there are balls left in reserve, in which case a new ball needs to be spawned, positioned correctly, and so on, or there are no balls left in reserve, in which case the "game over" message should become visible. There are at least three ways to set up the events for these conditions; we'll discuss each of these in turn.

The first possible arrangement is to have two separate events: the first with conditions *Ball.Count = 0* and *Reserve > 0* and the second with conditions *Ball.Count = 0* and *Reserve = 0*. This approach feels slightly redundant because of the repeated condition *Ball.Count = 0*. To eliminate the repetition, you can use a feature in Construct called *subevents*. A subevent is an event that appears indented underneath another event (which is called its *parent event*); the subevent conditions are checked only if their parent event's conditions are true. Therefore, another (and somewhat better) possible arrangement is to have an event with the condition *Ball.Count = 0*, and then two subevents, one with the condition *Reserve > 0* and the other with the condition *Reserve = 0*. However, for this particular game, this approach will have another issue, which is that the actions associated to *Reserve > 0* include decreasing the Reserve count by 1, so if the value of *Reserve* was initially 1, then both of the subevents would activate, and the game would end (which should not be the case). To avoid this scenario, you will use another feature in Construct, and that is a *System* condition called *Else*. An event with the *Else* condition will be true and run its actions only if the condition of the previous event was false. (For those familiar with traditional programming languages, this is similar to if-else statements.) Thus, the final arrangement of events that will be considered (and the one that you will implement) is to use subevents and replace the *Reserve = 0* condition with an *Else* condition.

At this point, you will now create the conditions for the events in the style described earlier and add the actions afterward. In the event sheet, create a new event with the condition *System - Compare two values*, setting it to check whether *Ball.Count* is equal to 0. To create a subevent, right-click the area in the event to the left of the condition, and from the pop-up menu that appears, select Add and then *Add sub-event* (or use the keyboard shortcut key S). The add condition window will appear; add the condition *System - Compare variable*, and set it to check whether Reserve is greater than 0. Once again, right-click the *Ball.Count = 0* event to create another subevent, this time with the condition *System - Else*. For the subevent with the condition *Reserve > 0*, add the following actions:

- Add *System - Variables: Subtract from*, subtracting 1 from *Reserve*.

- Add *System - Create Object*, creating a Ball object on the Main layer, with X coordinate Paddle.X and Y coordinate Paddle.Y - 24 (the coordinates position the ball directly above the center of the paddle).

- Add *Ball - Angle: Set angle*, and set it to 280 degrees.

- Add *MessageStart - Set visible*, and set it to Visible.

- Add *Ball - Pin to object*, and select *Paddle* with mode Position Only.

- Add *Ball - Bullet: Set enabled*, and select Disabled.

In particular, notice that these last two actions are the same that appear in the layout start event, which effectively attaches the ball to the paddle and freezes it in place until the player clicks a mouse button. For the event with the condition *System - Else*, add the action *MessageEnd - Set Visible*, and select *Visible*. In contrast, to congratulate the user upon destroying all bricks, create a new event with the condition *System - Compare two values*, and set it to check whether *Brick.Count* is equal to 0; add the action *MessageWin - Set Visible*, and select *Visible*. In addition, you need to make sure that the win and lose messages cannot appear on the screen at the same time; to the *Else* condition, add the inverted condition *MessageWin - Is visible*, and to the *Brick.Count* equals 0 condition, add the inverted condition *MessageLose - Is visible*. These events and subevents should appear as shown in Figure 8-5; notice in particular that the subevents appear indented underneath their parent event. Also add an action to the *Every tick* event that sets the text of *TextReserve* to Balls left: " & Reserve. Save and test your work; let the balls fall past the paddle and check whether the reserve ball functionality works as expected.

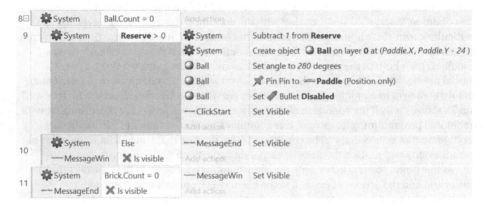

Figure 8-5. *Event and subevents for when balls are lost and winning the game*

Items

In this section, we will discuss a variety of items that are randomly released when bricks are destroyed. These items move downward toward the bottom of the screen, and if caught by the player, they can affect gameplay in a variety of ways. Some items will increase the size of the paddle or the speed of the ball. Other items will give game objects abilities. For example, the ball may be able to cause explosions that destroy nearby bricks, or the paddle may be able to fire laser beams (for a limited time) that destroy individual bricks. Other standard items spawn additional balls on the screen or add extra reserve balls. Having a great variety of gameplay-changing items is important in a game such as this, because without them, the gameplay would quickly become monotonous and dull.

In what follows, you will implement the items listed earlier; additional item ideas will be discussed in the "Side Quests" section later in this chapter. To begin, create a new sprite called Item with the image item-blank.png (from the Items folder in the assets archive). Change the size to 48,48, position the sprite outside the layout, add the behaviors *Destroy outside layout* and *Bullet*, and change the Bullet properties *Speed* to 200 and *Set angle* to No. For each type of item you create, a new animation will be added to the Item sprite. When an item is generated, one of the animations will be randomly selected, and when the paddle collides with an Item sprite, the name of the animation will be used to determine the effect the item will have. In the event sheet, locate the event with the condition *Brick - On destroyed*, and create a subevent for this event with the condition *System - Compare two values*, checking whether random(0, 100) is less than 50. Add the actions *Brick - Spawn another object*, spawning an Item object on the Main layer, and *Item - Bullet: Set angle of motion*, setting it to 90 degrees (this is in the downward direction). Later, after you have added item types, you will add one more action to this event that will randomly set the animation. Create a new event with condition *Paddle - On collision with*, and select Item; add the action *Item - Destroy*. For each new item type you add to the game, you will add a subevent to this event, which determines how gameplay is affected.

Items Affecting the Ball

First, you will implement a variety of items that affect the ball, in order of increasing complexity. The corresponding events will be shown in Figure 8-6 at the end of this section.

The simplest ball-related item adds 1 to the reserve ball count variable. Add a new animation to the Item object named BallExtra, using the image ball-extra.png. In the subevent that spawns items (under *Brick - On destroyed*), add the action *Item - Set animation*, and enter "BallExtra". Then, in the event with the condition where the Paddle collides with an Item, add a subevent with the condition *Item - Animation: Is playing*, and for the animation name, enter "BallExtra" (remembering that the spelling and capitalization has to match the animation name exactly). Then add the action *System - Variables: Add to* and add 1 to *Reserve*. Save and run your game; when a brick is destroyed, there will be a 50 percent chance that an item is spawned, and when you collect it, you should see in the user interface that the reserve ball count has increased by 1. You have now created your first item!

The next simplest items to implement change the speed of the ball. Add two new animations to the Item object: one named BallSpeedUp, using the image ball-speed-up.png, and the other named BallSpeedDown, using the image ball-speed-down.png. Now there are a total of three animations to choose from when an item is spawned. To randomly choose one of the animations, you will use the choose function, which can take any number of inputs and which randomly selects one of them. Double-click the action that sets the Item animation to edit the action, and replace the text with choose("BallExtra", "BallSpeedUp", "BallSpeedDown"). Now, each time an item is spawned, one of these three animations will be randomly selected and set for the item object.[1] In the Paddle collision with Item event, add a subevent with the condition *Item - Animation: Is playing*, and for the animation name, enter `"BallSpeedUp"`. Next add the action *Ball - Bullet: Set speed*, and enter `Ball.Bullet.Speed * 1.25`. This will cause the ball to speed up by 25 percent. Add another subevent that checks whether the Item animation BallSpeedDown is playing, and as before, add an action that changes the ball's speed, this time entering `Ball.Bullet.Speed * 0.80`, which reduces the speed of the ball by 20 percent (which cancels out a 25 percent increase from a BallSpeedUp item). As usual, save and test your game to verify that these new powerups work as intended.

Next, you will add the MultiBall item, which creates an additional ball on screen. Add a new animation to the Item object called `MultiBall`, with the image `ball-spawn.png`. Adjust the action that sets the Item animation so that the MultiBall animation may be selected. In the Paddle collision with Item event, add a subevent that checks whether the Item animation MultiBall is playing, and add the action *Ball - Spawn another object*, and select *Ball*. This will have the effect that every ball that is currently on the screen will spawn another ball, effectively doubling the number of balls currently in play. This can rapidly lead to many balls on screen, and too many balls may cause the game to lag. For this reason, or for other gameplay considerations, you may want to add a second condition to this subevent called *System - Pick random instance*, and select the *Ball* object. This will cause the action to apply to only one of the balls onscreen, and thus the total number of balls would increase only by 1 when this item is collected.

Finally, you will implement the ability for the ball to create explosions that destroy multiple bricks. When the ball has this ability, it will be indicated by changing the color of the ball to orange; similarly, other ball abilities could be indicated by using additional colors. Add a new animation to the Ball object named `Orange` with the image `ball-orange.png`. Add a new sprite named `Explosion` with the image `explosion.png`. Add the behavior *Fade*, change the property *Fade out time* to 0.25, and move the Explosion object into the margin area of the layout. Add a new animation to the Item object called `FireBall`, with the image `ball-fire.png`. Edit the action that sets the Item animation so that the FireBall animation may be selected. In the Paddle collision with Item event, add a subevent that checks whether the Item animation FireBall is playing, and add the action *Ball - Set animation* to `"Orange"`. Finally, you will need two new events to activate the effect. First, create an event with two conditions; specifically, add *Ball - On collision with*, selecting *Brick*, and then add *Ball - Animation: Is playing*, entering `"Orange"`. To this event, add the action *Brick - Spawn another object*, and select *Explosion* on layer Main. Second, create an event with condition *Explosion - Is overlapping another object*, select *Brick*, and add the action *Brick - Destroy*.

When you are finished adding all the content described in this section, the corresponding events should appear as shown in Figure 8-6.

---

[1]Later, when you have added many item types and you want to test only the most recently added type, you can change this line to just the name of the new animation, which guarantees that particular type will be spawned. When the final version of the game is ready, you can then change this to choose between all the item types you have added.

3 ⇒ Brick	On destroyed		System	Add *100* to **Score**
				Add action
4	System	random(0, 100) < 50	Brick	Spawn Item on layer **"Main"** *(image point 0)*
			Item	Set Bullet angle of motion to *90* degrees
			Item	Set animation to **choose("BallExtra", "BallSpeedUp", "BallSpeedDown", "MultiBall", "FireBall")** (play from beginning)
12 ⇒ Paddle	On collision with Item		Item	Destroy
				Add action
13	Item	Is animation "BallExtra" playing	System	Add *1* to **Reserve**
				Add action
14	Item	Is animation "BallSpeedUp" playing	Ball	Set Bullet speed to *Ball.Bullet.Speed * 1.25*
				Add action
15	Item	Is animation "BallSpeedDown" playing	Ball	Set Bullet speed to *Ball.Bullet.Speed * 0.80*
				Add action
16	Item	Is animation "MultiBall" playing	Ball	Spawn Ball on layer **"Main"** *(image point 0)*
	System	Pick a random Ball instance		Add action
17	Item	Is animation "FireBall" playing	Ball	Set animation to **"Orange"** (play from beginning)
				Add action
18 ⇒ Ball	On collision with Brick		Brick	Spawn Explosion on layer **"Main"** *(image point 0)*
Ball	Is animation "Orange" playing			Add action
19 Explosion	Is overlapping Brick		Brick	Destroy

Figure 8-6. Events for items that affect the ball

Items Affecting the Paddle

Here, you will implement a variety of items that affect the paddle. As in the previous section, the corresponding events will be shown at the end, in Figure 8-7.

The simplest paddle-related items change the size of the paddle and are quite similar to the items that change the speed of the ball. Add two new animations to the Item object: one named PaddleExpand, using the image paddle-expand.png, the other named PaddleShrink, with the image named paddle-shrink.png. Adjust the action that sets the Item animation so that these new animations may be selected. In the Paddle collision with Item event, you will add two new subevents. The first subevent should check whether the Item animation PaddleExpand is playing and that the associated action is *Paddle - Set width* set to Paddle.Width * 1.25. The second subevent should check whether the Item animation PaddleShrink is playing and that the associated action is *Paddle - Set width* set to Paddle.Width * 0.80.

Finally, you will add the ability for the paddle to shoot lasers that can destroy bricks; however, since this ability will make the game easy, the ability will be active for only 5 seconds. First, add a new animation to the Item object named PaddleLaser with the image paddle-laser.png. Then, add a new Sprite object to the game named Laser with the image laser-red.png, change its size to 90,30, position it off-screen, and add the behaviors *Bullet* and *Destroy outside layout*. Next, add a new animation to the Paddle object named Red using the image paddle-red.png, and apply the same collision polygon settings as you did for the original paddle image. Now you are ready to set up the events that implement this ability. Adjust the action that sets the Item animation so that this new animation may be selected. In *Paddle collision with Item event*, add a subevent that checks whether the Item animation PaddleLaser is playing, and add the following three actions:

- Add the action *Paddle - Set animation* to "Red".

- Add the action *System - Wait*, and enter 5 seconds.

- Add the action *Paddle - Set animation* to "Default".

The *System - Wait a*ction is particularly useful here because it sets up a delay until the next action in the event is performed (but there is no effect on other events). Create a new event with two conditions: first add *Mouse - On any click* and then add *Paddle - Animation: Is playing*, entering "Red". Add the action *Paddle - Spawn another object*, and select *Laser* on layer Main. Next, add the action *Laser - Z Order: Move to bottom* (so it appears underneath the paddle and behind the walls). Next, add the action *Laser - Bullet: Set angle of motion*, setting it to -90 degrees (this is in the upward direction). Finally, create an event with the condition *Laser - On collision with another object*, select *Brick*, and add these actions: *Brick - Start fade*; *Brick - Solid: Set enabled* (select *Disabled*); and *Laser - Destroy*.

When you are finished adding all the content described in this section, the corresponding events should appear as shown in Figure 8-7. As usual, save and test your project to verify that the newly added item types work as expected.

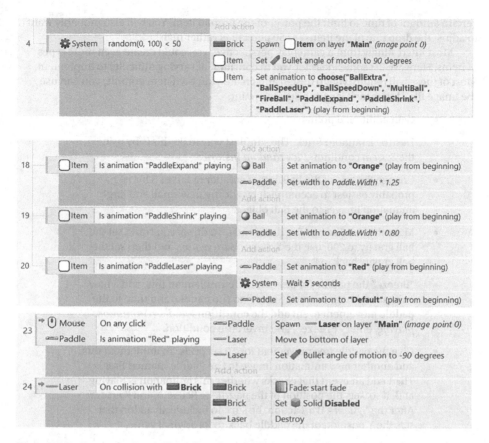

Figure 8-7. *Events for items that affect the paddle*

At this point, you have implemented all the basic mechanics for Rectangle Destroyer. Congratulations!

Side Quests

As usual, many of the standard features should be added to the game at this point: menus, audio, pause functionality, and so on. You could change the layout of the bricks to an interesting geometric pattern or even make the level resemble pixel art! You could also implement multiple levels; once all the bricks in a level are destroyed, the next level could be loaded. You could add a timer to the game, displayed in the user interface, and award the players a bonus at the end of the level depending on how quickly they destroy all the bricks. You could add a difficulty ramp, adding a small value to the ball speed every tick, so that the balls speed up slightly over time. You could add solid nonbrick obstacles to the level; you might even consider adding movement to these objects, with either the Sine or Rotate behavior. You might want to reset the ball to its original animation after a certain amount of time to limit the power of the fireball item. You will also probably want to adjust the drop rate of the items (as 50 percent is rather high).

Most interestingly from a gameplay perspective, you could create even more types of items. Here, we list some ideas for you to consider, of varying difficulty to implement. Most of these will require you to design and create your own item graphic; you can use the image file `item-blank.png` as a starting point.

- Gain additional points.

- Destroy a random brick. The simplest way to do this is by using the *System* condition *Pick random instance.*

- Change the size of the ball, either smaller or larger. This is probably easiest to accomplish by adding new small and large animation images to the Ball object.

- Make the ball "heavy" for 10 seconds. To do so, you could set the ball gravity to 200, use the *System - Wait action*, and then set the ball gravity back to 8.

- "Freeze" the paddle for 5 seconds. To implement this, add a new animation image (named Freeze) to the paddle, and then to the paddle movement event add the condition *Paddle - Animation: Is playing*, enter `"Freeze"`, and invert the condition.

- Give the paddle free movement for 10 seconds. To implement this, add another new animation image to the Paddle (named Free). Then add an event that checks whether this animation is playing and, if so, sets the position of the paddle to `Mouse.X` and `Mouse.Y`. After the *System - Wait* action, be sure to include an action that sets the Y position of the paddle back to its original value.

- Add a "safety net" along the bottom edge of the screen in the form of a solid object that is destroyed after it is hit; such an object will save a ball from falling off-screen once.

- Lose all reserve balls and destroy the paddle (thus causing the player to lose the game).

Summary

In this chapter, you created the game Rectangle Destroyer. You used animations to create multiple versions of objects (the Item object) and to indicate the current state or abilities of objects (the Ball and Paddle objects). Most important from a game design perspective, you spent a significant amount of time implementing items that alter the gameplay, which keeps the player experience changing and interesting.

In the next chapter, instead of destroying bricks with balls, you will destroy creatures with spells, as you create the top-down game Spell Shooter.

■■■

CHAPTER 9

Spell Shooter

In this chapter, you will be creating a top-down shooter game called Spell Shooter, shown in Figure 9-1, inspired by classic top-down shooters such as Gauntlet.

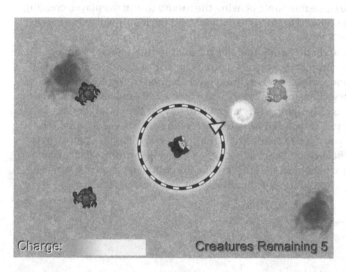

Figure 9-1. *The Spell Shooter game*

Introduction

In Spell Shooter, the player controls a wizard whose goal is to use his magical powers to banish evil creatures. The wizard shoots magical balls of energy, and if a creature is hit, that creature is destroyed. After a shot is fired, there is a "recharging period," which is a 1-second delay until the next shot is able to be fired; this gameplay mechanic is used to motivate players to carefully line up their shots. (If there were no such limitation in place, the average player might instead simply fire shots as quickly as possible hoping that some will hit their target.) The creatures randomly run between smokelike vortices, where they will hide for a short amount of time before running to the next.

The game world is large, and the player will most likely need to move around the area to locate some of the creatures. (To reduce this difficulty, one of the optional side quests explains how to implement a creature-locating compass spell.) Once the creatures are all destroyed, the player wins the game.

The wizard has eight-direction movement, controlled by the keyboard; for the convenience of the player, either the arrow keys or the W/A/S/D keys (or the E/S/D/F keys, for an international audience) can be used. Shots are aimed using the mouse and fired by clicking a mouse button. The user interface contains a progress bar that indicates when it is possible to fire the next shot. There is also a text display that shows how many creatures are left in the area. The optional compass spell, mentioned earlier, is activated when the spacebar is pressed, and a directional indicator fades in and out around the player.

This project uses many behaviors: *8-Direction, Scroll to, Bound to layout, Bullet, Destroy outside layout, Fade,* and *Sine.* Animations will be created from individual image files, as well as from spritesheets. Functions used include random, floor, and choose. New material includes the game mechanic of using the mouse to aim the player, creating variables for instances (as opposed to global variables), and the logic involved in making sprites navigate along a path.

To begin, download the zip file containing the graphics for this chapter from the book web site. In the layout properties, set the layout *Name* to Main, and set *Size* to 1600, 1200. As you have in previous projects, set up three layers named Background, Main, and UI. In the project properties, change the window *Size* to 800, 600 (and change the *Name* and *Author* properties as you like). Since the game world (layout size) is larger than the window size, it is important to stop the UI layer from scrolling off-screen (as you did in Chapter 7), and therefore you need to change the UI layer property Parallax to 0,0. In the layout area, create a TiledBackground named Background, using the image background. jpg, and position and resize the object so that it covers the entire layout area. Change its *Layer* property to Background. Your layout should appear as shown in Figure 9-2.

Figure 9-2. *The starting layout with a TiledBackground*

Player Setup and Mouselook

In this section, you will set up the wizard object and the mouse-based controls for aiming. In the layout, set the active layer to Main. Create a new sprite named Wizard. In the *Animation frames* image editor window, right-click and select the option to import animation frames from individual files (as you did in Chapter 5). Add the image files wizard-1.png, wizard-2.png, and wizard-3.png and delete the default empty frame. Change the animation properties *Speed* to 8, *Loop* to Yes, and *Ping-Pong* to Yes. When you're finished, close the image editor windows. In the layout area, change the wizard *Size* to 48,48, and position it in the center of the layout. Add the behavior *8-Direction* and change the property *Set angle* to No. (This will be particularly important, as the wizard should be able to move in one direction while facing a different direction.) Also add the behaviors *Scroll to* and *Bound to layout*.

Next, you will create some events that enable the player to use the W/A/S/D keys for movement, if desired, just as you did in Chapter 5. First, add a Keyboard object to the project. In the event sheet, create a new event with the condition *Keyboard - Key is Down*, and set *Key* to W. Add the action *Wizard - 8-Direction: Simulate Control*, and select *Up* from the list. Create additional events for the remaining keys and associated controls. When you are finished, these events should appear as in Figure 9-3. Test your game to check that when you hold each of the W/A/S/D keys, the wizard moves in the corresponding direction.

As it stands, the wizard's animation continues, even when the wizard is not moving. Next, you will create events to start and stop the wizard animation at the appropriate times. First, create a new event with the condition *Wizard - 8-Direction: Is moving*, and add the action *Wizard - Set animation*, with *Animation* set to "Default". Next, you need to stop the animation when the wizard is not moving. You could do this with an event that has an inverted *Is moving* condition, as you did in Chapter 4, but instead, you will use the newly learned *Else* condition, which has the same effect in this situation. Create a new event with the condition *System - Else*, and add the action *Wizard - Animation: Stop*. Since the *Else* event is directly below the *Is moving* event, this event will activate exactly when the wizard is not moving. These events are also shown in Figure 9-3.

Finally, you will implement the game mechanic that causes the wizard to face in the direction of the mouse; this is often referred to as *mouselook*. This control scheme is common in first-person and top-down shooter games. First, add a Mouse object to the project. In the event sheet, create a new event with the condition *System - Every tick*, and then add the action *Wizard - Rotate toward position*, setting *Degrees* to 10,[1] setting *X* to Mouse.X, and setting *Y* to Mouse.Y. When you are finished, this event should appear as in Figure 9-3. Save and test your game to check that when you move your mouse cursor around the game's window, the wizard rotates and faces toward the location of the mouse cursor.

---

[1]Setting *Degrees* to 10 *will result in a rotation rate of 600 degrees per second, provided that the program is running at 60 frames per second. To achieve more consistent performance across computers with lower frame rates, you could instead set this value to* 600 * dt.

1	⌨ Keyboard	**W** is down	🧙 Wizard	Simulate ⋮⋮ 8Direction pressing Up
			Add action	
2	⌨ Keyboard	**S** is down	🧙 Wizard	Simulate ⋮⋮ 8Direction pressing Down
			Add action	
3	⌨ Keyboard	**A** is down	🧙 Wizard	Simulate ⋮⋮ 8Direction pressing Left
			Add action	
4	⌨ Keyboard	**D** is down	🧙 Wizard	Simulate ⋮⋮ 8Direction pressing Right
			Add action	
5	🧙 Wizard	⋮⋮ 8Direction is moving	🧙 Wizard	Set animation to **"Default"** (play from beginning)
			Add action	
6	⚙ System	Else	🧙 Wizard	Stop animation
			Add action	
7	⚙ System	Every tick	🧙 Wizard	Rotate *10* degrees toward (*Mouse.X*, *Mouse.Y*)

Figure 9-3. *Events for changing the 8-Direction controls, wizard animation playback, and mouselook*

Creatures and Vortices

In this section, you will add the enemy creatures that the wizard is attempting to destroy and the vortices that these creatures run between (although the actually movement won't be implemented until the following section).

In the layout, create a new sprite named Creature. In the *Animation frames* window, import the frames from the sprite strip named monster.png, which has eight horizontal cells and one vertical cell. The animation frames need to be facing right to be aligned with the default angle of motion for the *Bullet* behavior, so the frames must be rotated to the right. To rotate all the animation frames by 90 degrees clockwise at once, hold *Shift* on your keyboard, and click the *Rotate 90° clockwise* button at the top of the *Edit image* window, as displayed in Figure 9-4. Each Creature frame should now be facing right. Set the animation properties *Speed* to 12, *Loop* to Yes, and *Ping-pong* to Yes. When you are finished, close the image editor. Add the *Bullet* behavior and change *Speed* to 300. Also, add the *Fade* behavior and set *Active at start* to No.

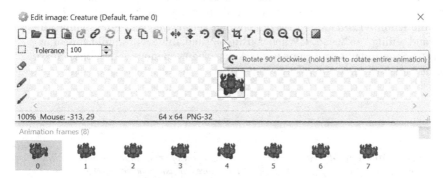

Figure 9-4. *Rotating the animation frames in the image editor*

118

Next, create a new sprite named Vortex. These sprites will be the locations that the Creatures move toward. In the *Animation frames* window, import the frames from the sprite strip named smoke.png, which has six horizontal cells and five vertical cells. Set the animation properties *Speed* to 30 and *Loop* to Yes. When you are finished, close the image editor. In the layout, change the size of the Vortex object to 160,160, and add the behavior *Sine* to the Vortex sprite. In the *Sine* behavior properties, set *Movement* to Size, *Period* to 4, and *Magnitude* to 32. This will give the Vortex sprite a pulsing effect.

Create five additional instances each of the Creature and Vortex objects, and spread them across the layout, as shown in Figure 9-5.

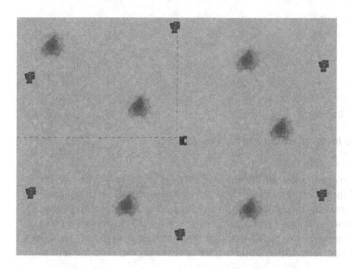

Figure 9-5. *Creature and Vortex instances spaced around the layout*

Instance Variables and Waypoint Logic

Next, you will set up the project so that the creatures randomly move between the vortices. For this to work, there needs to be a way to distinguish between the instances of the Vortex object and for each creature to keep track of which vortex it should be moving toward. Variables are an ideal way to store this information. Each instance needs to store its own related data, however, and thus global variables are not an optimal way to keep track of this information. Instead, Construct 2 allows you to create *instance variables*, which are variables that are associated to an object, where each instance can store and access its own values. Each instance effectively has its own copy of the variable, which it can then change at will. In what follows, you will create an instance variable for the Vortex objects named ID, which will serve as a unique identifier, and an instance variable for the Creature objects named Target, which will store the ID number of the vortex toward which it will be moving.

First, click the Vortex object in the object panel, and in the Properties panel, click the blue text *Instance variables*. The *Vortex: Instance variables* window will appear, containing space for local values to be stored, shown on the left side of Figure 9-6. Add a new instance variable by clicking the + icon. Name it ID, set *Type* to Number, set *Initial*

119

value to 0, and set *Description* to Unique identification number. Click *OK* and return to the layout editor. Your new instance variable should appear as shown on the right side of Figure 9-6. Click the *Creature* object in the object panel, repeat this process to create an instance variable named Target, and set *Description* to ID of the Vortex to move towards.

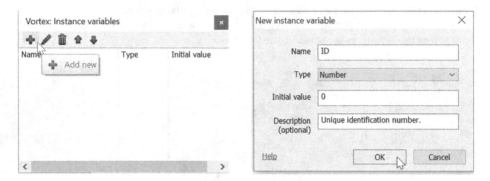

Figure 9-6. *Adding a new instance variable to the Vortex object*

In the layout editor, you can now set the value of the ID variables for the vortex instances (the creatures' target values will be set with an event described in a later section). Click a single vortex in the layout, and in the *Properties* panel, set the value of ID to 0. Click a different vortex, and set its ID value to 1. Repeat this process for each of the vortices in the layout until they each have one of the numbers from 0 to 5, as shown in Figure 9-7 (where text has been added in the figure to show the values for each instance).

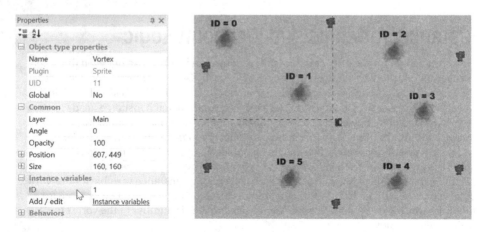

Figure 9-7. *Setting up the ID instance variable for the vortices*

Next, you will randomly set the Target values of the creatures at the beginning of the game. You could use the *System* condition *On start of layout*, but instead you will use the creature condition *On created*; this activates immediately for any creatures that are present at the beginning of the game and has the added advantage that if creatures are created later, their target values will also be set by this event. Create an event with the condition *Creature - On created*, and add the action *Creature - Instance variables: Set value*. Then set *Instance variable* to Target and *Value* to floor(random(Vortex. Count)). The floor function is used to round a decimal number to the nearest integer less than the number; for example, the expression floor(3.85) yields the number 3. It is necessary to round the random number since the vortex IDs are whole numbers, but the random function results in decimal values. Rounding down is important here since the largest vortex ID number will be one less than the total number of vortices, as the vortex numbering began at zero. When finished, this event should appear as in Figure 9-8.

Figure 9-8. *Event to give creatures random starting targets*

You will also need to create an event that rotates a creature toward its intended target vortex. You will use the *Rotate towards position* action, just as you did for rotating the wizard toward the mouse position. However, identifying the associated pairs of creatures and vortices is somewhat complicated and requires understanding of the Construct event "filter" system.

In general, actions are applied to the set of instances that meet the criteria specified in the condition (or conditions), and in particular, if there are no restrictions in the conditions, then all the instances will be affected at the same time. This fact was implicit and straightforward in earlier projects, but because of the complexity of this project, a more detailed discussion is in order.

At first thought, the correct condition to use for this event appears to be *Creature - Compare instance variable*, while checking whether Target is equal to Vortex.ID. However, this condition is insufficient. When the condition is being checked, the Construct software checks each creature instance one by one, selects the subset of creature instances (which is called *filtering*) whose Target variables matches the expression Vortex.ID, and then applies the corresponding action (or actions) to this subset. What is unclear is which Vortex instance's ID is being used for each of these comparisons. To clarify and correct the logic of this condition, you will use a *System* condition called For each, which effectively repeats an event once for each instance of the object.

With this understanding, you are ready to proceed. Create a new event with the condition *System - Loops: For Each*, and select *Creature*. Add the condition *Vortex - Compare instance variable*, and check whether *ID* is equal to Creature.Target. Finally, add the action *Creature - Rotate toward position*, set *Degrees* to 10, set *X* to Vortex.X, and set *Y* to Vortex.Y. The event should appear as shown in Figure 9-9.

Figure 9-9. *Event to set the creatures to rotate toward Vortex objects*

Next, you will implement a set of actions that occur when each creature reaches its intended destination. The creatures should hide (turn invisible) and stop moving for a random amount of time, select a new target vortex, and then become visible and start moving again. Create a new event with the condition *Creature - On collision with another object*, and select *Vortex*. To verify that the creature has collided with its actual target (rather than a vortex that was simply in the way), you will add a second condition called *Vortex - Compare instance variable*, and (as before) check whether *ID* is equal to `Creature.Target`. Next, add the following actions:

- Add *Creature - Set visible*, and set *Visibility* to `Invisible`.

- Add *Creature - Bullet: Set speed*, and set *Speed* to 0.

- Add *System - Variables: Add to*. For *Variable*, select *Target*, and for *Value*, enter `choose(1,2)`.

- Add *System - Wait*, and set *Seconds* to `random(1,3)`.[2]

- Add *Creature - Set visible*, and set *Visibility* to `Visible`.

- Add *Creature - Bullet: Set speed*, and set *Speed* to 300.

Note that some randomness was included when selecting the next target: by randomly choosing 1 or 2, the creature may either go to the next vortex in the sequence or go to the one after that. However, there are a limited number of possible target values; once the target value reaches the total number of vortices (Vortex.Count), the target number should "wrap around" and be reset to 0 or 1. To set this up, add a subevent with the condition *Creature - Instance variables: Compare value*, and check whether `Target` is greater than or equal to Vortex.Count. Then, add the action *Creature - Instance variables: Set value*, and set *Target* to `choose(0,1)`. When you are finished, the events should appear as shown in Figure 9-10. Save and test your project, making sure that the enemies move randomly, as expected.

Figure 9-10. *The events that will cause the creatures to move and hide along a random path*

---

[2]There is an alternative and more robust approach to queuing future actions for an object using the Timer object, which will be introduced in the next chapter.

Spell Shooting

In this section, you will create the spell-related game mechanics: the wizard will shoot a spell when a mouse button is clicked, and if the spell hits a creature, the creature will be destroyed. You will also implement the spell-charging delay described in the introduction of the chapter, as well as the charge progress bar and enemy count displayed in the user interface.

First, you need to add the spell object. Add a new sprite named Spell; in the *Animation frames* window, import animation frames from the sprite strip named swirling-yellow.png, which consists of four rows and five columns. Set the animation properties *Speed* to 30 and *Loop* to Yes. Close the image editor, and position the spell in the margins of the layout. Add the behavior *Bullet*, and change the bullet property *Speed* to 600. Also add the behavior *Destroy outside layout*. In the event sheet, create a new event with the condition *Mouse - On click* (keeping the default properties), add the action *Wizard - Spawn another object*, set *Object* to Spell, and set *Layer* to "Main". This event is shown in Figure 9-11.

Next, you will enable the player to destroy the creatures when they are hit by a spell. A sparklike special effect will be added as the creature fades out of existence. Add a new sprite named Spark; in the *Animation frames* window, add animation frames from the sprite strip named spark.png, which consists of four rows and four columns. Set the animation properties Speed to 16 and Loop to Yes. Close the image editor, position the spark in the margins of the layout, and add the behavior *Fade* (keeping the default properties). In the event sheet, create a new event with the condition *Spell - On collision with another object*, and select *Creature*. Also add the condition *Creature - Is visible*. Next, add the following actions:

- Add *Creature - Spawn another object*, set *Object* to Spark, and set *Layer* to "Main".

- Add *Spell - Destroy*.

- Add *Creature - Bullet: Set enabled*, and choose *Disabled*.

- Add *Creature - Start fade*.

This event is also shown in Figure 9-11. Save your project and run the layout; test that the wizard is able to shoot spells and that when they collide with a creature, a spark effect is generated, while the creature stops and fades away with the spark.

Figure 9-11. *Events related to casting spells*

Spell Charge and User Interface

In this section, you will implement the spell-charging game mechanic and begin creating the user interface. After firing a spell, a bar graphic that indicates the amount of charge will shrink, and after it regrows to its normal size, the wizard will be able to shoot another spell.

First, add a new Text object named TextCharge to the project. Place it on the UI layer, and position it in the bottom-left corner of the game window (as indicated by the dashed lines in the layout). Since this object will be the label for the charge bar, change the default text to Charge:. To make the text easier to read, change the font to Arial, bold, size 24. By adding the drop shadow effect from previous chapters, the text will be easier to see with contrasting backgrounds. Duplicate the TextCharge object, move it a few pixels down and to the right, and then change the font color to yellow to match the Spell object and create a coordinated color scheme.

Next, add a new Sprite object named Chargeometer with the image chargeometer. png. When the chargeometer grows, it should grow from left to right. This can be accomplished by changing the width of the object, but first one modification must be made. When sprites are rotated or scaled, it is with respect to a special point called the *origin*; by default, this point is located at the center of the sprite. This makes sense for most situations because objects typically rotate around their center (rather than around a corner) or grow equally in all directions from the center. Since we want the sprite to grow from left to right, the origin point location must be changed. Double-click the chargeometer to open the image editor windows, and click the second icon from the bottom to open the Image Points window. Here, right-click the list entry named *Origin*, and in the pop-up window, click *Quick assign* and then *Left*, as shown in Figure 9-12. You should see the Origin point moved to the left of the image.

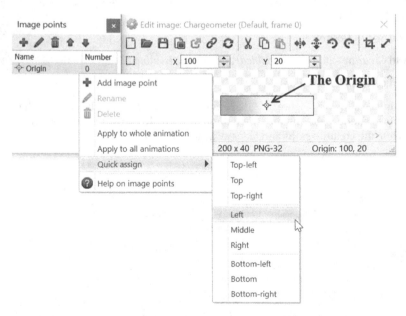

Figure 9-12. *Editing the Origin point location in the image points menu*

When you are finished, close the image editor. Place the Chargeometer object on the UI layer, and position it in the bottom-left area of the game window, directly to the right of the TextCharge object from earlier. Your TextCharge and Chargeometer objects should appear as shown in Figure 9-13.

Figure 9-13. *The TextCharge and Chargeometer objects in the layout*

For the chargeometer to return to its original width after being shrunk, its original size needs to be stored in a variable for later reference. Here, you can use a global variable (since there is only one instance of the chargeometer), but in theory, you could choose to use an instance variable instead. In the event sheet, right-click and add a global variable; set *Name* to OriginalWidth, with *Initial Value* set to 0. The value can be set when the game begins; create a new event with the condition *System - On start of layout*. Then create the action *System - Variables: Set value*, and set *OriginalWidth* to Chargeometer. Width.

Implementing the charging functionality requires a variety of additions to pre-existing events as well as the creation of entirely new events. First, to drain the charge, locate the event where the spell is spawned, and add the action *Chargeometer - Set width*, setting it to 0. To prevent the wizard from firing again before the charging period is finished, in the same event as before, add the condition *Chargeometer - Compare width*, and check whether it is equal to OriginalWidth. To continuously recharge the bar, you need to add a small fraction of its original width back during every tick. Since there is no *Add width* action, you can instead use the *Set width* action, setting the width to its current value plus a fraction of its original width. The fractional value you will use is the built-in Construct expression dt, which stands for "delta time" and stores the amount of time that passes during every tick. Typically, video games run at 60 frames per second, which means that each tick takes 1/60 of a second, and this is the value of dt. (The value of dt is automatically adjusted for games that run at slower rates.) Adding 1/60 of the width of the chargeometer back at a rate of 60 times per second means that the chargeometer will be restored to its original width in exactly one second. To set this up, locate the event with the condition *Every tick*, and to this event add the action *Chargeometer - Set width*, set to Chargeometer.Width + OriginalWidth * dt. Finally, to stop the charge bar from growing too large (larger than its original size), you need one more event. Create a new event with the condition *Chargeometer - Compare width*, and check whether it is greater than OriginalWidth; add the action *Chargeometer - Set width*, and set it to OriginalWidth. When you are finished, these events should appear as shown in Figure 9-14. Save and test your project to check that when you shoot, the chargeometer drains and recharges and that you can't shoot again until the bar has returned to its original size.

7	⚙ System	Every tick	🧙 Wizard	Rotate *10* degrees toward (*Mouse.X, Mouse.Y*)
			⊸ Chargeometer	Set width to *Chargeometer.Width + OriginalWidth * dt*

12	➡ (🖱) Mouse	On **Left** button **Clicked**	🧙 Wizard	Spawn ◯ **Spell** on layer **"Main"** *(image point 0)*
	⊸ Chargeometer	Width = OriginalWidth	⊸ Chargeometer	Set width to *0*

14	➡ ⚙ System	On start of layout	⚙ System	Set **OriginalWidth** to *Chargeometer.Width*
			Add action	

15	⊸ Chargeometer	Width > OriginalWidth	⊸ Chargeometer	Set width to *OriginalWidth*

Figure 9-14. *Events for draining and recharging the chargeometer*

Score and Game Over

Currently, the wizard is able to shoot spells and destroy creatures. In this section, you will improve the user interface so that it keeps players aware of their progress: a Text object that displays the number of creatures remaining to destroy, and a "you win" message that appears once all the creatures have been destroyed.

First, add a new Sprite object named MessageWin with the image YouWin.png. Position it in the center of the game window, set its *Layer* to UI, and set *Initial Visibility* to Invisible. Also, add a new Text object named TextScore to the project. Set Layer to UI, and position it in the bottom-right corner of the game window. Change its default text to Creatures Remaining: 0, and change the font to Arial, bold, size 24. Set the *Horizontal alignment* property to Right. Duplicate the object, move it a few pixels down and to the right, and set the font color to red to match the creatures. The area of the layout corresponding to the game window (the top-left region) should appear similar to Figure 9-15.

Figure 9-15. *The new user interface in the layout*

Next, locate the event with the condition *Every tick*, and add the action *TextScore - Set text*, set to `"Creatures Remaining: " & Creature.Count`. To configure the win message, create a new event with the condition *System - Compare two values*, set to check whether *Creature.Count* is equal to 0, and add the action *MessageWin - Set visible*. The events should appear as shown in Figure 9-16. Save and test your project; make sure that TextScore updates correctly and that your win message appears when you have destroyed all the creatures.

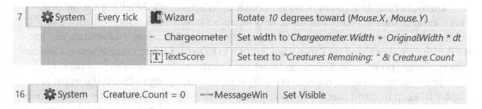

7	⚙ System	Every tick	🧙 Wizard	Rotate *10* degrees toward (*Mouse.X*, *Mouse.Y*)
			⊸ Chargeometer	Set width to *Chargeometer.Width + OriginalWidth * dt*
			[T] TextScore	Set text to *"Creatures Remaining: " & Creature.Count*

16	⚙ System	Creature.Count = 0	⟿ MessageWin	Set Visible

Figure 9-16. Events for updating the score and displaying the win message

Congratulations! You have now finished implementing the core mechanics of the Spell Shooter game.

Side Quests

In this optional section, you will learn how to add a compass-like mechanic to your game to assist the player in locating creatures that are off-screen, as well as some suggested additional features to explore.

Adding a Radar

Currently, the player must move around the layout to find creatures. In this section, you will create a compass display that is pinned to the player and appears for a brief time when the player presses the spacebar. The compass image contains an arrow that will point in the direction of the nearest creature. Using this feature will simplify the game for the player, possibly reducing any feeling of frustration from the difficulty of locating the quick and randomly moving creatures.

First, add a new Sprite object named `Compass` with the image `compass.png`. Position it directly centered on the wizard, as shown in Figure 9-17. Add the behavior *Fade*, and change the properties *Active at start* to No and *Destroy* to No. Also add the behavior *Pin*.

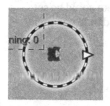

Figure 9-17. The compass object centered on the wizard

For the compass to fade in and out correctly, set its *Opacity* to 0, but don't do this until after you have positioned the compass correctly (because you won't be able to see it on the layout after you change this property). In addition, to pin the compass to the wizard, locate the event with the condition *On start of layout*, and add the action *Compass - Pin to another object*, setting *Pin to* to Wizard and setting *Mode* to Position only. Setting the mode correctly is particularly important in this case since you want the compass to be able to rotate independently from the wizard.

There is a condition you have not previously used before called *Pick nearest/furthest*. This condition selects a particular instance of an object based on its distance from a given point. Create a new event with the condition *Creature - Size & Position: Pick nearest/furthest*, set *Which* to nearest, and set *X* to Wizard.X and *Y* to Wizard.Y. Then add the action *Compass - Rotate toward position*, set *Degrees* to 10, set *X* to Creature.X, and set *Y* to Creature.Y.

Now that the compass rotation is configured, you are ready to create the event to display it. Keep in mind that, for the compass to work properly, it should be usable when there is at least one creature remaining. Create a new event with the condition *Keyboard - On key pressed*, and select the Space key. Add another condition called *System - Compare two values*, and set it to check whether *Creature.Count* is greater than 0. Add the action *Compass - Set opacity* to 100 and the action *Compass - Start fade*. The events should appear as shown in Figure 9-18.

14	⇒ 🔧 System	On start of layout	🔧 System	Set **OriginalWidth** to *Chargeometer.Width*
			◯ Compass	🪄 Pin Pin to 🧙 **Wizard** (Position only)

17	🦎 Creature	Pick nearest to (Wizard.X, Wizard.Y)	◯ Compass	Rotate *10* degrees toward (*Creature.X, Creature.Y*)
				Add action

18	⇒ ⌨ Keyboard	On **Space** pressed	◯ Compass	Set opacity to *100*
	🔧 System	Creature.Count > 0	◯ Compass	📊 Fade: start fade

Figure 9-18. *Events for rotating and displaying the compass*

On Your Own

You can add plenty of other additions and features to Spell Shooter. As usual, it would be wise to add polish to this game with standard features such as menus, audio, and pause functionality. To add to the difficulty level, you could add a lose condition: the player may lose the game if the wizard gets hit by creatures a given number of times. Also, keep in mind what you learned in Chapter 8 when designing Rectangle Destroyer. You are now able to add spawnable items to any of your previous games! Such an item could be set to appear once every 10 seconds at a random position on the layout and fade out after 5 seconds have passed.

Here are some item ideas that would work well in Spell Shooter:

- "SpeedUp" and "SpeedDown" items or obstacles that affect the wizard or creatures' speeds as you did in the previous chapter

- "Shrink" item that shrinks creatures, making them harder to vanquish

- "Burst" spell item that shoots three spells at once

- "Rapid" spell that takes less time to recharge

- "CreatureNest" item that spawns more creatures if you touch them

You could also add a countdown timer, which adds a sense of urgency to the player's quest to destroy all the creatures, and if the player doesn't destroy all the creatures within the time limit, the player loses the game. With a timer in place, a ranking or rating system could be added that evaluates the player's performance depending on how quickly the wizard vanquished the creatures.

Summary

In this chapter, you created the game Spell Shooter. You learned how to implement the mouselook game mechanic and combined it with traditional W/A/S/D-style controls to give the player the ability to shoot while moving around the screen. To create random movement patterns, you learned how to use instance variables and waypoint logic, together with the random and choose functions. To create more balanced gameplay, you implemented a rechargeable shooting mechanic. You also added a rotating compass feature to assist the player in locating difficult-to-find creatures. The "Side Quests" section discussed extra features such as a lose condition, items, a timer, and a rating system.

In the next chapter, you will leave the magical world of spells and creatures and instead shoot at enemy planes flying over the ocean as you create the game Airplane Assault.

CHAPTER 10

■ ■ ■

Airplane Assault

In this chapter, you will be creating another top-down shooter game called Airplane Assault, shown in Figure 10-1, that was inspired by the classic survival-based game 1942.

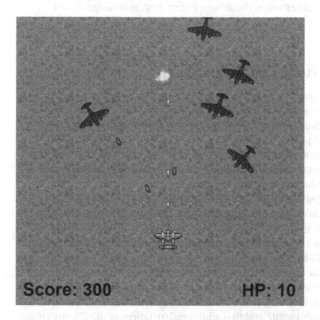

Figure 10-1. *The Airplane Assault game*

In Airplane Assault, the player controls a plane whose goal is to destroy as many enemy planes as possible for points. The player's plane shoots small bullets, and if an enemy is hit, that enemy is destroyed. In contrast to Spell Shooter, the player will have a limited amount of health, which is reduced when hit by an enemy plane bullet. If the player's health reaches zero, then the plane will be destroyed, and the game will be over. During gameplay, enemies will spawn every few seconds, move in a random pattern between waypoints, and face and attack the player with their own bullets. The player will need to move around the screen to line up shots and avoid enemy bullets at the same time. This game is endless; the implicit goal of the player is to earn a high score.

© Lee Stemkoski and Evan Leider 2017
L. Stemkoski and E. Leider, *Game Development with Construct 2*,
DOI 10.1007/978-1-4842-2784-8_10

The player plane has eight-direction movement, controlled by the arrow keys. Shots are fired by pressing the spacebar. The user interface contains two Text objects that display the player's current health points and score.

This chapter assumes you are familiar with the Sprite, TiledBackground, Text, and Keyboard objects; the *8-Direction, Bound to layout, Bullet,* and *Destroy outside layout* behaviors; animations; global and instance variables; and the functions random, floor, and choose. The *Flash* behavior will be introduced to give the player a moment of invincibility after being hit. The *Timer* behavior will also be introduced to enable enemy planes to periodically fire at the player. You will learn about the angle function, which makes it easy to determine the angle between two objects or locations. Instance variables will be used in a new way: to add health points to objects.

To begin, download the zip file containing the graphics for this chapter from the book web site. In the layout properties, set the layout *Name* to Game, and set *Size* to 800, 800. As you have in previous projects, set up three layers named Background, Main, and UI. In the project properties, change the window *Size* to 800, 800. Add a TiledBackground object named Water using the image water.png, and resize it so it covers the entire layout area.

Player, Waypoint, and Enemy Setup

In this section, you will add the player plane object, the enemy planes that the player must shoot, and the Waypoint objects that determine the path that the enemy planes follow. In the layout, set the active layer to Main. Create a new sprite named Player, with the image player.png, and position it near the bottom of the layout. Change its *Angle* property to 270, and position it in the lower center of the layout. Add the behavior *8-Direction* and change the property *Set angle* to No. (The player will face only upward during gameplay.) Also add the behavior *Bound to layout.*

Next, add a new sprite named Waypoint. This Waypoint object will be almost identical to the Vortex waypoint from the Spell Shooter game, except in Airplane Assault the waypoints will be invisible in the final version. Since a graphic isn't needed, use the image editor tools such as the bucket or paintbrush to fill the image area with a solid color. Change the size of the sprite to 32-by-32 pixels. When you are finished, close the image editor windows. Create another new sprite named Enemy, with the image enemy-plane.png. Add the *Bullet* behavior, and change the properties *Speed* to 200 and *Set angle* to No, since the enemies will be facing the player rather than their direction of movement. Create five additional instances of the Waypoint sprite and two additional instances of the Enemy sprite, organizing them in the layout, as shown in Figure 10-2.

Add an instance variable named ID to the Waypoint object, set *Type* to Number, *Initial value* to 0, and *Description* to Unique identification number. Then, to the Enemy object, add an instance variable named Target, set *Type* to Number, set *Initial value* to 0, and set *Description* to ID of the Waypoint to move towards. In the layout editor, click a single waypoint in the layout, and in the *Properties* panel, set the value of ID to 0. Click another waypoint and set its ID value to 1. Repeat this for each waypoint in the layout until they each have one of the numbers from 0 to 5 (each number occurring exactly once), as shown in Figure 10-2.

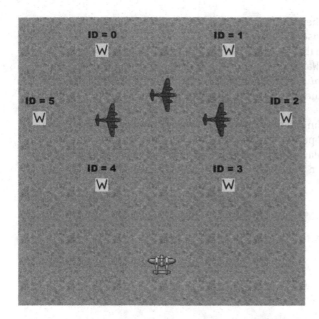

Figure 10-2. *The player, enemies, and waypoints with IDs in the layout*

Next, you will randomly set the Target values of the enemy airplanes at the beginning of the game as you did in Spell Shooter with the event condition *On created*. First, in the event sheet, create an event with the condition *Enemy - On created*, and set the action *Enemy - Variables: Set value*. Then set *Instance variable* to Target, and set *Value* to floor(random(Waypoint.Count)).

You will now create movement events that rotate and move enemies toward their intended target waypoints, with the *For Each* and *ID* comparison conditions. Create a new event with the condition *System - Loops: For Each*, and select *Enemy*. Add another condition called *Waypoint - Compare instance variable*, and check whether the ID is equal to Enemy.Target. In Spell Shooter, you used the *Rotate towards position* action to rotate sprite images toward vortex waypoints and also to move them toward these waypoints using the *Bullet* behavior (in that project, the *Bullet* property *Set angle* was set to Yes). In Airplane Assault, the enemy plane sprite images will rotate to face the player while they are moving in a different direction toward waypoints. To accomplish this, you will use two actions: *Rotate towards position* and *Bullet: Set angle of motion*. With *Set angle of motion*, you will use the angle function, which takes as input the *X* and *Y* coordinates of two locations (a total of four inputs altogether) and returns the angle between those locations. Add the action *Enemy - Rotate toward position*, set *Degrees* to 10, set *X* to Player.X, and set *Y* to Player.Y. Add another action *Enemy - Set angle of motion*, and set *Angle* to angle(Enemy.X, Enemy.Y, Waypoint.X, Waypoint.Y).

Next, you will add the events for when an enemy reaches its destination, at which point they should select their next target (which should involve some randomness). Create a new event with the condition *Enemy - On collision with another object*, and select *Waypoint*. To verify that the enemy has collided with its actual target, add a second condition called *Waypoint - Compare instance variable*, and again check whether the ID

133

is equal to Enemy.Target. Add the action *Enemy - Variables: Add to*. For *Variable*, select Target, and for *Value* enter choose(1, 2).

You also need to make sure that the value of the Target variable does not exceed the total number of waypoints (Waypoint.Count). Add a subevent with the condition *Enemy - Compare instance variable*, and check whether *Target* is greater than or equal to Waypoint.Count. Then, add the action *Enemy - Variables: Set value*, and set *Target* to choose(0,1).

When you are finished adding all the content described in this section, the corresponding events should appear as shown in Figure 10-3. Save and test your project. Make sure you can move your player with the arrow keys and that the enemies move randomly while facing the player.

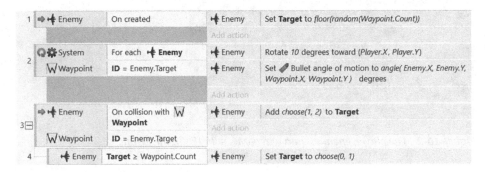

Figure 10-3. *Events to set the enemies to rotate toward waypoints*

Shooting and Spawning Enemies

In this section, you will add bullets for the player and enemies to shoot at each other and explosions that appear when they hit. You will also add random enemy spawning as well as configure the Timer behavior to set up a randomly periodic event that causes enemy planes to shoot.

First, in the layout, now that you have verified the enemy movement between waypoints works as expected, you no longer need to see the waypoints on the screen; click the Waypoint object in the object panel (so that all instances are selected) and set *Initial visibility* to Invisible. Next, create a Keyboard object. Then add two new sprites: one named PlayerBullet with the image bullet-gold.png and another named EnemyBullet with bullet-silver.png. Add the *Bullet* and *Destroy Outside Layout* behaviors to both. Position the bullets in the margins of the layout. Add another new sprite named Explosion; in the *Animation frames* window, import animation frames from the sprite strip named explode-animation.png, which consists of four rows and four columns. Set the animation properties *Speed* to 30, and set *Loop* to No. Close the image editor and position the explosion in the layout margins.

In the event sheet, create a new event with the condition *Keyboard - On key pressed*, and select the *Space* key. Add the action *Player - Spawn another object*, select PlayerBullet, and set *Layer* to "Main". Next, create a new event with the condition *PlayerBullet - On collision with another object*, and select *Enemy*. Add the following three actions: *PlayerBullet - Destroy*, *Enemy - Spawn another object* to spawn an Explosion object on the Main layer, and *Enemy - Destroy*. To remove explosions from the game once their animations are complete, create one more event with the condition *Explosion - Animations: On any finished*, and add the action *Explosion - Destroy*.

Since randomness adds to the challenge and replayability factor of this game, you will add periodically spawning enemies at random positions above the layout. In addition, you will implement a random shooting rate to prevent enemies from shooting at the same time; having enemies act differently from each other adds to the realism of the game.

To do this, you will use the *Timer* behavior, a new action named *Start timer*, and a new condition named *On timer*. The *Start timer* action determines when the corresponding *On timer* condition will register as true; both the condition and the action contain a Tag parameter, which is used to set up the association by giving these the same value. The *Start time* condition contains two additional parameters: Duration, which is used to specify how much time will pass until the *On timer* condition is first activated, and Type, which can be set to Once (which activates the condition one time) or Regular (will periodically activate the condition). In this game, every time an enemy spawns, it will start a timer called Shoot, which will repeat at a random rate, between 0.5 and 1.0 seconds. When an enemy's *On timer* condition activates, it will shoot a bullet toward the player.

In the layout, select the *Enemy* object, and add the behavior *Timer*. Then, move the enemy objects into the margins above the layout. In the event sheet, create a new event with the condition *System - Every X seconds*, and set *Interval* to 1. Add the action *System - Create object*, set *Object* to Enemy, set *Layer* to "Main", set *X* to random(100, 700), and set *Y* to -100. In the event with the condition *Enemy - On created*, add the action *Enemy - Start timer*, set *Duration* to 0.5 + random(0.5), set *Type* to Regular, and set *Tag* to "Shoot". Next, create a new event with the condition *Enemy - On timer* and set *Tag* to "Shoot". Then add the action *Enemy - Spawn another object* to spawn an EnemyBullet object on the Main layer.

When you are finished adding all the content described in this section, the corresponding events should appear as shown in Figure 10-4. Save and test your project. Make sure you can shoot bullets with the spacebar key to destroy enemies and that enemies are shooting toward you at random rates.

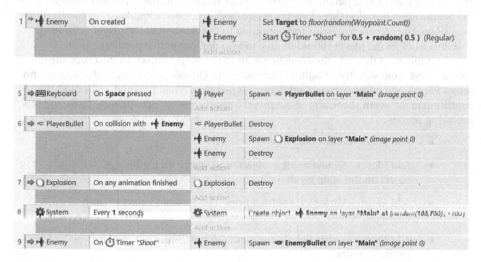

Figure 10-4. Events for shooting and spawning more enemies

Score, Health, Invincibility, and Game Over

In this section, you will implement player health and invincibility game mechanics, create the scoring system and user interface, and add the "game over" message that appears when the player runs out of health. After the player is hit by an enemy bullet, the player will lose one health point, and a Text object will update to indicate the player's current health.

First, add a new Text object named TextScore to the project. Set its *Layer* to UI, and position it in the bottom-left corner of the game window. Change the default text to Score: 0. To make the text easier to read, change the font to Arial, bold, size 24, and set the font color to black. Add another new Text object named TextHP to the project. Set its *Layer* to UI, and position it in the bottom-right corner of the game window. Change its default text to HP: 0, and change the font to Arial, bold, size 24. Also set the *Horizontal alignment* property to Right.

You will add health points as an instance variable to the player object since they are associated to a value intrinsic to the player, in contrast to the score, which is associated to the game as a whole. Add an instance variable named HP to the *Player* object, set *Type* to Number, *Initial value* to 10, and *Description* to Player health points. In the event sheet, create a new global variable named Score with the initial value 0. Then create an event with condition *Enemy - On destroyed* and action *System - Variable: Add to*, adding 100 to Score. Create another event with the condition *System - Every tick* and the two actions TextScore - *Set text to "Score: " & Score* and TextHP - *Set text to "HP: " & Player.HP*.

When an enemy bullet collides with the player and the player is not currently invincible (which occurs for a brief period after having been damaged), a small explosion should appear to indicate the damage, the player's health should decrease by 1, and the player sprite should flash for 1 second to indicate invincibility. To implement the invincibility feature, you will use the *Flash* behavior, a new action called *Flash*, and a new condition called *Is flashing*. The action *Flash* will then cause the object associated to alternate between visible and invisible at a specified rate. The visibility duration is specified by the *On time* parameter, the invisibility duration by the *Off time* parameter, and the overall effect duration (how long the entire flash sequence should last) by the *Duration* parameter. You can use the *Is flashing* condition to check whether the player is flashing and thus whether the player should be able to take damage at that particular time.

To implement this, add the *Flash* behavior to the Player object. In the event sheet, create a new event with the condition *EnemyBullet - On collision with another object*, and select *Player*. Add another condition *Player - Is flashing*. When finished, right-click this condition in the event sheet, and select *Invert* from the menu that appears. Then add the following actions:

- Add *EnemyBullet - Destroy*.

- Add *Player - Spawn another object*, and spawn an Explosion object on the Main layer.

- Add *Player - Variables: Subtract from*. For Variable, select HP, and for Value, enter 1.

- Add *Enemy - Flash*. For *On time* and *Off time,* enter 0.1, and for *Duration* enter 1.

Finally, you will implement the "game over" functionality. In the layout, add a new sprite named GameOver with the image gameover.png. Positon it in the center of the layout, set its *Layer* to UI, and set *Initial Visibility* to Invisible. When the player's health reaches 0 (or below), the "game over" message will be displayed, the player will be destroyed, and a giant explosion will appear (many times larger than the default size). In addition, enemies should stop spawning, and any remaining enemies will rotate toward and fly off the bottom of the layout (since there is no player object remaining to shoot at). For the enemies to rotate and move differently, the For each event that currently rotates and moves enemies should be restricted to work only while the player exists (or is onscreen); otherwise, they will interfere with the "game over" sequence of movements discussed earlier. In the event sheet, locate the For each event, and add the condition *Player - Is on-screen*. Also, add this condition to the *Every 1 second* event to stop enemy planes from spawning after the player is destroyed. Then create a new event with the condition *Player - Compare instance variable*, and check whether HP is less than or equal to 0. Then add the following actions:

- Add *GameOver - Set visible*, and set it to Visible.

- Add *Player - Spawn another object*, and spawn an Explosion object on the Main layer.

- Add *Explosion - Set scale*, and set it to 8.

- Add *Player - Destroy*.

- Add *Enemy - Angle: Set angle*, and set *Angle* to 90 degrees.

- Add *Enemy - Bullet: Set angle of motion*, and set *Angle* to 90 degrees.

When you are finished adding all the content described in this section, the corresponding events should appear as shown in Figure 10-5. Save and test your project. Make sure you receive points for destroying enemies and that you can lose health and flash upon taking damage. Also test that when you run out of health, the game ends properly.

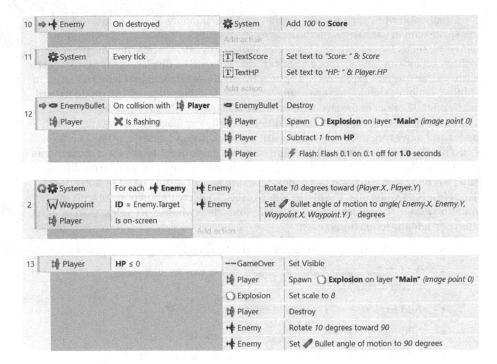

Figure 10-5. *Events for score, player health, and game over*

Congratulations! You have now finished implementing the core mechanics of the Airplane Assault game.

Side Quests

In this optional section, you will add endless vertical scrolling along the vertical axis to your water background, similar to the effect from the Plane Dodger game, with a few key differences. This will add a sense of global movement to the gameplay. A list of suggested additional features will also be presented for your consideration.

Endless Vertical Scrolling

First, in the layout, for the Background sprite, change the *Position* property to 0, 0, and set *Size* to 800, 800. Add the *Bullet* behavior, change *Speed* to 200, and change *Set angle* to No (because this object should not be rotated). Create another instance of Background, and set its *Position* to 0, -800. The layout should appear as shown in Figure 10-6.

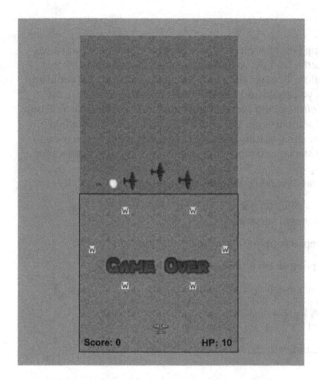

Figure 10-6. *The layout adjusted for endless vertical scrolling*

In the event sheet, create a new event with the condition *System - On start of layout*, add the action *Water - Set angle of motion*, and set *Angle* to 90. Next, you will create the event that shifts Background above the layout after it moves off-screen on the bottom. Create another event with the condition *Water - Size & Position: Is on-screen*. When finished, right-click this condition in the event sheet and select *Invert* from the menu that appears. Add the condition *Water - Compare Y*, and check whether the Y coordinate is greater than 800. Finally, add the action *Water - Move at angle*, with *Angle* set to 270 and *Distance* set to 2 * Water.Height. When you are finished, these events should appear as in Figure 10-7. Save and test your project; the background image should appear to scroll forever, with no noticeable gap between the two images.

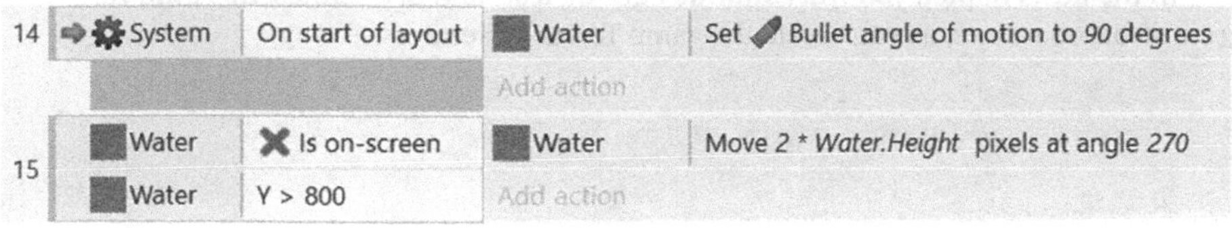

14	⇒ 🔧 System	On start of layout	▨ Water	Set 🖊 Bullet angle of motion to *90* degrees
			Add action	
15	▨ Water	✖ Is on-screen	▨ Water	Move *2 * Water.Height* pixels at angle *270*
	▨ Water	Y > 800	Add action	

Figure 10-7. *Events for endless vertical scrolling*

On Your Own

Airplane Assault is a great starting point for applying many features and items you have learned so far. Adding menus, audio, and pause functionality would certainly give this game a more polished presentation. To make the game a bit more difficult, you could add enemy health points. To do this, you could add a health point instance variable to the enemy and, in the *Enemy - On collision with PlayerBullet event*, replace the *Destroy* action with one that subtracts a health point instead. You could then add an event for when the Enemy's health is less than or equal to 0 and proceed to destroy them as you used to do. You could also add falling obstacles and items that positively or negatively affect the player's characteristics such as speed.

Here, we list some other ideas of varying difficulty to implement:

- Adjusting the player's collision polygon to be smaller (thus increasing their chances of survival)

- Adding analog gamepad support (discussed in Chapter 5)

- Gaining additional points from a "Bonus Points" item

- Adding an item to increase the player's health points

- Adding a dangerous, instant destruction item that would destroy the player on contact

- Adding an explosive bullet to shoot and explode after a delay, with range damage

- Implementing *SpawnRate* and *EnemySpeed* variables from Plane Dodger for difficulty ramp

Summary

In this chapter, you created the game Airplane Assault. You used the *Timer* behavior to implement time-based, repeated enemy shooting with a random interval. To give the player multiple chances to battle, you learned how to add health points and how to use the *Flash* behavior to add invincibility. In the "Side Quests" section, you added endless vertical scrolling to the background for a more immersive experience. The "Side Quests" section also discussed other additions including enemy health points, analog gamepad support, items, and a difficulty ramp.

In the next chapter, you will continue fighting a stream of enemies, this time via ground-based turrets, as you create the game Tower Defenders.

CHAPTER 11

■ ■ ■

Tower Defenders

In this chapter, you'll create Tower Defenders, a top-view game where the player places various towers to defend a base from attacking enemies, as shown in Figure 11-1.

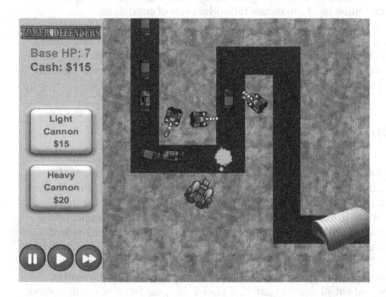

Figure 11-1. The Tower Defenders game

In Tower Defenders, the player places cannons (or other defensive structures) alongside a road, which automatically attack enemies traveling along the road toward the player's base. Destroying enemies increases the player's resources (or "cash"), which can then be used to purchase additional turrets. As time progresses, enemies spawn more frequently, and more difficult enemies may appear. Every time an enemy reaches the player's base, the base loses one health point; if all health points are lost, the game is over. Since an unlimited number of enemies can spawn, the ultimate goal of the player is to survive as long as possible.

Since cannons have a limited field of view, turret placement is important in this game; the player should choose locations within the range of as much road area as possible, but at the same time, it is important to fit as many turrets as possible in the available area. Cash management is also a key feature in this game: the player must decide which type of cannons to invest in. Less expensive cannons are generally less powerful; they may have weaker bullets, may have a smaller range, or may take longer between shots, compared to more expensive turrets.

In developing this game, a significant amount of time will be spent on the user interface. In addition to text displays, there are also clickable buttons that enable the player to purchase new cannons. Once a cannon is purchased, there will be a colored disk centered on the mouse that indicates the range of the turret and whether it may be placed at the current mouse location.

This game will make use of Sprite, TiledBackground, Text, and Mouse objects; global and instance variables; subevents; else conditions; and the waypoint-based logic from previous chapters. You will learn how to use the *Turret* behavior, which rotates an object toward a preset target and fires bullets at regular intervals. You will also implement a shoplike game mechanic to purchase cannons. To place the purchased cannons, you will learn how to implement a mouse-based drag-and-drop mechanic. You will also learn how to create "or" condition blocks to reduce redundant sets of conditions.

To begin, download the zip file containing the graphics for this chapter from the book web site. In the layout properties, set the layout *Name* to Main, and set *Size* to 800, 600. As you have in previous projects, set up three layers named Background, Main, and UI. In the project properties, change the window *Size* to 800, 600. Also, on the *View* tab select the *View grid* and *Snap to grid* check boxes.

Level Setup

In this section, you will set up the level and create a path for the enemies to follow. First, create a TiledBackground named BackgroundUI, with the image white-pixels. png. Change its size to 192,608, and position it on the left side of the layout. Then, in the Background layer, create a TiledBackground named BackgroundDirt, with the image dirt.png; change its size to 608,608, and position it on the right side of the screen so that it fills the remaining area in the layout. Finally, create a TiledBackground named Road with the image road.png; this object will be used to create the path along which the enemies will move. Create multiple instances of the Road object and position them to form a road from the top edge of the dirt area to another edge; make sure the road is 64 pixels (2 squares) wide at all times. Figure 11-2 shows one possible road configuration.

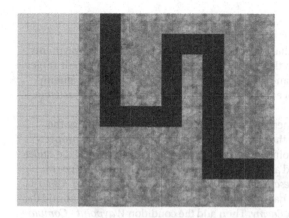

Figure 11-2. *Setup for the background graphics and the road*

Next, you'll need to configure the spawn point and waypoints that the enemy objects will follow. Set the layout's active layer to Main. Create a new sprite named SpawnPoint; draw any image you like in the image editor (as it won't be visible while the game is being played), resize it to 32,32, and place it in the margin of the layout by the beginning of the road. Create a new sprite named Waypoint (again, with a drawn image), and create an instance variable with *Name* set to ID, *Type* set to Number, *Initial value* set to 0, and *Description* set to Unique identification number. Create additional instances of this object, place one in the center of each corner of the road, and place one beyond the end of the road in the margins of the layout. Change the values of the instance variables of the Waypoint objects so that they start at 0 and increase by 1 at each corner. When finished, change the size of the Waypoint objects to 8,8. Figure 11-3 illustrates the placement and numbering of the waypoints for the road configuration in Figure 11-2.

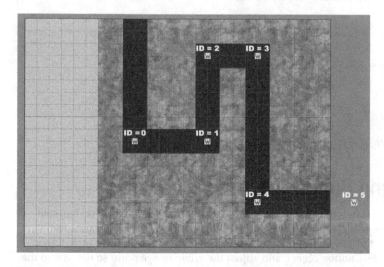

Figure 11-3. *Waypoint positions and numbering*

Enemy Movement

In this section, you will add enemies that will follow the path indicated by the waypoints. In contrast to previous chapters, when the enemy arrives at a waypoint, its current Target value will be increased by 1 (rather than by a random value). In addition, a new enemy will spawn every second. Also, as each enemy is created, its angle should be adjusted to move downward.

First, create a new sprite named Enemy, with the image truck.png, and change the name of the animation to Truck. Close the image editor window and change the property Angle to 90. Place it above the SpawnPoint object in the margin of the layout. Add the *Bullet* behavior, and change *Speed* to 200. Add an instance variable named Target, set *Type* to Number, set *Initial value* to 0, and set *Description* to ID of the Waypoint to move towards.

Movement along the waypoints is handled by two events. First, create an event, add the condition *System - For Each*, and select *Enemy*. Then add the condition *Waypoint - Compare instance variable*, and check whether *ID* is equal to Enemy.Target. Add the action *Enemy - Rotate toward position*, set *Degrees* to 15, set *X* to Waypoint.X, and set *Y* to Waypoint.Y. Second, create another event, and first add the condition *Enemy - On collision with another object*, and select *Waypoint*. Then add the condition *Waypoint - Compare instance variable*, and again check whether *ID* is equal to Enemy.Target. Add the action *Enemy - Variables: Add to*, select *Target*, and enter 1. Finally, to periodically spawn enemies, create another event with the condition *System - Every X seconds*, and for *Interval*, enter 5. Add the action *SpawnPoint - Spawn another object*, and select *Enemy*. In addition, add the action *Enemy - Set angle*, and set *Angle* to 90 degrees. When you are finished, the enemy-related events should appear as in Figure 11-4. Save and test your project, making sure that the enemies spawn and move along the path until the end and then move outside the layout. Once you have verified that everything works as expected, click the Waypoint object in the object panel (so that all instances are selected) and set *Initial visibility* to Invisible. Note that the enemies aren't automatically destroyed when they move off-screen; this will be addressed later in the chapter when you add the player's base.

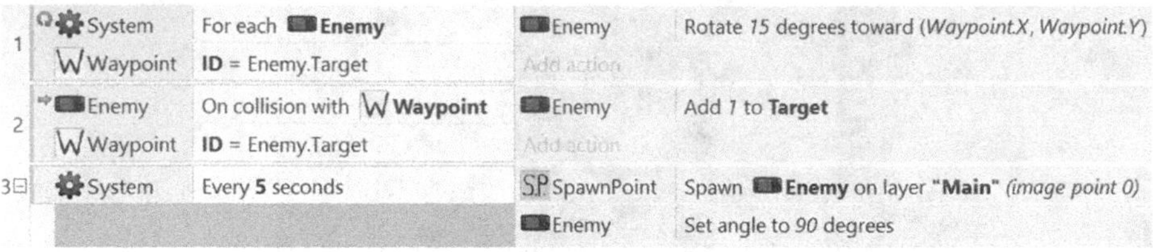

1	System	For each **Enemy**	Enemy	Rotate *15* degrees toward *(Waypoint.X, Waypoint.Y)*
	Waypoint	ID = Enemy.Target	Add action	
2	Enemy	On collision with **Waypoint**	Enemy	Add *1* to **Target**
	Waypoint	ID = Enemy.Target	Add action	
3	System	Every **5** seconds	SP SpawnPoint	Spawn **Enemy** on layer **"Main"** *(image point 0)*
			Enemy	Set angle to *90* degrees

Figure 11-4. Events for enemy movement and spawning

Cannons and Bullets

You are now ready to implement cannons, most of whose functionality will be handled by the Turret behavior. Add a new Sprite object named Cannon with the image turret-light.png. Rename the animation to Light. Adjust the collision polygon to form a box around the base of the Cannon object, and adjust the origin image point so that it is in the middle of the base, as shown in Figure 11-5.

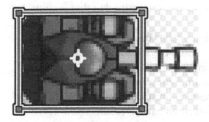

Figure 11-5. *Collision polygon for the Cannon sprite*

When you are finished, close the image editor windows. Position the cannon on the dirt, near a corner of the road. Add the behavior Turret. The *Turret* behavior will give the cannon the ability to aim at enemies and shoot bullets, which need to be set up now as well. Create another new sprite named Missile with the image message.png, add the behavior *Bullet* and the behavior *Destroy* outside layout, and position the sprite in the margin area. Select the Cannon object again. The *Turret* behavior properties that you need to adjust are explained and their new values are given in the following list:

- *Range*: This is how close enemies must be to be detected. Set this to 100.

- *Rotate Speed*: This is how quickly the cannon can rotate (in degrees per second) toward its target. Set this to 360.

- *Predictive aim*: When set to No, the turret will rotate toward the target's current position; when set to Yes, the turret will rotate to a position ahead of the current target, taking into account the speed of the turret projectile and the speed and direction of the target. (However, the turret may still miss its intended target if the target changes direction suddenly.) Set this to Yes.

- *Projectile speed*: This value is used as described earlier when Predictive aim is set to Yes. In general, this should be set to the speed of the projectile objects that the turret will spawn. Set this to 400.

You will now set up instance variables to add health to enemies and a power level (which indicates the amount of damage inflicted on contact) to the missiles, which will be set by the cannons. Select the Enemy object, add an instance variable named HP, set *Type* to Number, set *Initial value* to 2, and set *Description* to Enemy health points. Then select the Cannon object, add an instance variable named Power, set *Type* to Number, set *Initial value* to 1, and set *Description* to Used to set Missile Power. Then, select the Missile object, add an instance variable named Power, set *Type* to Number, set *Initial value* to 1, and set *Description* to Value to subtract from enemy HP.

The objects that the cannon will target and the projectiles that the cannon will fire are specified with events. Create a new event with the condition *System - On start of layout*, add the action *Cannon - Turret: Add object to target*, and select *Enemy*. Add another event with the condition *Cannon - Turret: On shoot*, add the action *Cannon - Spawn another object* (select Missile), add the action *Missile - Instance variables: Set value*, and set *Power*

145

to Cannon.Power. These events, as well as the following events described in this section, should appear as shown in Figure 11-6.

To make it easier for the player to see when an enemy has been damaged, you will add an animated explosion effect. Add a new sprite named Explosion; in the *Animation frames* window, import animation frames from the sprite strip named explosion.png, which consists of six rows and six columns. Set the animation property *Speed* to 60 and *Loop* to No. Close the image editor and position the explosion sprite in the layout margins.

To make the missiles damage the enemies as described earlier, create a new event with the condition *Missile - On collision with another object*, and select Enemy. Then add the following actions:

- Add *Enemy - Variables: Subtract from*, select *HP*, and for *Value* enter Missile.Power.

- Add *Missile - Spawn another object*, and select *Explosion*.

- Add *Explosion - Set size*, and set both *Width* and *Height* to 32.

- Add *Missile - Destroy*.

To destroy enemies whose health has reached 0, create a new event with the condition *Enemy - Compare instance variable*, and check whether HP is less than or equal to 0. Then add the following actions:

- Add *Enemy - Spawn another object*, and select Explosion.

- Add *Explosion - Set size*, and set both *Width* and *Height* to 64.

- Add *Enemy - Destroy*.

Finally, two more events will complete this section. First, explosions whose animations are complete should be removed from the layout, so create an event with the condition *Explosion - On any animation finished* and the action *Explosion - Destroy*. Second, missiles should not appear in the area of the layout corresponding to the user interface, so create an event with the condition *Missile - On collision with another object*, select *BackgroundUI*, and add the action *Missile - Destroy*. Figure 11-6 shows the events described in this section.

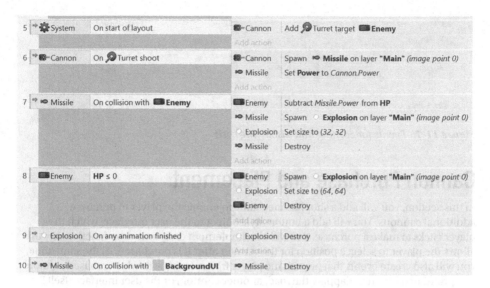

5	System	On start of layout	Cannon	Add Turret target **Enemy**
				Add action
6	Cannon	On Turret shoot	Cannon	Spawn **Missile** on layer **"Main"** *(image point 0)*
			Missile	Set **Power** to *Cannon.Power*
				Add action
7	Missile	On collision with **Enemy**	Enemy	Subtract *Missile.Power* from **HP**
			Missile	Spawn **Explosion** on layer **"Main"** *(image point 0)*
			Explosion	Set size to *(32, 32)*
			Missile	Destroy
				Add action
8	Enemy	HP ≤ 0	Enemy	Spawn **Explosion** on layer **"Main"** *(image point 0)*
			Explosion	Set size to *(64, 64)*
			Enemy	Destroy
				Add action
9	Explosion	On any animation finished	Explosion	Destroy
				Add action
10	Missile	On collision with **BackgroundUI**	Missile	Destroy

Figure 11-6. Events for cannon setup and enemy health

Earning Cash

Next, you will begin to implement the cash mechanic that will be used for purchasing additional cannons later, which will become important as the enemy spawn rate increases (which will be implemented later). To begin, in the event sheet, create a new global variable named Cash with initial value 0, and for *Description* enter Used to buy cannons. To help distinguish the user interface area from the gameplay area, you will add a decorative logo. Create a new sprite named Logo with the image tower-defenders-title.png, set its size to 192,32, and position it on top of BackgroundUI, in the top-left area of the layout, as shown in Figure 11-1. Then create a new *Text* object named TextCash, and set its position to 0, 96. Change its default text to Cash: $0; set the font to Arial, bold, size 22; and set the font color to green. Also set both the *Horizontal alignment* and *Vertical alignment* properties to Center.

Select the Enemy object, add an instance variable named Cash, set *Type* to Number, set *Initial value* to 4, and set *Description* to Cash added when destroyed. In the event sheet, locate the Enemy.HP <= 0 event, and add the action *System - Variables: Add to*, adding the value *Enemy.Cash to* the Cash variable. Create a new event with the condition *System - Every tick* and action *TextCash - Set text to "Cash: $" & Cash*. The events in this section should appear as shown in Figure 11-7.

147

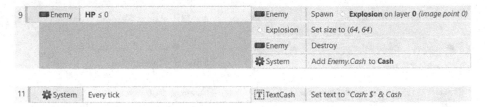

9	■ Enemy	HP ≤ 0		■ Enemy	Spawn ○ **Explosion** on layer **0** *(image point 0)*
				○ Explosion	Set size to *(64, 64)*
				■ Enemy	Destroy
				✹ System	Add *Enemy.Cash* to **Cash**
11	✹ System	Every tick		[T] TextCash	Set text to *"Cash: $"* & *Cash*

Figure 11-7. *Events for earning and displaying cash*

Cannon Purchase and Placement

In this section, you will add a shoplike mechanic to enable the player to purchase additional cannons. You will add a button-style object to the user interface, which the player clicks to make a purchase. You will also implement drag-and-drop functionality that allows the player to select a position for the cannon after it is purchased. At the same time, you will also create events that prevent the player from placing a newly purchased cannon in a prohibited area (overlapping the road, another cannon, or the user interface itself).

The purchasing buttons will created from a combination of a Sprite object and a Text object to avoid having to create new sprite images with prerendered text for each individual button. Add a new sprite named PurchaseButton with the image button. png. Position it in the center of the BackgroundUI, and set its size to 160,128. Add two instance variables, one named Type (with Type set to Text, *Initial value* set to Light, and *Description* set to Cannon animation name) and the other named Price (with *Type* set to Number, *Initial value* set to 15, and *Description* set to Cash needed to purchase cannon). Next, add a new Text object named TextPrice, and position it on the purchase button. Change its default text to Light Cannon $15; set the font to Arial, bold, size 16; and set its font color to green. Also set both the *Horizontal alignment* and *Vertical alignment* properties to Center. You may want to resize the Text object so that each word appears on a separate line. The user interface should appear in the layout as shown in Figure 11-8.

Figure 11-8. *Adding a button to the user interface*

The next mechanic to implement is cannon spawning and placement. The cannon being dragged will be set to the position of the mouse (similar to the paddle movement in the Rectangle Destroyer game), but because there are typically multiple cannons onscreen, the correct one needs to be uniquely identified. For this purpose, select the Cannon object, and add a new instance variable named Dragging, set *Type* to Number, set *Initial value* to 0, and set *Description* to 0 = Fixed in place, 1 = Dragging.

You will next set up a translucent circle that appears when a cannon is purchased, which serves two purposes: the size of the circle indicates the range of the cannon, and the color of the circle indicates whether the cannon may be placed at the current mouse position (green for "yes" and red for "no"). Create a new sprite named Circle with the image circle-green.png, and change the name of the animation to Green. Add a new animation named Red, using the image circle-red.png. Close the image editor, and set the properties *Layer* to UI, *Opacity* to 50, and *Initial visibility* to Invisible. Since the circle indicator will be visible only while the player is in the process of placing the cannon, the circle's visibility can be used in one of the conditions that check whether the player is currently able to purchase a cannon (the player cannot purchase another cannon while in the process of placing one).

With these steps completed, you are now ready to create the event that enables the player to purchase a cannon. To begin, add the Mouse object to the project. In the event sheet, create a new event with the following conditions:

- Add *Mouse - On object clicked*, and select *PurchaseButton*.

- Add *Global* and *Local Variables - Compare variable*, and check whether *Cash* is greater than or equal to PurchaseButton.Price.

- Add *Circle - Is Visible*; this condition needs to be inverted.

Next, add the following actions to the event:

- Add *System - Variables: Subtract from*, select *Cash*, and for *Value* enter PurchaseButton.Price.

- Add *PurchaseButton - Spawn another object*, select *Cannon*, and set *Layer* to "UI".

- Add *Cannon - Set animation*, and enter PurchaseButton.Type.

- Add *Cannon - Variables: Set value*, select *Dragging*, and for *Value* enter 1.

- Add *Cannon - Turret: Set enabled*, and select *Disabled*.

- Add *Circle - Set size*, and set both *Width* and *Height* to Cannon.Turret.Range * 2.

- Add *Circle - Set visible*, set to Visible.

This event appears in Figure 11-9.

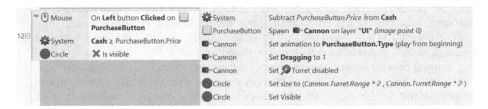

Figure 11-9. *Event for purchasing cannons*

The next event to create implements the drag mechanic, which sets the purchased cannon (and the indicator circle) to the position of the mouse. While this is happening, the color of the circle needs to change depending on whether the cannon can be placed in the current position. The cannon may *not* be placed if it overlaps the road, the user interface, or another cannon. The first two of these conditions are straightforward to check, but the third is not, because of the way conditions "filter" the set of instances under consideration. It may seem like you should be able to simply check this with a pair of conditions: *Cannon - Compare instance variable* (check whether Dragging equals 1) and *Cannon - Is overlapping another object* (select *Cannon*). However, after the first condition is evaluated, only those cannons whose Dragging variable equals 1 will be considered when checking the second condition, which is not what you need to happen. To avoid these complexities, a new sprite will be introduced to indicate the areas currently occupied by cannons.

Create a new sprite named Taken, fill in the sprite with any color, close the image editor, and set *Initial visibility* to Invisible. Resize and position the sprite so that it exactly covers the cannon currently placed on the layout. In the event sheet, create a new event with the condition *Cannon - Compare instance variable* (and check whether Dragging equals 1). Add the action *Cannon - Set position*, setting X and Y to Mouse.X and Mouse.Y, respectively, and add the action *Circle - Set position to another object*, selecting *Cannon*. To this event, add a subevent with the condition *Cannon - Is overlapping another object*, select *BackgroundUI*, add the action *Circle - Set animation*, and enter "Red". Next, you could create additional events with similar conditions to check the other overlap cases, but since each one of these events would contain the same action, it is more efficient to use an "or" block, in which case only one of the listed conditions needs to be true to activate the actions. To make this event an "or" block, right-click the area in the event to the left of the condition, and from the pop-up menu that appears, select Make 'Or' block. Add the condition *Cannon - Is overlapping another object*, and select *Road*; then add the condition *Cannon - Is overlapping another object*, and select *Taken*. You will notice that the word *or* appears between the conditions you have added. Finally, add a second subevent to this event, with the condition *System - Else*. Then add the action *Circle - Set animation*, and enter "Green". This event should appear as in Figure 11-10.

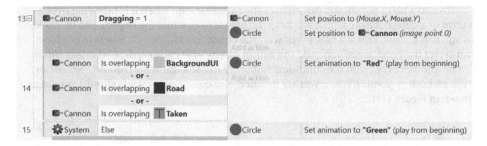

Figure 11-10. *Event for dragging cannons and updating the circular placement indicator*

Finally, you need to implement the drop mechanic. Thanks to your previous work, this step is relatively straightforward since the color of the circle indicates whether the cannon may be placed. There are a few actions that you need to remember: enable the *Turret* behavior, and then set the Dragging variable to 0, make the Circle invisible, and spawn a Taken instance to mark the selected location as unavailable in future cannon placements. Create a new event with the following conditions:

- Add *Mouse - On click* (keep the default properties).

- Add *Cannon - Variables: Compare value*, set to check whether Dragging is equal to 1.

- Add *Circle - Animation: Is playing*, set to check whether Green is playing.

Then add the following actions:

- Add *Cannon - Move to layer*, and enter "Main".

- Add *Cannon - Variables: Set value*, select *Dragging*, and for *Value* enter 0.

- Add *Cannon - Turret: Set enabled*, and select *Enabled*.

- Add *Cannon - Spawn another object*, and select *Taken*.

- Add *Circle - Set visible*, set to Invisible.

This event should appear as shown in Figure 11-11.

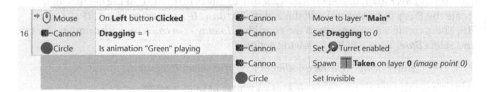

Figure 11-11. *Event for placing cannons*

151

To add a bit of polish, you can change the mouse cursor when it is hovering over a button to a different icon, which will help the player notice that the objects can be clicked. To add this feature, create a new event with the condition Mouse - Cursor is over object, and select the PurchaseButton. Add the action *Mouse - Set cursor style*, and select *Hand*. Create another event with the condition *System - Else*, add the action *Mouse - Set cursor style*, and select *Normal*. When you are finished, the cursor style events should appear as shown in Figure 11-12.

17	( ) Mouse	Cursor is over ☐ **PurchaseButton**	( ) Mouse	Set cursor to **Hand**
		Add action		
18	⚙ System	Else	( ) Mouse	Set cursor to **Normal**

Figure 11-12. Events for setting mouse cursor style

At this point, if you haven't done so recently, you should certainly save your game and test the purchasing mechanic and the drag-and-drop functionality. To speed up the testing project, you should change the initial value of the global variable Cash to a large number (so that you don't have to wait to earn money to make purchases); just remember to set it back to the original value when you're done testing!

Game Ending and Difficulty Ramp

In this section, you will add the Base object that the player will defend from incoming enemies. The base will be placed at the end of the road path and will have a limited number of health points, which will be displayed in the user interface. Every enemy that reaches the base will reduce the base's health by 1, and when its health reaches 0, the game is over. To keep the game challenging, a difficulty ramp will be added to increase the enemy spawning rate, similar to the implementation from the Plane Dodger game.

To begin, in the layout, add a new Sprite object named Base with the image base. png, and position it at the end of the path made by the road. To the Base object, add an instance variable named HP, set *Type* to Number, set *Initial value* to 10, and set *Description* to Health points. Next, add a new Text object named TextBaseHP, and set its position to 0, 64. Change its default text to Base HP: 10; set the font to Arial, bold, size 22; set the font color to red, and set the *Horizontal alignment* to Center. Add another new sprite named GameOver with the image game-over.png. Position it in the center of the game area, set its *Layer* to UI, and set *Initial Visibility* to Invisible. Next, in the event sheet, locate the *Every tick event* and add the action *TextBaseHP - Set text to "Base HP: " & Base. HP*. Then, create a new event with the condition *Enemy - On collision with another* object, and select *Base*. Then add the following actions:

- Add *Enemy - Spawn another object*, and select *Explosion*.

- Add *Explosion - Set size*, set to a *Width* of 64 and *Height* of 64.

- Add *Enemy - Destroy*.

- Add *Base - Spawn another object*, and select *Explosion*.

- Add *Explosion - Set size*, set to a *Width* of 128 and *Height* of 128.

- Add *Base - Variables: Subtract from*, select *HP*, and for *Value* enter 1.

To destroy the base when it runs out of health, create a new event with the condition *Base - Compare instance variable*, and check whether HP is less than or equal to 0. Then add the following actions:

- Add *GameOver - Set visible*, set to *Visible*.

- Add *SpawnPoint - Destroy*.

- Add *Base - Destroy*.

When you are finished, the base-related and "game over" events should appear as shown in Figure 11-13. Save and test your project. Make sure that enemies damage the base and that when the base runs out of health, the game ends.

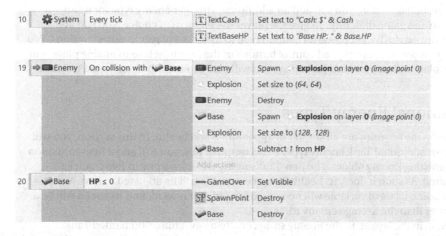

Figure 11-13. *Events for "game over"*

As the game stands, enemies spawn at a constant interval, and this game is trivially easy once a few turrets are in place. To increase the challenge, you will create and use a global variable named SpawnRate to adjust this rate. First, in the event sheet, create a new global variable named SpawnRate with an initial value of 5, and for *Description*, enter Seconds until next enemy spawns. Locate the Every 1 seconds event, double-click its condition, and change Interval to SpawnRate. Then, create a new event with the condition *System - Every X seconds*, and for Interval enter 5. Add the condition *System - Variables: Compare varia*ble, set to check whether *SpawnRate* is greater than or equal to 0.50. Then add the action *System - Variables: Subtract from*. For *Variable* select *SpawnRate*, and set Value to 0.25. The difficulty ramp events should appear as shown in Figure 11-14. Save and test your project. Make sure that enemies spawn at a gradual and increasing rate, and notice the game's new difficulty.

Figure 11-14. *Events for difficulty ramp*

Congratulations! You have now finished implementing the core mechanics of the Tower Defenders game.

Side Quests

In this optional section, you will add an additional, stronger enemy type for more variation and game difficulty. To give the player the element of choice, you will add a new, more expensive yet powerful cannon type to assist the player in dire situations. You will also implement time speed control buttons in the user interface to enable players to pause, play, and fast-forward gameplay. You will also explore other suggested features.

Additional Enemy Types

Currently, the enemies are all similar in appearance and health. In this section, you will create an additional Tank enemy type. To accomplish this, you will add a new animation to the existing Enemy object. The new Tank enemy will have a one in five chance of appearing. As soon it does, its health instance variable will be adjusted to have an extra health point, its Cash variable will be set to 6 for a higher reward, and its speed will be a bit slower than the average enemy truck.

First, in the layout, to the Enemy sprite, create a new animation named Tank, using the image tank.png. Then in the event sheet, locate the event where enemies are spawned. To this event, add a subevent with the condition *System - Compare two values*, set to check whether random(0, 100) is less than or equal to 20. Then add the following actions:

- Add *Enemy - Set animation*, and enter "Tank".

- Add *Enemy - Variables: Set value*, select *HP*, and for *Value* enter 3.

- Add *Enemy - Variables: Set value*, select *Cash*, and for Value enter 6.

- *Enemy - Bullet: Set speed*, and enter 180.

When you are finished, these events should appear as in Figure 11-15. Save and test your project. Make sure that every once in a while, a slower and stronger enemy Tank appears, rewarding you with more cash upon its destruction.

Figure 11-15. *Events for adding a Tank enemy type*

Additional Cannon Types

In the game's current state, the player has one choice in terms of cannon purchase. In this section, you will add a new Heavy cannon choice that will be more expensive, will be stronger, and will have more range than the current Light cannon. Create another instance of the PurchaseButton object, position it below the original, set its *Type* variable to Heavy, and set its *Price* variable to 20. Then create another instance of the TextPrice object, change its default text to Heavy Cannon $20, and position it on the new PurchaseButton. At this point, your user interface should resemble the one shown at this beginning of this chapter, in Figure 11-1. Next, double-click the Cannon sprite, and create a new animation named Heavy, using the image turret-heavy.png. When you are finished, close the image editor windows.

The purchase event must be adjusted to coordinate the values and properties of the cannon based on its type. In particular, you will increase the power of the heavy cannon type (which is reasonable, given its higher cost). Locate the event containing the condition where the PurchaseButton is clicked, and add a subevent with the condition *Cannon - Animation: Is playing*, set to check whether Heavy is playing. Then, add the action *Cannon - Variables: Set value*, select *Power*, and for *Value* enter 2. When you are finished, the subevent should appear as in Figure 11-16. Save and test your project; you should now be able purchase and place stronger "heavy cannons" for a cost of $20.

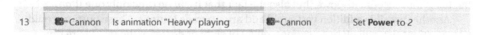

Figure 11-16. *Subevent for configuring the heavy cannon type*

Time Speed Control

In this section, you will implement time speed control buttons that enable players to pause or speed up the game. These buttons will all be created in similar fashion to the buttons created in Chapter 5. To begin, in the layout, create three new sprites, with the names ButtonPlay, ButtonPause, and ButtonFast, using the images button-play.png, button-pause.png, and button-fast.png, respectively. Change the size of each of these sprites to 60, 60 and arrange them near the bottom of the BackgroundUI object. Then, in the event sheet, create a new event with the condition *Mouse - On object clicked*, and select the ButtonPause. Add the action *System - Set time scale*, and enter 0. Create two more similar events, but for clicking the ButtonPlay and ButtonFast objects and setting the timescales to 1 and 1.5, respectively. When you are finished, the time speed control events should appear as in Figure 11-17. Save and test your project. You should be able to pause, play, and speed up the game. Notice during speedup, enemies spawn faster, which adds a layer of difficulty.

Figure 11-17. *Events for time speed control*

On Your Own

As usual, you should add menus and audio to this project. With the dynamic shoplike mechanic and customizable variables you have created in Tower Defenders, there is plenty of room for possible additions and features. You could create new cannon types with different speeds, firing rates, range, and power; you will have to take all these features into account when selecting the price for each new cannon type to keep the gameplay balanced.

Another addition you could consider is a Land Mine object. Such an object would be very different from cannons and would not involve the turret behavior at all; such an object should be able to be placed only on the road (and not overlapping dirt or walls). When an enemy collides with it, it should do a great deal of damage to the enemy, but the land mine itself should also be destroyed. The logic for purchase and placement would be similar to that for cannons, but it will require its own set of events because of the different overlapping conditions. You will have to determine a fair cost for the Land Mine object that takes into account its power but also the fact that it can be used only one time.

Another possible addition you could add are upgrade buttons. These buttons could trigger actions that will increase cannon range of sight or decrease the rate of fire time for the cannons. Their cost should be typically high. (You will need to store these adjusted values in global variables, update all the currently existing turret properties, and use the global variables when initializing newly created turrets.)

Summary

In this chapter, you created the game Tower Defenders. You were introduced to the Turret behavior to implement dynamic aiming and firing cannon objects. You then learned how to create a game economy, which fueled a shoplike mechanic for purchasing additional cannons. In doing this, you learned how to add buttons and how to implement drag-and-drop mechanics to place cannons on the playing field. You also learned how to use the "or" block feature to reduce event redundancy. The "Side Quests" section discussed potential game additions including implementing more enemy types, more turret types, and speed control buttons for the user interface.

In the next chapter, instead of destroying enemies that travel across the screen, you will focus on avoiding enemies as you run around a maze while collecting coins, as you create a game called Maze Runman.

CHAPTER 12

■ ■ ■

Maze Runman

In this chapter, you'll create Maze Runman, a top-down collection game where the player maneuvers around a maze trying to collect coins while avoiding being caught by ghosts, as shown in Figure 12-1.

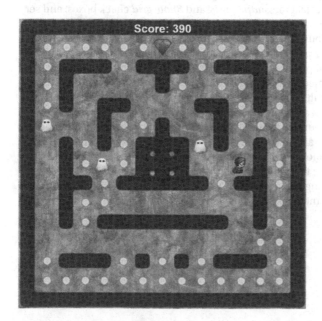

Figure 12-1. The Maze Runman game

In Maze Runman, the player controls a character, named Runman, whose goal is to collect all the coins scattered around a haunted maze. Three ghosts will move around the maze; two of them will chase Runman, while the third will wander around at random. If Runman is hit by a ghost, the game is over. The player must plan their route carefully, keep an eye on the ghosts, and be ready to change their route quickly.

© Lee Stemkoski and Evan Leider 2017

L. Stemkoski and E. Leider, *Game Development with Construct 2*,
DOI 10.1007/978-1-4842-2784-8_12

Runman can travel in four directions, and movement is controlled by the arrow keys. Coins are collected on contact. This chapter assumes you are familiar with using the Sprite, TiledBackground, Keyboard, and Tilemap objects; using the *Bullet*, *Timer*, and *Fade* behaviors; creating image-based animations; and using the floor and random functions. In this chapter, you will learn how to implement precise grid-aligned movement with the *Bullet* behavior. You will also learn about the Array object, a data structure that will be used to store the possible directions in which each ghost may move. There will also be a discussion about how to create "intelligent" ghosts, which will appear to respond to the player's movement and, at times, may even seem to be setting up "ambushes" for the player. Since the logic underlying the game mechanics in this chapter is quite complex, you will also learn how to create groups in the event sheet to keep the events more clearly organized. Also in this chapter, conditions and actions will be expressed more briefly than in previous chapters: event group headings will be included only occasionally to avoid confusion, and if a condition or action requires only one parameter, it will be given in parentheses.

To begin, download the zip file containing the graphics for this chapter from the book web site. In the *View* tab, select the *Snap to grid* and *Show grid* check boxes, and set the grid width and grid height both to 16. Set both the layout size and the window size to 480, 480. As you have in previous projects, set up three layers named Background, Main, and UI. In the Background layer, add a TiledBackground object named Background with the image dirt.png. Resize and position this object so that it covers the entire layout. Then add a TileMap object named Walls with the image wall-tileset.png. These tiles are 32-by-32 pixels, so the default properties for the tilemap do not need adjustment. Using the Tilemap editor, design a mazelike level using any arrangement you like, provided that the layout is surrounded by a wall (which will prevent Runman and the ghosts from moving off-screen), and make sure that there are no dead-end paths (these would interfere with the ghost movement events, as will be explained later). Figure 12-2 shows one possible level design; this figure displays a 32-by-32 grid to more clearly illustrate the tiles used in creating the level. When you are finished, click the selection tool in the *Tilemap* panel, and lock the Background layer via the Layer panel.

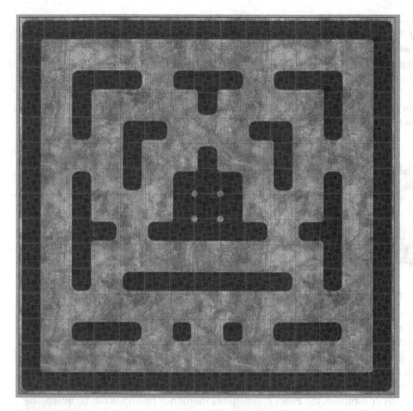

Figure 12-2. Background and tilemap maze setup

Player Setup and Grid-Based Movement

In this section, you will set up the Runman character and grid-based movement. The process for setting up the Runman sprite's animations is identical to how you set up the Cleaner sprite's animations in the Cleanup Challenge game in Chapter 4. To begin, set the active layer to Main, and create a new sprite named Runman; in the *Animation frames* window, load the spritesheet general48.png (with three horizontal cells and four vertical cells), and set the Animation properties Speed to 6, Loop to Yes, and Ping-pong to Yes. Then duplicate this animation three times so that there are four animations in total. Next, rename the animations to South, West, East, and North. Select the animation named *South* in the list; in the *Animation frames* window, click each frame that does *not* correspond to the character walking south (those initially numbered 3 through 11); and press the *Delete* key. Repeat this process for the West, East, and North animations, deleting the frames not required within each of the animations.

Next, you need to adjust the sprite's collision polygon to a smaller shape and adjust the sprite's origin to be aligned with the grid. These adjustments must be applied to all frames of all animations for consistency and to prevent glitches. Select the South animation, and adjust the collision polygon (adding and repositioning vertices as necessary) until it is

161

roughly circular, as illustrated in Figure 12-3. After this adjustment, right-click the polygon and select *Apply to all animations*. Next, in the *Image points* window, adjust the origin image point using the Quick-assign tool (as you did with the Chargeometer object in the Spell Shooter game in Chapter 9) so that the origin point is at the bottom-left corner of the sprite, also shown in Figure 12-3. After this adjustment, right-click the *Origin in the Image points* window, and select *Apply to all animations*. When you are finished, close the image editor windows. Change the size of the sprite to 32,32, and position it at any open grid square except for those with an adjacent wall on the right.

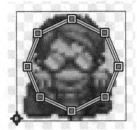

Figure 12-3. *The Player sprite's circular collision polygon*

The next mechanic you will implement is grid-based movement: the characters in this game can move only in straight lines in four directions (north, south, east, and west) and can change directions only from the center of each grid square. Determining when a character has reached the center of a grid square is difficult since character positions are updated only 60 times per second, and because of the automatic approximation of decimal values by computers, the exact coordinates might not be obtained. To overcome this dilemma, you will use a formula from physics: speed = distance/time. You will know both the speed (it will be set to 100 pixels/second) and the distance between tiles (32 pixels). Therefore, you can use this formula to calculate how long it will take a character to travel from one grid square to the next since the formula can be rewritten as time = distance/speed. A timer will be set up to go off regularly at this time interval, and on the corresponding tick (and only then), the character will have the opportunity to change direction. At the same time, the character might not be located at the exact center of a tile when the timer goes off (because of the aforementioned rounding errors), so the character's position will also be adjusted at this instant, as shown in Figure 12-4, to avoid accumulating errors that could result in glitches at a later time.

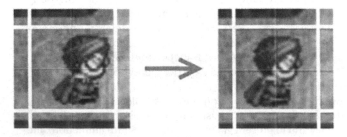

Figure 12-4. *Adjusting Runman's position to be centered in a grid square*

To begin, select the Runman object and add the behaviors *Bullet* and *Timer*. Set the *Bullet* properties *Speed* to 100 and *Set angle* to No. Also, since Runman will move to the right by default, in the *Properties* panel change *Initial animation* to East. (Incidentally, this is also why you avoided placing Runman with a wall directly to his right.) In what follows, you will use groups to keep sets of events organized and easy to locate in the event sheet. Groups are basically headers that display a line of text; events are added to a group by adding them as subevents to the group, just as you would add a subevent to another event. In the event sheet, right-click in the margins, select *Add group*, and set *Name* to Player Movement. To this group, add an event with the condition *System - On start of layout*. In accordance with the formula discussed earlier, add the action *Runman - Timer - Start timer*, set *Duration* to 32/100, set *Type* to Regular, and set *Tag* to "Grid".

The next event to be added will realign Runman to the center of the grid square to which he is closest. Since the grid square positions are located at multiples of 32, Runman's X and Y position should be set to the nearest multiple of 32 whenever the timer activates. To determine which multiple of 32 is closest, you can divide the current position by 32, round it to the closest whole number, and then multiply it by 32. For example, given the number 95, the closest multiple of 32 is 96 = 3 * 32. The key part in this calculation is figuring out the multiplier, which is 3 in this case. We know that 96 / 32 is exactly 3, while 95 / 32 is 2.96875, which is only approximately 3. Using the round function converts this approximate decimal into the desired exact value 3, and then you can simply multiply this by 32 to get the position to which Runman should be adjusted. To implement this calculation in the event sheet, in the *Player Movement* group, add a subevent with condition *Runman - On timer*, and set *Tag* to "Grid". Add the action *Runman - Set X*, setting X to round(Runman.X / 32) * 32, and add the action *Runman - Set Y*, setting Y to round(Runman.Y / 32) * 32. When you are finished, the events should appear as in Figure 12-5.

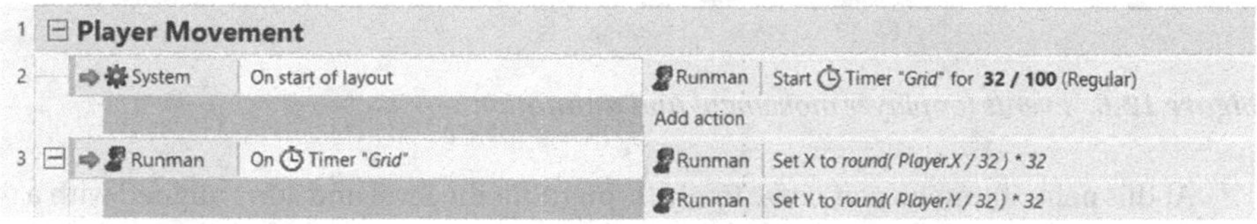

Figure 12-5. *The Player Movement group and events for grid alignment*

Next, you will implement events that enable the player to change Runman's direction, provided that no walls are blocking the way. This type of check is called *preventative collision detection*, meaning that rather than waiting for a collision to happen (and responding accordingly), you will check to see whether the player is holding down an arrow key corresponding to a direction in which a tile exists; if so, Runman will be prevented from moving in that direction in the first place. Potential collisions such as these can be detected with a condition named *Is overlapping at offset*. To begin, in the layout, add a *Keyboard* object. Then, in the event sheet, add a subevent to the *On timer* event you created previously. Create two conditions for this new event: *Keyboard - Key is down* (Right arrow) and the inverted condition *Runman - Is overlapping at offset* (Walls, at an *Offset X* of 32 and an *Offset Y* of 0). Add two actions to this event: *Runman - Bullet: Set angle of motion* (0) and *Runman - Set Animation* ("East"). Next, you will create three more subevents in the *On timer* event with the same conditions and actions, but with the parameter values changed as follows:

- Check whether the player is holding down the left arrow key and for an overlap at the values *Offset X* of -32 and *Offset Y* of 0; set the angle of motion to 180 and the animation to "West".

- Check whether the player is holding down the up arrow key and for an overlap at the values *Offset X* of 0 and *Offset Y* of -32; set the angle of motion to -90 and the animation to "North".

- Check whether the player is holding down the down arrow key and for an overlap at the values *Offset X* of 0 and *Offset Y* of 32; set the angle of motion to 90 and the animation to "South".

When you are finished, these events should appear as in Figure 12-6.

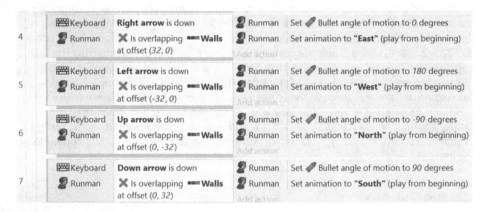

Figure 12-6. *Events for player movement and animation*

At this point, Runman can move freely throughout the level and stays aligned with a grid. However, the wall tiles you added in the tilemap do not currently function as walls; Runman can travel right through them. To get the precisely desired effect, you will *not* add the *Solid* behavior; instead, you will create another set of events to implement this feature. These events will check the direction in which Runman is traveling (by checking the name of the currently playing animation), and if there is a wall ahead, Runman's movement, animation, and timer will all be stopped. If the player presses a key while Runman is not moving (indicated by a speed of 0), then his speed will be restored to its original value, the *On timer* event will be activated again immediately, and the recurring timer will be set up again.

To start implementing these features, add a new subevent to the *On timer* event, with two conditions: *Runman - Animation: Is playing* ("East") and *Runman - Is overlapping another object* (Walls, with Offset X set to 32 and *Offset Y* set to 0). To this event, add three actions: *Runman - Bullet: Set speed* (0), *Runman - Animation: Stop*, and *Runman - Timer:*

Stop timer ("Grid"). Next, you will create three more subevents in the *On timer* event with the same conditions and actions, but with the parameter values of the conditions changed as follows:

- Check whether the West animation is playing and for overlap at *Offset X* of -32 and *Offset Y* of 0.

- Check whether the North animation is playing and for overlap at *Offset X* of 0 and *Offset Y* of -32.

- Check whether the South animation is playing and for overlap at *Offset X* of 0 and *Offset Y* of 32.

You will also need an event as described earlier that starts Runman moving again after he has stopped. Create a new subevent in the *Player Movement* group (but it should *not* be a subevent of the *On timer* event) with the condition *Keyboard - On any key pressed* and the condition *Runman - Bullet: Compare speed* (0). Add the three actions *Runman - Bullet: Set speed* (100), *Runman - Timer: Start timer* (*Duration* set to 0, *Type* set to Once, *Tag* set to "Restart"), and *Runman - Timer: Start timer* (*Duration* set to 32/100, *Type* set to Regular, *Tag* set to "Grid"). The extra Restart timer needs to be created to activate the *On timer* event again right away (the Grid timer cannot be used for both these purposes at the same time). Finally, the *On timer* event needs to be adjusted so that either of the named timers can activate it; to this end, right-click the event, select *Make "or" block*, and then add a second condition called *Timer - On Timer* ("Restart"). When you are finished, these events should appear as in Figure 12-7. Save the project and preview your game to make sure that the movement works as expected and that Runman is blocked by the walls.

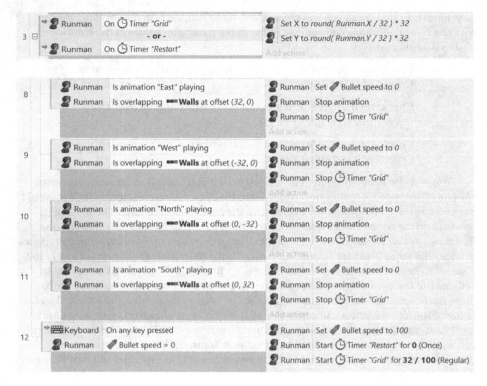

Figure 12-7. *Events for tilemap wall functionality*

Enemies and Intelligent Movement

In this section, you will implement enemy ghosts with intelligent movement patterns that will chase the player around the maze. These ghosts will also be subject to grid-based movement; the implementation will be similar to the previous section but simpler, as the ghosts will not stop moving. To begin, create a new sprite named Ghost; in the *Animation frames* window, load the spritesheet ghost.png (three horizontal cells and one vertical cell), and set the *Animation* properties *Speed* to 6, *Loop* to Yes, and *Ping-pong* to Yes. As you did with the Runman sprite, adjust the collision polygon shape and origin image point, as shown in Figure 12-8, and after each of these changes, select the right-click menu option *Apply to whole animation*. When you are finished, close the image editor windows. Change the size to 28,28, add the *Bullet* and *Timer* behaviors, set *Bullet Speed* to 90 (so it is just a bit slower than Runman), and change *Set angle* to No. Create two more instances of the Ghost object, and position them each on an empty tile space (but not with a wall directly to the right, as before).

Figure 12-8. *The Ghost sprite's collision polygon*

In the event sheet, right-click and create a new group named Ghost Movement. In this group, create an event with the condition *System - On start of layout*, and add the action *Ghost - Timer: Start Timer* (with *Duration* set to 32/90, *Type* set to Regular, and *Tag* set to "Grid"). Then create an event with the condition *Ghost - On Timer* ("Grid") and the condition *System - For Each (Ghost)*. Add the action *Ghost - Set X*, setting *X* to round(Ghost.X / 32) * 32, and add the action *Ghost - Set Y*, setting Y to round(Ghost.Y / 32) * 32.

Before creating any more events, it is necessary to introduce a new feature of Construct: the Array object. Arrays are "data structures" that can be used to store a list (or a grid) of values. Here, arrays will be used to store the directions of movement available to each ghost each time they reach the next grid square, and one of the stored directions will be selected according to the programmed pattern for each ghost. To begin, in the layout, add a new object, an Array object named Directions, and then return to the event sheet.

In the *Ghost - On timer* event, add an action called *Directions - Set Size*, and set *Width* to 0, *Height* to 1, and *Depth* to 1. Since you are interested only in storing a list of values (as opposed to a 2D or 3D grid of values), Height and Depth should always be set to 1. The width refers to the number of values being stored in the list, and setting it to 0 effectively "resets" or "clears out" the list, preparing it for reuse when analyzing the options for each of the ghosts.

Next, you will add values to the array, corresponding to the angles of movement for the available directions. One of the requirements for a direction to be considered available is that there must be no overlap with a wall in that direction. Additionally, ghosts are not permitted to reverse direction because otherwise ghosts would behave erratically, hovering back and forth between positions as they attempt to align themselves horizontally or vertically with Runman. Directions satisfying these conditions are added, or "pushed," onto the array. For example, if there is no wall to the right (offset (32,0)) and the ghost is not moving to the left (motion angle 180), then moving to the right is a valid option, and the corresponding angle (0) will be added to the array. To implement this, create a subevent to the *Ghost - On timer* event, with the inverted condition *Ghost - Is overlapping at offset* (Walls, *Offset X* set to 32, *Offset Y* set to 0) and the condition *System - Compare two values* (check whether *Ghost.Bullet.AngleOfMotion* is *not* equal to 180). Add the action *Directions - Manipulation - Push* (set *Where* to Back, *Value* to 0, and *Axis* to X).

Create three more events with the same conditions and actions, with the parameter values changed as follows:

- If there is no overlap at offset (-32, 0) and the angle of motion is not 0, then push 180 onto the array.

- If there is no overlap at offset (0, -32) and the angle of motion is not 90, then push -90 onto the array.

- If there is no overlap at offset (0, 32) and the angle of motion is not -90, then push 90 onto the array.

When you are finished, the *Ghost Movement* group should appear as in Figure 12-9.

13	Ghost Movement				
14	➡ ✪ System	On start of layout		🔵 Ghost	Start 🕐 Timer *"Grid"* for **32 / 90** (Regular)
					Add action
15	➡ 🔵 Ghost	On 🕐 Timer *"Grid"*		🔵 Ghost	Set X to *round(GhostX / 32) * 32*
	↺✪ System	For each 🔵 **Ghost**		🔵 Ghost	Set Y to *round(GhostY / 32) * 32*
				▦ Directions	Set size to *(0, 1, 1)*
					Add action
16	🔵 Ghost	✘ Is overlapping ▬▬**Walls** at offset *(32, 0)*		▦ Directions	Push back *0* on X axis
	✪ System	Ghost.Bullet.AngleOfMotion ≠ 180			Add action
17	🔵 Ghost	✘ Is overlapping ▬▬**Walls** at offset *(-32, 0)*		▦ Directions	Push back *180* on X axis
	✪ System	Ghost.Bullet.AngleOfMotion ≠ 0			Add action
18	🔵 Ghost	✘ Is overlapping ▬▬**Walls** at offset *(0, -32)*		▦ Directions	Push back *-90* on X axis
	✪ System	Ghost.Bullet.AngleOfMotion ≠ 90			Add action
19	🔵 Ghost	✘ Is overlapping ▬▬**Walls** at offset *(0, 32)*		▦ Directions	Push back *90* on X axis
	✪ System	Ghost.Bullet.AngleOfMotion ≠ -90			Add action

Figure 12-9. Events for ghost grid alignment and adding available directions to the array

Before adding the events that correspond to the different movement patterns that the ghosts will follow, you need to add an instance variable to the ghosts to distinguish between them. Select the ghost object, and add an instance variable named Pattern, with *Type* set to text, *Value* set to Vertical, and *Description* set to Vertical, Horizontal, or Random. Then, select an instance of one of the ghosts, set its Pattern variable to Horizontal, and select another one and set its *Pattern* variable to Random so that each of the three ghosts has a different value. When changing direction, the ghost with *Pattern* set to Vertical will choose to move either north or south, depending on whether Runman is located to the north or south of the ghost (and provided the ghost is currently able to move in that particular direction). If this ghost has the same Y coordinate as Runman, then it will choose to move either east or west, following similar criteria. The ghost with *Pattern* set to Horizontal follows similar logic but prioritizes moving east or west, while the ghost with Pattern set to Random will simply choose one of its currently available directions at random.

Before implementing these movement patterns, you will set up a "default" direction for the ghosts to follow, in case no good option is available (where "good" is defined from the perspective of the ghosts, as a direction that moves them closer to Runman).

Add a subevent to the *Ghost - On timer* event, with the condition *System - Every tick* and the action *Ghost - Bullet: Set angle of motion*, set to `Directions.At(0)`. The Array action *At* retrieves a value stored in the array at a given position (or *index*); array positions are numbered starting with 0 (a standard convention in computer science).

Next, you will implement the vertical pattern of movement described earlier. To the *Ghost - On timer* event, add a subevent with the condition *Ghost - Compare instance variable* (check whether *Pattern* is equal to `"Vertical"`). To this event, you will add a set of four subevents that compare the position of the ghost to Runman, and if a good move exists in the array of directions, then the ghost's angle of motion will be changed to that value. For example, if the ghost's *X* coordinate is less than Runman's *X* coordinate (Runman is to the right of the ghost) and the angle 0 is currently in the Directions array (indicating that the ghost is able to move to the right), then the ghost angle of motion will be set to 0. Similar events will be created for the other possible directions. It should be noted here that events that appear later in this list correspond to the movements that will take priority because their actions can override previous actions; it is as if these later events "have the final word" in what happens in the game. Create a new subevent with the condition *Ghost - Compare X* (check whether it is less than `Runman.X`) and the condition *Directions - Contains value* (0), and add the action *Ghost - Bullet: Set angle of motion* (0). Create three more subevents with the same conditions and actions, but change the parameter values as follows:

- Check whether the ghost X value is greater than `Runman.X` and whether *Directions* contains the value 180, and set the angle of motion to 180.

- Check whether the ghost *Y* value is less than `Runman.Y` and whether *Directions* contains the value 90, and set the angle of motion to 90.

- Check whether the ghost *Y* value is greater than `Runman.Y` and whether *Directions* contains the value -90, and set the angle of motion to -90.

When you are finished, the events should appear as in Figure 12-10.

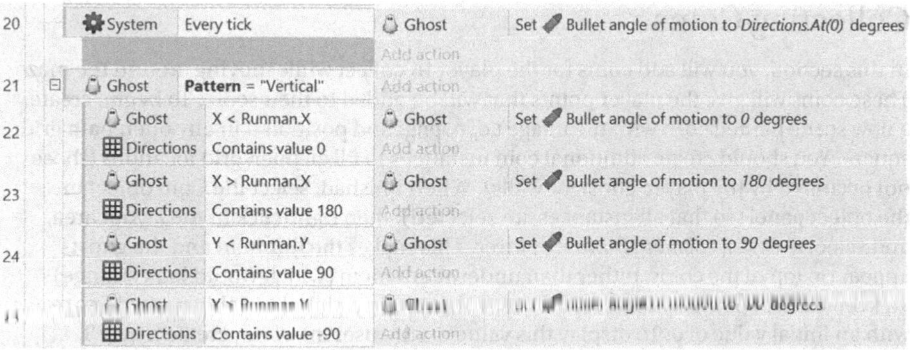

Figure 12-10. *Events for vertical pattern ghost movement*

The events controlling the ghost following the horizontal pattern are extremely similar to the previous events. Copy and paste the event with the condition *Pattern = "Vertical"* and its subevents. In the new copy of the events, edit the condition to check whether *Pattern* is equal to "Horizontal", and click and drag to rearrange the subevents so that the events comparing the X values appear last, as shown in Figure 12-11. Finally, to implement the random movement pattern, you will need to write only a single event. Add a new event with the condition *Ghost - Compare instance variable*, and check whether *Pattern* is equal to "Random". For the action, you need to generate a random number between 0 and the width of (number of elements in) the Directions array, use the floor function to truncate the decimal digits (since array positions are whole numbers), and extract the array element at that position. This is accomplished by adding the action *Ghost - Bullet: Set angle of motion*, set to Directions.At(floor(random(Directions. Width))). When finished, these events should appear as shown in Figure 12-11. Save and test your project, and verify that all three ghosts move in different patterns, as expected. (To check an individual pattern more easily, you could delete the other ghost instances temporarily and simply add them back to the project later.)

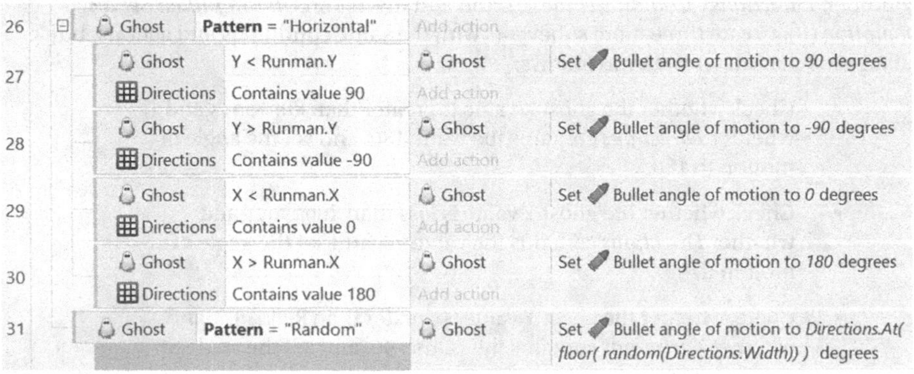

26	⊟	🜄 Ghost	**Pattern** = "Horizontal"	Add action		
27		🜄 Ghost	Y < Runman.Y	🜄 Ghost	Set 🗲 Bullet angle of motion to *90* degrees	
		▦ Directions	Contains value 90	Add action		
28		🜄 Ghost	Y > Runman.Y	🜄 Ghost	Set 🗲 Bullet angle of motion to *-90* degrees	
		▦ Directions	Contains value -90	Add action		
29		🜄 Ghost	X < Runman.X	🜄 Ghost	Set 🗲 Bullet angle of motion to *0* degrees	
		▦ Directions	Contains value 0	Add action		
30		🜄 Ghost	X > Runman.X	🜄 Ghost	Set 🗲 Bullet angle of motion to *180* degrees	
		▦ Directions	Contains value 180	Add action		
31		🜄 Ghost	**Pattern** = "Random"	🜄 Ghost	Set 🗲 Bullet angle of motion to *Directions.At(floor(random(Directions.Width)))* degrees	

Figure 12-11. *Events for horizontal and random pattern ghost movement*

Collecting Coins

In this section, you will add coins for the player to collect while moving around the maze. These coins will give the player points that will be added to their score. To begin, create a new sprite named Coin with the image coin.png, and position it in any open path grid square. You should create additional coin instances to fill all open grid locations (those not occupied by the player, ghost, or walls). When finished, select the Coin object in the object panel (so that all instances are selected); then right-click in the layout area, and select *Z-Order - Send to bottom of layer*. This makes the Runman and the ghosts appear on top of the coins, rather than underneath them (which would look strange). To keep track of points earned, in the event sheet, add a global variable named Score with an initial value of 0. To display this value on the user interface, create a new Text object named TextScore, set its *Layer* to UI, and position it in the top-center of the game window, over the top bounding wall. Change the default text to Score: 0. Change the font to Arial, bold, size 14, and change the font color to a bright yellow (since it matches the color of the coins and is also easily visible against the dark wall). Your user interface and style of coin placement should be similar to example layout shown in Figure 12-12.

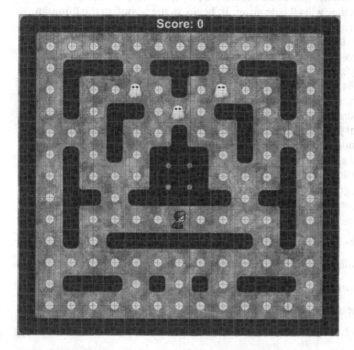

Figure 12-12. *The user interface and coin placement in the layout*

You can now set up the corresponding events for collecting coins and updating the text displayed. First, in the event sheet, right-click the empty area in the event sheet to create a new group named Coin Events. Next, to this group, add a new subevent with the condition *Runman - On collision with another object* (Coin), add the action *System - Variables: Add to* (add 10 to Score), and add the action *Coin - Destroy*. Add another event to this group, with the condition *System - Every tick* and the action *TextScore - Set text* ("Score: " & Score). When finished, these events should appear as in Figure 12-13.

32	⊟ **Coin Events**			
33	↱ 🐾 Runman	On collision with ● **Coin**	⚙ System	Add *10* to **Score**
			● Coin	Destroy
			Add action	
34	⚙ System	Every tick	T TextScore	Set text to *"Score: "* & *Score*

Figure 12-13. *Events for collecting coins*

Game End

In this section, you will implement end-of-game conditions that indicate whether the player has lost or won. When the game has ended, the player and ghosts' movement will be stopped, and then they will all fade away. To begin, in the layout, to the Runman object, add the behavior *Fade*, and set *Active at start* to No. Then, click *Ghost* in the object panel (so all instances are selected) and similarly add the *Fade* behavior, and set *Active at start* to No. Create two new sprites: one named MessageLose using the image text-lose. png and one named MessageWin using the image text-win.png. Set their Layer properties to UI, set Size to 416 by 64, set "Initial visibility" to Invisible, and center both within the window bounds. Next, you will add the "game over" sequence event that will fade the player and the ghosts upon player collision with a ghost. Since you will want to fade away all ghosts in the game, not just the one filtered by the collision condition, you will add an additional System condition called *Pick all* to reset the event's filter for the ghosts so that the actions are applied to all ghosts (not just the one that collided with the player). First, in the event sheet, right-click the empty area in the event sheet to create a new group named Game End. To this group, add a new subevent, add the condition *Runman - On collision with another object* (Ghost), and add the condition *System - Pick all* (Ghost). Add the following actions:

- *MessageLose - Set visible* (Visible)

- *Runman - Bullet: Set enabled* (Disable)

- *Runman - Start fade*

- *Ghost - Bullet: Set enabled* (Disable)

- *Ghost - Start fade*

You will now add the winning sequence event, which will occur when all coins have been collected (or equivalently, when no coins remain). To the *Game End* group, add another subevent called *System - Compare two values* (check if *Coin.Count* is equal to 0); then add the same actions as in the previous event, but change *MessageLose* to MessageWin in this new event. The "game end" events should appear as in Figure 12-14.

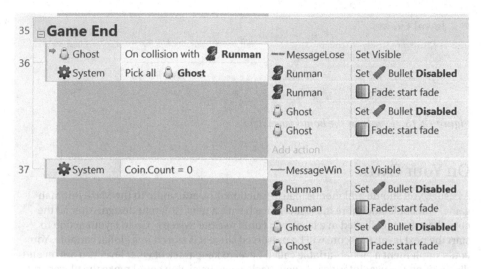

Figure 12-14. Events for the end of the game

Congratulations! You have now finished implementing the core mechanics of the game Maze Runman.

Side Quests

In this optional section, you will add a special collectable jewel item that will repeatedly spawn at a specified location for the player to collect, giving the player repeated chances for extra points. Additional features will also be suggested at the end of this section.

Adding a Jewel Bonus Item

To add more variety to the maze, you will add a special collectable jewel item that will repeatedly spawn at a specified location (designated by a SpawnPoint sprite), and on collection, the jewel should grant the player a bonus of 100 points. To begin, add a new sprite named JewelSpawn with any drawn image (this sprite will be invisible during gameplay), and resize it to 32, 32. Find a location of a coin in the middle of the maze, delete that particular coin instance, and position the JewelSpawn at that location. Then, set *Initial visibility* to Invisible. Next, add a new sprite named Jewel, with the image jewel.png, and position it in the layout margins. Add the *Fade* behavior to the jewel, and set *Wait time* to 9. Every 20 seconds a jewel should spawn, and the player will have 10 seconds to collect it before it disappears. In the event sheet, create a new group named Jewel Events. To this group, add a new event with the condition *System - Every X seconds* (20) and the action *JewelSpawn - Spawn another object* (Jewel). Add another event to this group with the condition *Runman - On collision with another object* (Jewel); add the action *System - Variables: Add to* (add 100 to *Score*), and add the action *Jewel - Destroy*. When you are finished, the events should appear as in Figure 12-15.

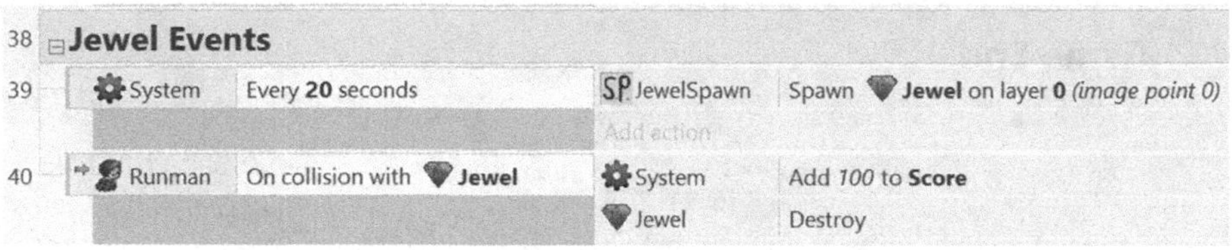

38	⊟**Jewel Events**					
39	⚙ System	Every **20** seconds		⚐ JewelSpawn	Spawn ◈ **Jewel** on layer **0** *(image point 0)*	
				Add action		
40	⬆⬇ Runman	On collision with ◈ **Jewel**		⚙ System	Add *100* to **Score**	
				◈ Jewel	Destroy	

Figure 12-15. Events for the bonus jewel item

On Your Own

As usual, you should add menus, pause functionality, and audio to the Maze Runman game. You could add more maze levels, each with a new, different design. After all the coins have been collected in a level, you could use the System - Go to layout action to start the next level; the score will be preserved since it is stored in a global variable. You could implement a global variable called Level to keep track of what level you are on and display it on the user interface. As you reach a new level, you could make the player and ghosts have higher speeds to ramp up the difficulty. In addition, to compensate for this higher difficulty, more points could be awarded for collecting coins in higher levels.

You could design and create more types of enemies besides ghosts. For example, you could create a Spider enemy, whose movement (limited to either vertical or horizontal) is controlled by the Sine behavior; its position and magnitude (a multiple of 32) would have to be determined and set manually for each instance to prevent it from appearing to move through walls. You could also add different types of jewel that appear at the spawn point (randomly selected by the choose function, similar to the Item objects from the Rectangle Destroyer game), with each jewel worth different point values. You could even implement a "runaway" moving jewel, controlled by a similar set of events as the ghosts, with the comparisons reversed so that the jewel moves away from Runman instead of toward him. This jewel could be set to disappear after a certain time interval, adding to the challenge. If the player catches this jewel, then the player should earn a great number of points.

Summary

In this chapter, you created the game Maze Runman. By using a tilemap, you created a maze for the player to strategically navigate, while collecting coins and avoiding ghosts. You learned how to implement precise grid-based movement by combining the *Bullet* and *Timer* behaviors. You were introduced to the Array object, which helped you store multiple values. By accessing the array data, you created events that simulated intelligent behavior for the ghosts and created variations on their movement patterns. Throughout the chapter, you organized events by using groups in the event sheet. The "Side Quests" section discussed how to create a regularly reappearing jewel for bonus points and suggested a variety of other features you could add to your game.

In the next chapter, you'll create another game where the player collects coins and dodges enemies: a side-view, platformer-style game called Jumping Jack.

CHAPTER 13

■ ■ ■

Jumping Jack

In this chapter, you will create a side-perspective platform-style game called Jumping Jack, shown in Figure 13-1, inspired by classic arcade and console games such as Super Mario Bros.

Figure 13-1. The Jumping Jack game

In Jumping Jack, the player controls Jack the Koala, whose goal is to navigate a level, collecting coins and dodging or defeating enemies along the way, until he reaches the flag at the end of the level. Enemies come in two varieties: the flying type, which fly back and forth between two given points, and the ground type, which move along the ground and reverse direction whenever they encounter a wall. Enemies can be destroyed by jumping on top of them, but otherwise they damage the player on contact. After being hit three times, the player loses the game. The environment itself contains a variety of interactive elements, such as ladders that can be climbed, springboards that launch the koala into the air, platforms that can be jumped through from underneath, brick blocks that can be destroyed by colliding with them from underneath, and keys that can be collected to allow the koala to pass through locked blocks. The "Side Quests" section describes additional potential features such as adding a countdown timer.

The player controls the koala using the arrow keys to walk and climb ladders and using the spacebar to jump. The user interface displays the number of coins collected, the health of the koala, and whether any keys have been collected. This project uses the Tilemap, Sprite, TiledBackgrounds, and Keyboard objects, and it uses the behaviors *Scroll to*, *Pin*, *Fade*, *Bullet*, *Solid*, and *Flash*. The koala character uses a new behavior called *Platform* for standard platform controls, as well as the 8-Direction behavior for climbing ladders. The behavior *JumpThru* is introduced to create a special type of one-way solid. The Function object will be introduced to avoid repeating code, and the Particle object will be introduced for a brick-breaking visual effect.

To begin, download the assets for this chapter from the book web site. Set the layout size to 1600, 640 and the window size to 800, 640. On the *View* tab, select the *Snap to grid* and *Show grid* check boxes, and set the grid width and grid height both to 16. Add three additional layers to your project (for a total of four layers), naming them Background, Map, Main, and UI. The reason for using four layers in this project (as opposed to three, as you have in previous projects) is that the background image needs to scroll more slowly than the tilemap for a parallax effect (as in the Plane Dodger game in Chapter 6), so it must be in a separate layer. At the same time, to avoid accidentally selecting or modifying the tilemap once it is complete (as discussed when developing the Racecar 500 game in Chapter 7), the tilemap should be in its own layer so that it can be locked later. For the Background layer, set *Parallax* to 50, 0; this will cause the Background layer to scroll at half the speed as the Map and Main layers while the player navigates the level. For the UI layer, set *Parallax* to 0,0; this will fix the UI in place, as desired.

Level Design

In this section, you will set up a basic level. In the Background layer, add a TiledBackground object named Background with the image background.png. Resize and position this object so that it covers the entire layout. In the Map layer, add a TileMap object named Map with the image platform-tiles.png. These tiles are 32-by-32 pixels, so the default properties for the tilemap do not need to be adjusted. However, you should adjust the collision polygons for the nonsquare tiles, as you did for the Racecar 500 game in Chapter 7. In the layout, add some ground tiles across the bottom of the map. Also, create some walls (at least six blocks high) on each side to stop the player from falling off the sides of the level. (Alternatively, you could create invisible solid objects to place at either end to serve the same purpose.) Feel free to add a staircase or two in the middle for variety and perhaps some floating platforms. Many other objects will be added later in the chapter, so do not feel compelled to fill the tilemap at this time; leave plenty of open space available. When you are finished, the layout should appear similar in style to Figure 13-2.

When you are finished, add the *Solid* behavior to the tilemap, click the selection tool in the Tilemap panel, and lock the Background and Tilemap layers.

Figure 13-2. Background and basic tilemap setup

Player Setup

The next goal is to set up the koala character that the player controls. Set the active layer to Main, and add a new sprite named Koala. In the image editor, set up the following animations with the given names, images from the koala folder, and animation properties (when applicable):

- Name: Stand. Image: stand.png.

- Name: Jump. Image: jump.png.

- Name: Walk. Images: walk-1.png, walk-2.png, walk3.png. Set *Speed* to 6, *Loop* to Yes, and *Ping-pong* to Yes.

- Name: Climb. Images: climb-1.png, climb-2.png. Set *Speed* to 6 and *Loop* to Yes.

When you are finished, you need to adjust the collision polygon so that it is consistent across all frames of all animations; otherwise, strange glitches may occur. Select the Stand animation, and adjust the collision polygon (deleting and repositioning vertices as necessary) until it is a rectangle, somewhat thinner than the image itself, as illustrated in Figure 13-3. Make sure that the left and right sides of the collision polygon are perfectly vertical. For precise measurements, when a vertex is selected, its coordinates are displayed at the bottom of the image editor window, and its position can be adjusted pixel by pixel with the arrow keys. When you are finished, right-click the polygon, and in the menu that appears, select *Apply to all animations*.

Figure 13-3. *Collision polygon for the Koala sprite*

For the Koala object, set *Size* to 32,50, and add the behaviors *Platform*, *Scroll to*, and *8-Direction*. The *Platform* behavior handles walking and jumping. However, the ability to climb ladders must be managed separately. For example, when climbing a ladder, gravity does not affect the player, and the player can also move up and down. This can be efficiently handled by using two behaviors, enabling one and disabling the other when appropriate. Set the *Platform* properties *Max speed* to 120 and *Default controls* to No. Set the *8-Direction* properties *Max speed* to 120, *Set angle* to No, and *Initial state* to Disabled. There are no conditions that check whether these behaviors are enabled, so you will store this information with an instance variable. Add an instance variable and set *Name* to State, *Type* to Text, *Initial value* to Normal, and *Description* to Normal or Climbing.

The reason you disabled the default Platform controls is that you will reserve the up and down arrow keys for climbing, and the spacebar (or another key of your choice) can be used for jumping. Next, you will implement these alternative controls. At the same time, you will use the *Appearance: Set mirrored* action to reflect the sprite image so that the koala is facing in the direction that it is moving. In the layout, add a Keyboard object and then open the event sheet. Because of the large number of events in this project, you will use groups to keep your events organized. In the event sheet, add a group named Player Movement, and add the following subevents in this group (be sure to use the *Platform* action *Simulate control,* not the *8-Direction* action):

- Add the condition *Keyboard - Key is down* (Left arrow), add the action *Koala - Platform: Simulate control* (Left), and add the action *Koala - Appearance: Set mirrored* (Mirrored).

- Add the condition *Keyboard - Key is down* (Right arrow), add the action *Koala - Platform: Simulate control* (Right), and add the action *Koala - Appearance: Set mirrored* (Not Mirrored).

- Add the condition *Keyboard - On key pressed* (Space), and add the action *Koala - Platform: Simulate control* (Jump).

The completed events should appear as shown in Figure 13-4.

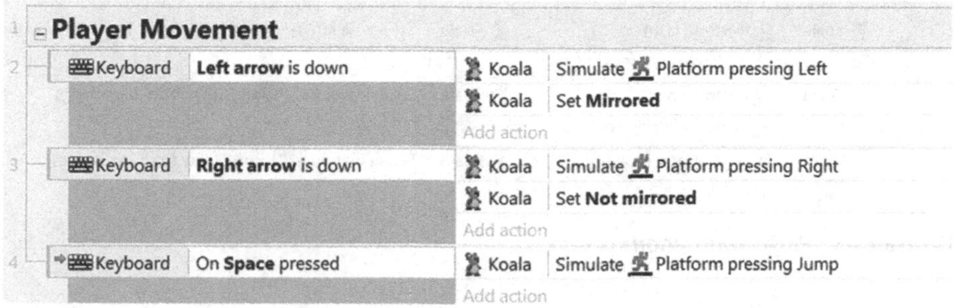

⊟ **Player Movement**			
⌨Keyboard	**Left arrow** is down	🐨 Koala	Simulate 🐨 Platform pressing Left
		🐨 Koala	Set **Mirrored**
		Add action	
⌨Keyboard	**Right arrow** is down	🐨 Koala	Simulate 🐨 Platform pressing Right
		🐨 Koala	Set **Not mirrored**
		Add action	
⌨Keyboard	On **Space** pressed	🐨 Koala	Simulate 🐨 Platform pressing Jump
		Add action	

Figure 13-4. Player movement events

This is a good point to save and test your game. At this point, check that the controls move the koala as expected and that the screen scrolls along with the koala (and the background scrolls at half-speed). The koala should face the direction it is moving in, but the animations have not been activated yet; you set these up (except for climbing) next. As you will see, the Platform behavior has a great number of conditions that check the movement and surroundings of the object, and these are quite useful for activating the correct animation.

In the event sheet, add a new group named Player Animation. In this group, add a subevent with the condition *Koala - Compare instance variable*, and check whether *State* equals Normal. Create three subevents to this condition as follows:

- Add the condition *Koala - Platform: Is on floor*, add the inverted condition *Koala - Platform: Is moving*, and add the action *Koala - Set Animation* ("Stand").

- Add the condition *Koala - Platform: Is on floor*, add the condition *Koala - Platform: Is moving*, and add the action *Koala - Set Animation* ("Walk").

- Add the inverted condition *Koala - Platform: Is on floor*, and add the action *Koala - Set Animation* ("Jump").

The completed events should appear as in Figure 13-5. Once again, save and test your game and confirm that the animations appear as expected.

5	– Player Animation				
6	☐ 🐨 Koala	**State** = "Normal"		Add action	
7		🐨 Koala	🏃 Platform is on floor	🐨 Koala	Set animation to **"Stand"** (play from beginning)
		🐨 Koala	✖ 🏃 Platform is moving	Add action	
8		🐨 Koala	🏃 Platform is on floor	🐨 Koala	Set animation to **"Walk"** (play from beginning)
		🐨 Koala	🏃 Platform is moving	Add action	
9		🐨 Koala	✖ 🏃 Platform is on floor	🐨 Koala	Set animation to **"Jump"** (play from beginning)
				Add action	

Figure 13-5. *Player animation events*

Ladders and Climbing

In this section, you will implement the ladder-climbing mechanic. This is complicated because of the need to switch between two different behaviors, determine the different conditions in which the player will want the koala to start or stop climbing, and handle the animations. To reduce the repetition of particular sets of actions, you will also learn how to use the Function object. To start, create a new TiledBackground object named Ladder, using the image ladder.png. You are using a TiledBackground rather than a Sprite object so that the pattern of rungs repeats as you resize the object. Resize and position the Ladder object so that it is 32 pixels wide and so it reaches from the ground to the top of one of your tilemap platforms, as shown in Figure 13-6. Also, add the behavior Jump-thru to the ladder. This behavior allows other objects to pass though from below, but not from above, a mechanic that is used in many platform-style games.

Figure 13-6. *Setting up a ladder next to a tilemap platform*

When switching from the platform behavior to the *8-Direction* behavior for climbing, two of the required actions are to disable the *Platform* behavior and to enable the *8-Direction* behavior. In addition, the koala's *State* variable should be set to keep track of the control scheme being activated (in this case, "Climbing"). One subtle point that needs to be taken into account is the koala's motion at the moment when a movement behavior is disabled. Both the *Platform* and *8-Direction* variables independently keep track of the koala's velocity in the *X* and *Y* directions in variables named *VectorX* and *VectorY*. Whenever you disable a behavior, you should set both of these values to 0. Otherwise, when the behavior is reenabled later, these variables will be restored to their original values at the moment the behavior was disabled, causing unexpected motion in some direction.

As will be discussed later, you will see that there multiple combinations of conditions for which the koala should start climbing or stop climbing. To avoid entering the same set of actions repeatedly, you will use the Function object. The Function object has many uses, one of which is to activate another event in the event sheet. In the layout, add the Function object to the project. Much like the Keyboard or Audio object, this does not add anything to the layout, but it enables extra conditions and actions in the event sheet. In the event sheet, in the *Player Movement* group, add a new subevent with the condition *Function - On Function*, and set *Name* to "ClimbStart". This event can be activated at a later time by a Function object action named Call function, as you will see. Next, add the following actions to the event you just created:

- *Koala - Platform: Set enabled* (Disabled)
- *Koala - Platform: Set Vector X* (0)
- *Koala - Platform: Set Vector Y* (0)
- *Koala - 8-Direction: Set enabled* (Enabled)
- *Koala - Instance variables: Set value*, with *State* set to "Climbing"

Add another subevent in this group, again with the condition *Function - On Function*, but this time set *Name* to "ClimbStop". Add the following set of actions, which closely correspond to the set of actions earlier:

- *Koala - 8-Direction: Set enabled* (Disabled)
- *Koala - 8-Direction: Set Vector X* (0)
- *Koala - 8-Direction: Set Vector Y* (0)
- *Koala - Platform: Set enabled* (Enabled)
- *Koala - Instance variables: Set value*, with *State* set to "Normal"

When you are finished, the events should appear as in Figure 13-7. You can save your project, but there is nothing new to test at this time, as no other events have activated these functions yet.

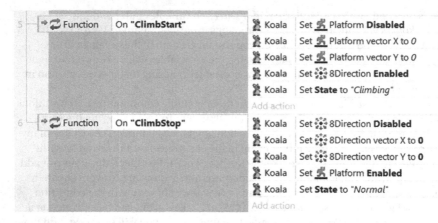

Figure 13-7. *Functions that switch the Platform and 8-Direction behaviors*

Next, we will discuss the conditions for which one of these functions should be activated. The most obvious cases are that when the koala is overlapping a ladder and the player presses either the up arrow or down arrow key, the ClimbStart event should be called, and whenever the koala is not overlapping a ladder, then the ClimbStop event should be called. However, there are two subtle additional scenarios to consider. First, if the koala is climbing down and reaches the ground, then the player probably wants the koala to stop climbing. If the koala is standing on top of the ladder and the player presses down, then the player probably wants to start climbing.

The logical difficulty with checking these last two scenarios is that they both involve the area directly below the koala's feet. The most straightforward way to be able to check these conditions is to create a sprite that serves as a "sensor" for this area, as follows. Create a new sprite named Below, and use the image editor drawing tools to fill in the box with a solid color and draw a letter *B*. When you are finished, close the image editor windows, change the property *Size* to 24,18, and set *Initial visibility* to Invisible. Position the sprite so that it appears a few pixels below the bottom of the Koala sprite, as shown in Figure 13-8 (you may need to temporarily disable the *Snap to grid* option to line it up accurately, or press the Alt key while dragging to ignore the grid positioning). Add the *Pin* behavior to the Below object. To active the *Pin* object, in the event sheet, create a new event with the condition *System - On start of layout*, and add the action *Below - Pin to object* (Koala). In addition, since the ladder was added after the koala, the koala will appear underneath the ladder. To remedy this, add a section action to the event: *Koala - Z Order: Move to top*. This event should appear as in Figure 13-9.

Figure 13-8. *Placement of the Below sprite*

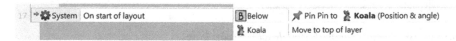

Figure 13-9. *Events to activate on start of layout*

Now you are ready to add the events that activate and deactivate the climbing behavior. In the group *Player Movement,* add the following five subevents, which are also shown in Figure 13-10:

- Add the condition *Keyboard - On key pressed* (Up arrow), add the condition *Koala - Is overlapping another object* (Ladder), and add the action *Function - Call function* ("ClimbStart").

- Add the condition *Keyboard - On key pressed* (*Down* arrow), add the condition *Koala - Is overlapping another object* (*Ladder*), and add the action *Function - Call function* ("ClimbStart").

- Add the inverted condition *Koala - Is overlapping another object* (Ladder), and add the action *Function - Call function* ("ClimbStop").

- Add the condition *Keyboard - Key is down* (Down arrow), add the condition *Below - Is overlapping another object* (Map), add the inverted condition *Below - Is overlapping another object* (Ladder), and add the action *Function - Call function* ("ClimbStop").

- Add the condition *Keyboard - On key pressed* (Down arrow), add the condition *Below - Is overlapping another object* (Ladder), add the inverted condition *Below - Is overlapping another object* (Map), add the action *Function - Call function* ("ClimbStart"), and add the action *Koala - Move at angle*, with *Angle* set to 90 and *Distance* set to 2.

	Keyboard	On **Up arrow** pressed		⟳ Function	Call **"ClimbStart"** ()
7	🐨 Koala	Is overlapping ⊟ **Ladder**		Add action	
8	Keyboard	On **Down arrow** pressed		⟳ Function	Call **"ClimbStart"** ()
	🐨 Koala	Is overlapping ⊟ **Ladder**		Add action	
9	🐨 Koala	✖ Is overlapping ⊟ **Ladder**		⟳ Function	Call **"ClimbStop"** ()
				Add action	
10	Keyboard	**Down arrow** is down		⟳ Function	Call **"ClimbStop"** ()
	Ⓑ Below	✖ Is overlapping ⊟ **Ladder**		Add action	
	Ⓑ Below	Is overlapping ▦ **Map**			
11	Keyboard	On **Down arrow** pressed		⟳ Function	Call **"ClimbStart"** ()
	Ⓑ Below	Is overlapping ⊟ **Ladder**		🐨 Koala	Move 2 pixels at angle 90
	Ⓑ Below	✖ Is overlapping ▦ **Map**		Add action	

Figure 13-10. *Events to activate and deactivate climbing*

In the last two events listed, the overlapping map conditions are present to stop the koala from trying to start climbing when the solid tilemap is in the way and to stop the koala from falling off the ladder too soon in the situation where the bottom of the ladder is not next to solid tiles from the tilemap. In addition, the extra action in the last event is necessary because the Jump-thru behavior on the ladder prevents the koala from passing through it from above, so an initial adjustment is required. Finally, in some platform games, pressing the jump button also causes the player to stop climbing and "fall down" (return to the *Platform* controls); you can add this feature as a sixth event if desired.

Although you could test the climbing mechanic at this time, the koala would appear strange while climbing because the events that activate the climb animation have not yet been set up; this will be your next step. In the *Player Animation* group, add a new subevent with the condition *Koala - Compare instance variable*, and check whether State equals `"Climbing"`. Create two subevents to this condition as follows:

- Add the condition *Koala - 8-Direction: Is moving*, and add the action *Koala - Set Animation* (`"Climb"`).

- Add the condition *System - Else*, and add the action *Koala - Animation: Stop.*

Figure 13-11 shows these events. Now is an excellent time to save and test your game and verify that the climbing mechanic works as desired. However, when climbing up the ladder, the player will have to be careful to align the koala so that its head does not hit a tilemap tile while climbing, which, having the Solid behavior, would prevent further movement. Try every combination of movement that can trigger these events: standing on the ground and climbing up the ladder, standing on top of the ladder and climbing down, climbing the ladder starting from midjump, falling off the ladder by climbing to either side, and so on.

Figure 13-11. *Events to activate the climbing animation*

Overall, climbing ladders is a difficult and complicated mechanic to implement well, so congratulations on completing this section!

Additional Game Objects

In this section, you will create a variety of objects for the koala to interact with, which will make the gameplay much more interesting. In particular, you will add a flag (which it is the koala's goal to reach), platforms that can be jumped through, coins to collect along the way, springboards that launch the koala into the air, bricks that can be broken, coins to collect along the way, and keys that let the koala pass through locked blocks. Although many of these objects could be considered optional, it is worth implementing them all to learn how the game mechanics work, and later you can make a final decision on which of these to include. To keep your code organized, in the event sheet, create a new group named Object Interaction. All the events you create in the following sections should be subevents in this group unless stated otherwise.

Goal Flag

The player needs to have a goal; in this game, you will create a flag that the koala is trying to reach. Create a new sprite named Flag; in the *Animation frames* window, load the spritesheet flag.png (two horizontal cells and one vertical cell), and set the *Animation* properties *Speed* to 5 and *Loop* to Yes. Make sure the Flag object is on the Main layer, and place it near the end of your level. Create another new sprite, named MessageComplete, using the image message-complete.png. Place it on the UI layer; to center it in the window, make its X coordinate 400 (since a sprite's location is measured from its center by default and the window is 800 pixels wide). Its Y coordinate can be anything you want, although you should avoid overlapping the other elements on the UI layer. Set the property *Initial visibility* to Invisible. Then, in the event sheet, add a new event with the condition *Koala - On collision with another object* (Flag), add the action *Koala - destroy*, and add the action *MessageComplete - Set visible* (Visible). Figure 13-12 shows this event.

Figure 13-12. *Event to display a message after reaching the goal*

Jump-Through Platforms

Jump-through platforms are a common feature in many platform-style games; in some, they are used as an alternative to ladders that enable the player to reach higher areas in the level. Since the Construct game engine provides a *Jump-thru* behavior (which you have used previously in the section on ladder mechanics), this is fairly straightforward. Recall that the *Jump-thru* behavior enables an object to act as a solid from above, while enabling the player to move (or jump) through it from below. In the layout, create a new TiledBackground object named Platform using the image log-bridge.png. You are using a TiledBackground object instead of a Sprite object so that the image repeats, similar to the Ladder object. Add the *Jump-thru* behavior. In the layout, change the height of your platform to 16 pixels, but make the width anything you like.

Optionally, you may want to give the players the ability to jump down through platforms, which is conveniently an action provided with the Platform behavior. An intuitive control scheme to activate jumping down is when the koala is standing on a platform and the player presses the jump button while holding the down arrow key. To configure this event, locate the event in the *Player Movement* group that contains the action *Platform - Simulate control* (Jump). To this event, add a subevent with the condition *Keyboard - Key is down* (Down arrow) and the condition *Koala: Compare instance variable* (check whether *State* is equal to "Normal"). Then add the action *Koala - Platform: Fall through*. Figure 13-13 shows this subevent.

Figure 13-13. *Event for jumping down through Platform objects*

Another optional feature to add to the platform objects is movement, which is most easily accomplished by adding the *Sine* behavior and setting the *Sine* property *Movement* property to Horizontal or Vertical. To make each platform move a greater distance, you can increase the value of the *Magnitude* property, but you will need to increase the *Period* property by the same factor if you want to keep the same speed of movement. If you add the *Sine* behavior but you still want some platforms to remain stationary, set their *Magnitude* value to 0.

Springboards

With the default *Platform* behavior property values, the koala can jump to a height of nearly five (32-pixel) tiles. To overcome walls or other barriers higher than this, you could design a route involving ladders or platforms. To add some variety, you could also create a springboard, which is an object that launches a character into the air when the character lands on it. To implement this, create a new sprite named Springboard; in the *Animation frames* window, load the spritesheet springboard.png (three horizontal cells and one vertical cell), and set the Animation properties *Speed* to 8, *Loop* to Yes, and *Ping-pong* to Yes. Adjust the collision polygon for each frame of the animation to fit the image displayed in each frame. In the event sheet, create a new event with the condition *Below - On collision with another object* (Springboard), and add the action *Koala - Platform: Set Vector Y* (-1000). Vector Y indicates motion in the vertical axis; the negative value indicates the upward direction. Figure 13-14 shows this event. Feel free to experiment with the value of Vector Y until you are satisfied with the jump height.

Figure 13-14. Event to implement a springboard game mechanic

Breakable Bricks

Destructible objects are another type of classic platform game objects. In this section, you will implement breakable bricks, which can be destroyed by the koala if he jumps into them from underneath or, equivalently, if the area above the koala collides with the brick. To detect collisions in this area, you will create another sprite (named *Above*) that will be invisible and pinned to the koala, similar to the Below sprite. To provide visual feedback to the player when the brick is destroyed, you will create an animated effect that resembles brick fragments falling down. Since it is difficult to find a spritesheet with this particular sequence of images, you will learn how to simulate this effect with a Particle object.

First, create a new sprite named Brick using the image brick.png. Open the collision polygon editor, right-click to bring up the corresponding menu, and select *Set to bounding box*. This is important to keep the koala from "snagging" or getting caught on the corners if he were to walk across the top of a row of bricks. Create a few new instances of this object, and position them around the level within the jumping range of the koala.

Create a new sprite named Above; use the image editor drawing tools to fill in the box with a solid color and draw a letter *A*. When you are finished, close the image editor windows, change the size to 16,16, and set *Initial visibility* to Invisible. Position this sprite above the head of the koala sprite. Add the *Pin* behavior. In the event sheet, locate the *On start of layout* event, and add the action *Above - Pin to object* (Koala).

Next, you will set up a Particle object. Particle objects generate particle systems, which are large numbers of copies of a single small image (each of which is called a *particle*) that move independently to simulate visual effects; these are often used to create animations of smoke, fire, star fields, and so forth. There are a great number of properties that can be configured for the Particle object, only some of which will be discussed in the text that follows. In the layout, create a new Particle object named Fragments; in the image editor, open the image fragment.png. Close the image editor, and position the fragments object in the left margin of the layout area. The relevant particle object properties that you need to modify are briefly defined, and their values should be set as listed here:

- *Type*: This can be Continuous (to create a constant spray of particles over a period of time) or One-shot (which generates a set number of particles at a single instant in time); set this to One-shot.

- *Rate*: If *Type* is set to Continuous, this represents the number of particles generated per second. If *Type* is set to One-shot, this represents the total number of particles generated. Set this to 6.

- *Spray cone*: This represents the range of directions (specified in degrees) in which the particles can be fired; the angle of motion for each particle will be a random number between 0 and this number. Set this to 120.

- *Speed*: This is how fast the particles move initially; set this to 300.

- *Size*: This is the initial size of the particles; set this to 16.

- *Gravity*: This represents the downward acceleration of the particles. For consistency, this value should match the value for the platform behavior, so you should set this to 1500.

- *Acceleration*: This represents the change in speed per second; this is not needed for the intended effect, so set this to 0.

- *Speed randomizer*: This specifies a random adjustment to the speed of the particles; since this is also unnecessary for this effect, set this to 0 as well.

- *Destroy mode*: This determines when the particle will be destroyed: after fading out, after a certain amount of time passes, or after the particles stop moving. Set this to Timeout expired.

- *Timeout*: This is the time in seconds until the particles will be destroyed; set this to 3 (so that the particles will have enough time to fall past the bottom edge of the layout).

Finally, you can set up the event that enables the koala to destroy the bricks. In the event sheet, create a new event with the condition *Above - On collision with another object* (Brick), and add the following three actions:

- Add *Brick - Spawn another object* (Fragments, on the "Main" layer).

- Add *Fragments - Set angle* (270) so that the particle spray cone direction faces upward.

- Add *Brick - Destroy*.

When finished, this event should appear as in Figure 13-15.

Figure 13-15. *Event to create breakable bricks with a particle effect*

Coins

A standard feature in many platformer games is the ability to collect some type of object, such as coins. They may be worth a certain number of points, or collecting a certain number may yield some type of award to the player, such as an extra life. Players can use them as a benchmark of their skill and have the personal goal of collecting more than their personal best, with the ultimate goal of collecting them all. As they have the potential to serve so many purposes, you will learn how to implement collectible coin objects in this game.

To begin, create a new sprite named Coin, and in the image editor *Animation frames* window, load the spritesheet coin.png (six horizontal cells and one vertical cell). Set the *Animation* properties *Speed* to 8 and *Loop* to Yes. Close the image editor windows, and in the layout, change the property Size to 24,24. Create a few additional instances of the Coin object. To keep track of the number of coins collected by the koala, add an instance variable to the koala named Coins with an initial value of 0. To display this value on the user interface, create a new Text object named TextCoins with *Text* set to 0, and change the font to Arial, bold, size 36. Change the font color to a golden yellow to match the coins themselves. For visual simplicity, instead of displaying the word *Coins* in the Text object, you will add an icon to the UI instead. Create a new sprite named IconCoin with the image icon-coin.png. Make sure that TextCoins and IconCoin are both on the UI layer, and position them in the upper-left area of the layout, with the icon to the left of the text. (Figure 13-18 shows how they will be positioned, after you have added some other user interface elements later.) The final addition to the layout will be a sparkle animation that will appear every time a coin is collected; this gives visual feedback to the player. On the Main layer, create a new sprite named Sparkle, and in the image editor *Animation frames* window, load the spritesheet from the sparkle folder named sparkle-yellow.png (four horizontal cells and eight vertical cells). Set the animation property *Speed* to 60.

With these objects added, you can now set up the corresponding events. First, create a new event with the condition *Koala - On collision with another object* (Coin), and add these three actions: *Koala - Instance variables: Add to* (add *1* to Coins), *Coin - Spawn another object* (*Sparkle*, on layer "Main"), and *Coin - Destroy*. Create another event with the condition *Sparkle - Animation: On any finished,* and add the action *Sparkle - Destroy*. Finally, create an event with the condition *System - Every tick*, and add the action *TextCoins - Set Text* (Koala.Coins). When finished, these events should appear as in Figure 13-16.

26	Koala	On collision with Coin	Koala	Add *1* to **Coins**
			Coin	Spawn **Sparkle** on layer **"Main"** *(image point 0)*
			Coin	Destroy
			Add action	
27	Sparkle	On any animation finished	Sparkle	Destroy
			Add action	
18	System	Every tick	TextCoins	Set text to *Koala.Coins*

Figure 13-16. Events related to the coin-collecting mechanic

189

Keys and Locked Blocks

A feature common in many genres of games are locked doors, which are obstacles in the level that require the player to obtain a key in order to pass. Locks temporarily block further progress and can be used to help guide the player through a level, motivating the player to more fully explore a level to locate and obtain the necessary key. In this game, the locked doors will be solid-colored blocks (with a keyhole), and if the player obtains the correspondingly colored key, these blocks will unlock (disappear) on contact. There will be an icon in the user interface whose appearance changes once the player has obtained the key. To keep track of whether the player has collected a key (or any other objects), one often uses a variable, but for simplicity in this project, you will use the UI icon animation name for this purpose. As with the coins earlier, you will also create another colored sparkle effect to provide visual feedback when the player has collected the key.

To begin, create a new sprite named KeyBlue with the image key-blue.png. (For organizational purposes, you will find this image, as well as the other key-related images, in the key folder.) Close the image editor, change the size to 32,32, and position the key somewhere easily accessible in your layout. Create a new sprite named LockBlue with the image lock-blue.png. Just as you did for the Brick objects earlier (and for the same reasons), you need to adjust the collision polygon of the LockBlue object so that it is set to the bounding box. Once this is done, close the image editor, and change the brick size to 32,32. Add the behaviors *Solid* and *Fade*, and change the properties *Active at start* to No and *Fade out time* to 0.25. Create a new sprite named IconKeyBlue with the image key-blue-icon-0.png; this will be the default image displayed on the user interface. Add another animation named Collected, with the image key-blue-icon-1.png; this will be shown after the key is collected. Make sure that IconKeyBlue is on the UI layer, and position it in the layout near the upper-right area of the window bounds (indicated by a dashed line, shown in Figure 13-18). Finally, add a new animation to the Sparkle object named Blue using the spritesheet sparkle-blue.png and using the same settings as when you created the original sparkle animation.

You will set up two events for this mechanic, one for collecting the key and the other for removing the locks. First, create a new event with the condition *Koala - On collision with* (KeyBlue). Although only two actions are strictly necessary (destroying the key and updating the corresponding icon image), you will implement additional actions for visual feedback and to draw the player's attention to the changed state of the UI icon. Add the following actions:

- *KeyBlue - Spawn another object* (Sparkle on layer "Main")

- *Sparkle - Set animation* ("Blue")

- *KeyBlue - Destroy*

- *System - Wait* (1 second)

- *IconKeyBlue - Spawn another object* (Sparkle on layer "UI")

- *Sparkle - Set animation* ("Blue")

- *IconKeyBlue - Set animation* ("Collected")

Create another event with the condition *Koala - On collision with another object* (LockBlue) and the condition *IconKeyBlue - Animation: Is playing* ("Collected"); add the action *LockBlue - Start Fade* and the action *LockBlue - Solid: Set enabled* (Disabled). When you are finished, these two events should appear as shown in Figure 13-17.

Figure 13-17. *Events related to the key and lock mechanic*

If you want, you can create additional colored locks and keys, where each key unlocks the blocks of the same color, using the same setup as described earlier. Additional images for this purpose (keys, locks, icons, and sparkle effects) are included in the graphics collection for this chapter.

Enemies

In this section, you will implement two different types of enemy creatures to provide a more active challenge for the player. The first enemy will be an airborne creature named Fly that flies (as the name implies) back and forth between two locations using the waypoint-style mechanics used in the Spell Shooter and Airplane Assault games, but with no randomness included. The second enemy will be a ground-based creature named Slime that is subject to gravity (just as the koala is) and moves across the ground until encountering a wall, at which point it turns around and moves in the opposite direction. Both types of enemy have many features in common: they will use an instance variable to keep track of their current travel direction, they can both be destroyed if the koala jumps on top of them, and they both damage the koala if he collides with them in any other manner.

Before implementing the enemies themselves, you will set up the health mechanic for the player. Select the Koala object, and add a new instance variable named Health with an initial value of 3. To display this value on the user interface, create a new Text object named TextHealth with Text set to 3, and change the font to Arial, bold, size 36. Change the font color to red. As before with the coins, you will add an icon to the user interface instead of displaying the word *Health*. Create a new sprite named IconHeart with the image icon-heart.png. Make sure that TextHealth and IconHeart are both on the UI layer, and position them in the upper-central area of the layout, between the coin and key display. At this point, the user interface is complete and should resemble

191

Figure 13-18. Add the Flash behavior to the koala; this will be used for a temporary invincibility mechanic when the koala is damaged, similar to the setup for the plane in the Airplane Assault game. Finally, in the event with the condition *System - Every tick*, add the action *TextHealth - Set text* (`Koala.Health`).

Figure 13-18. *The final layout of icons and text in the user interface area*

Next, you will implement the fly enemy. Create a new sprite named `Fly`, and in the image editor *Animation frames* window, load the spritesheet `fly.png` (two horizontal cells and one vertical cell). Set the animation properties *Speed* to 8 and Loop to Yes. Close the image editor. Add the *Bullet* behavior, set *Speed* to 100, and set *Set angle* to No. Add an instance variable named `Direction`, of type *Text*, with an initial value of `Left` and description `Left or Right`. Next, create a new sprite named `FlyPoint`, using the image editor tools to fill in the background, draw the letter *F*, and change the size to 32-by-32 pixels. Add an instance variable to this object named `Move`, of type *Text*, with an initial value of `Left` and a description of `Used to set Fly Direction to Left or Right`. Change the property *Initial visibility* to `Invisible`. In the layout, create another instance of the FlyPoint object, and change its Move value to Right. In the layout, arrange the Fly object and the two FlyPoint objects in a horizontal line. The FlyPoint object with Move set to Right should be on the left, the Fly object should be in the center, the FlyPoint object with Move set to Left should be on the right, and about 100 pixels of space should separate each of these objects.

Now you will set up the events for fly movement, which are based on logic similar to waypoints from earlier chapters. The idea is that if Direction is set to Left, then the sprite image should face to the left and the angle of motion should be set to 180; corresponding actions occur when Direction is set to Right. Whenever a Fly object collides with a FlyPoint object, the Fly's Direction variable should be set to the FlyPoint's Move variable. (This is why the FlyPoint on the left side has its Move variable set to Right, because that is the new direction that the Fly should begin moving in after it collides with the FlyPoint.) In turn, the angle of motion of the Fly object will be set according to the value of its Move variable. To keep your events organized, start by creating a new group named `Enemies`; the events in this section should be added as subevents to this group unless stated otherwise. Create a new event with the condition *Fly - Compare instance variable*, and check whether *Direction* is equal to `"Left"`. Add the action *Fly - Appearance: Set Mirrored* (`Mirrored`), and add the action *Fly - Bullet: Set angle of motion* (180). Create another new event with the same set of conditions and actions, but change the parameters to check whether Direction is equal to `"Right"`, set the mirroring to `Not mirrored`, and set the angle of motion to 0. Figure 13-19 shows these events.

There are two events needed for interaction between the Fly and Koala objects. If the koala lands on top of the fly, the fly should be destroyed, and the koala bounces off by a small amount. Any other collision between the koala and fly will damage the koala, causing the koala to lose one health point and to flash for two seconds, during which period the koala cannot take additional damage. Create a new event with the condition *Below - On collision with another object* (Fly) and the condition *Koala - Platform: Is falling*. Add the action *Fly - Destroy* and the action *Koala - Platform: Set Vector Y* (-400). Create another new event with the condition *Koala - On collision with another object* (Fly), and add the inverted condition *Koala - Is flashing*. Add the action *Koala - Instance variables: Subtract from* (subtract *1* from Health) and the action *Koala - Flash* (change *Duration* to 2 seconds). These events are also shown in Figure 13-19.

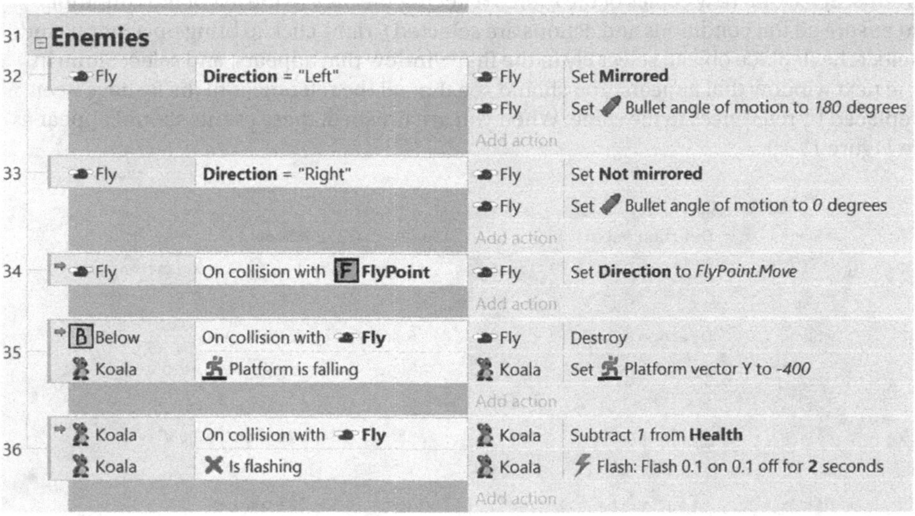

31	⊟ **Enemies**			
32	● Fly	**Direction** = "Left"	● Fly	Set **Mirrored**
			● Fly	Set 🖊 Bullet angle of motion to *180* degrees
			Add action	
33	● Fly	**Direction** = "Right"	● Fly	Set **Not mirrored**
			● Fly	Set 🖊 Bullet angle of motion to *0* degrees
			Add action	
34	⇨ ● Fly	On collision with **F** FlyPoint	● Fly	Set **Direction** to *FlyPoint.Move*
			Add action	
35	⇨ **B** Below	On collision with ● **Fly**	● Fly	Destroy
	🐨 Koala	🐨 Platform is falling	🐨 Koala	Set 🐨 Platform vector Y to *-400*
			Add action	
36	⇨ 🐨 Koala	On collision with ● **Fly**	🐨 Koala	Subtract *1* from **Health**
	🐨 Koala	✖ Is flashing	🐨 Koala	⚡ Flash: Flash 0.1 on 0.1 off for **2** seconds
			Add action	

Figure 13-19. *Events related to the Fly enemy*

Next, you will set up the Slime enemy. Create a new sprite named Slime, and in the image editor *Animation frames* window, load the spritesheet slime.png (two horizontal cells and one vertical cell). Set the animation property *Speed* to 4 and *Loop* to Yes. Close the image editor. Add the *Platform* behavior, and set *Max speed* to 60 and *Default controls* to No. Add an instance variable named Direction, of type Text, with an initial value of Left and a description of Left or Right. Since the Platform behavior has conditions that check for walls to the left or right, it is not necessary to create an object analogous to the FlyPoint object to detect when the slime needs to change direction.

The slime movement events are analogous to the fly movement events, except that instead of setting the bullet angle of motion, you will simulate the platform control in the corresponding direction. Changing the value of the Direction variable will occur when the slime is next to a wall. The events that result in the slime being destroyed or the koala taking damage are identical to the corresponding events for the fly, except that the references to the Fly object are replaced with the Slime object. To begin implementing these features, create a new event with the condition *Slime - Compare instance variable*, and check whether *Direction* is equal to "Left". Add the action *Slime - Appearance: Set Mirrored* (Mirrored), and add the action *Slime - Platform: Simulate control* (Left). Create another new event with the same set of conditions and actions, but change the parameters to check whether *Direction* is equal to "Right", set the mirroring to Not mirrored, and set

193

the simulated control to Right. Next, create an event with the condition *Slime - Platform: Is by wall* (left), add the action *Slime - Instance variables: Set value*, and set *Direction* to "Right". Create another event with the same condition and action, but change the parameters to check whether there is a wall to the right, in which case the value of *Direction* should be set to "Left".

Finally, you will create the events that handle interaction between the koala and the slime. Since these events are so similar to the events for the Fly object, the quickest way to create them is to copy and paste a new copy of each of the corresponding fly-related events. Select the new copies of the events (clicking the area to the left of the condition to ensure all the conditions and actions are selected), right-click to bring up a menu, and select the Replace object; select Fly in the first window that appears, and select Slime in the next window that appears. You should see that all the references to the fly have been replaced by references to the slime. When you are finished, these events should appear as in Figure 13-20.

37	Slime	Direction = "Left"	Slime	Set **Mirrored**	
			Slime	Simulate Platform pressing Left	
			Add action		
38	Slime	Direction = "Right"	Slime	Set **Not mirrored**	
			Slime	Simulate Platform pressing Right	
			Add action		
39	Slime	Platform has wall to left	Slime	Set **Direction** to *"Right"*	
			Add action		
40	Slime	Platform has wall to right	Slime	Set **Direction** to *"Left"*	
			Add action		
41	B Below	On collision with **Slime**	Slime	Destroy	
	Koala	Platform is falling	Koala	Set Platform vector Y to *-400*	
			Add action		
42	Koala	On collision with **Slime**	Koala	Subtract *1* from **Health**	
	Koala	X Is flashing	Koala	Flash: Flash 0.1 on 0.1 off for **2** seconds	

Figure 13-20. *Events related to the Slime enemy*

Finally, there needs to be a "game over" message that appears when the koala's health reaches 0. Create a new sprite named MessageGameOver using the image message-game-over.png. Set its Layer to UI, set *Initial visibility* to Invisible, and center it within the window bounds, as you did for the MessageComplete object earlier in the chapter. Then add the event *Koala - Compare instance variable* to check whether Health is less or equal than 0, and add the action Koala - Destroy and the action *MessageGameOver - Set visibility* (Visible). This event is shown in Figure 13-21.

| 43 | 🐨 Koala | Health ≤ 0 | 🐨 Koala | Destroy |
| | | | ‑‑ MessageGameOver | Set Visible |

Figure 13-21. Event to display the "game over" message

At this point, you now have a complete platformer game, with a great variety of obstacles, enemies, and win and lose conditions. This is the longest and most complex project you have encountered in this book thus far, so congratulations for reaching this point!

Side Quests

With the number of features you have added to this project, the first improvement you may want to consider is designing an interesting level, combining the features in various ways. You could create a mazelike level where the player has to search for a key to unlock a group of blocks surrounding the goal flag. You could add difficult jumps requiring great precision or many enemies for an extra challenge. You could add scenic elements (such as clouds and bushes) to the level, similar to the recommendation from the Racecar 500 game.

Pits are a feature that many platform games add; pits are holes in the ground that cause the player to lose if they fall through. Your instinct may be to add the *Destroy outside layout* behavior to the koala. However, this would have the unfortunate side effect of also destroying the player if they jumped above the top edge of the layout, which could easily happen, depending on your particular level design. If you want to implement this gameplay mechanic, one approach is to a new sprite named Pit, resizing it to be longer than the entire map and placing it in the margins of the layout, about 100 pixels below the bottom edge of the level. Create a corresponding event that checks whether the koala has collided with the Pit sprite and, if so, sets the koala's health to 0. At that point, the "game over" event will handle displaying the MessageGameOver object.

Another item you could add is a heart item that adds one to the koala's health when it is collected. You could set up a heartbeat-like pulsing animation with the Sine behavior set to change the size of the object. A few heart items could be strategically placed around the level in difficult-to-reach locations, or they could be occasionally spawned when an enemy is destroyed, similar to the item-spawning mechanic from the Rectangle Destroyer game. Locate the event where an enemy is destroyed, and create a subevent with a condition that compares a randomly generated number to a fixed number.

Currently, only enemies cause the koala to lose health points. You could add an environmental hazard, such as spikes, that damage the player on collision. Since you don't want the player to be able to walk through the spikes, you probably want to add the Solid behavior to the sprite. However, to stop the player from simply walking across the spikes damage-free after the first collision, you may instead want to replace the collision condition with checking for overlap with the Below sprite (which is sufficient if the spikes can only be fallen onto from above).

To add a sense of tension, you may want to consider adding a countdown timer, analogous to the timer you added in the Racecar 500 game; if the time reaches 0, then the player instantly loses the game. With this addition, you could also consider adding a Clock item, which adds to the total time remaining, thus making it easier to complete the level in time. The Clock item also opens up a possibility for a particularly challenging level design: you could design a level and initially set the timer to an amount that is insufficient to complete the level, thus forcing the player to pick up one or more Clock items along the way.

Finally, a common feature in many platform-style games are item blocks, which typically contain coins (or could contain other items such as hearts, keys, clocks, etc.) that are spawned when the block is hit from below. The blocks typically have two animations: a flashing animation, such as the one generated by the spritesheet shown on the left side of Figure 13-22, and an empty image, as shown on the right side of Figure 13-22. The event condition to set up is similar to the condition for breaking bricks: the Above sprite should collide with the item block, and you will also need to add the condition that checks whether the flashing animation is playing. The associated actions would be for the system to spawn an object directly above the item box (similar to the paddle spawning a ball in the Rectangle Destroyer game), and the item box should set its animation to the blank image. To be able to spawn different types of items, additional item block objects could be created (using the same animations, so as to not give away anything to the player), or if you want to have only one item block object, a random number could be generated to determine what is spawned, or an instance variable could be used to determine which time of item to spawn.

Figure 13-22. Item block graphics: a flashing block animation (left) and an empty block image (right)

These are just a few ideas to get you started; many more possibilities exist. Feel free to experiment and test your creations. Most important, have fun!

Summary

In this chapter, you created the platform-style game Jumping Jack. This game built on concepts and skills from most of the previous projects. Two new behaviors were introduced: *Platform* for standard platform controls and *Jump-Thru* for solidlike objects that characters can move or jump through from underneath. The Function object was introduced to reduce repeated code, and the Particle object was introduced to create an animated effect based on a single small image. Ladder-climbing mechanics were implemented, and many interactive objects were added to the level. Enemies with different movement patterns were also created to add an active challenge for the player. Finally, a great number of ideas for additional features were suggested in the "Side Quests" section.

In the next chapter, you will create the final game project in this book: Treasure Quest, a top-down perspective adventure game, inspired by the classic console game The Legend of Zelda.

CHAPTER 14

■ ■ ■

Treasure Quest

In this chapter, you will create a top-down adventure-style game named Treasure Quest, shown in Figure 14-1, inspired by classic games such as The Legend of Zelda.

Figure 14-1. *The Treasure Quest game*

In Treasure Quest, the player controls a character named Hero whose goal is to find and collect the treasure chest. Along the way, there will be obstacles such as rocks that block the hero's progress and enemies that attack the hero. The hero has a sword, which can be swung to destroy enemies (or any bushes that block the hero's path). Coins are sometimes dropped by defeated enemies (or can be found hidden around the level), and

© Lee Stemkoski and Evan Leider 2017
L. Stemkoski and E. Leider, *Game Development with Construct 2*,
DOI 10.1007/978-1-4842-2784-8_14

they can be used to purchase objects such as hearts (which restore a health point) or bomb bags (which contain a number of bombs, which can then be used to destroy rocks). There are three varieties of enemies: one that flies randomly through the air, one that moves randomly on the ground, and one that actively seeks out and chases the hero. In this project, the game world is spread out across multiple layouts.

The player moves the hero with the arrow keys, swings the sword with the spacebar key, and places bombs with the *B* key (after they are obtained). For simplicity, the purchasing mechanic is handled by placing items behind doors that open (disappear) on contact if the hero has enough coins. The user interface displays the hero's health and the number of coins and bombs currently held. Because of the complexity of this game, a sign object is introduced; if the hero touches the sign, the corresponding message is displayed on the user interface. This can be used to inform the player of the control scheme, to explain game mechanics (for example, how doors work), to provide navigational information (for example, "the bomb shop is to the south"), to give the player hints about how to complete the level, and so forth.

The chapter assumes familiarity with most of the topics presented in earlier chapters, including most types of objects, behaviors (*8-Direction, Solid, Bullet, Fade, Rotate, Flash, Timer*), instance and global variables, and functions. In the event sheet, groups, subevents, and "or" blocks will be used frequently. The *Line of sight* and *Persist* behaviors will be introduced, as well as the *Global* property for objects and layers, which enables them to continue existing when switching to a new layout (which is particularly important for the hero and the user interface). Many new mechanics will be introduced, such as switching between layouts and creating an "item shop." Since you have gained great experience in using Construct by this point, the style in this chapter is less guided and emphasizes game design concepts rather than the details of setting up events (although the events will be fully displayed in the chapter figures, as usual).

To begin, download the assets for this chapter from the book web site. Set the layout size to 960, 960 and the window size to 480, 480. Change the layout name to Field and the event sheet name to Game Events. In the *View* tab, select the *Snap to grid* and *Show grid* check boxes, and set the grid width and grid height both to 16. Add three additional layers to your project (for a total of four layers), and name them Map, Walls, Main, and UI. For the UI layer, set *Parallax* to 0,0; this will fix the UI in place, as desired.

Level Design

In this section, you will set up the level, using a tilemap for the background image. Unlike some of the previous projects (such as Racecar 500 and Jumping Jack), you will not add the *Solid* behavior to the tilemap. Instead, you will create *wall sprites*, which will be invisible and have the *Solid* behavior attached; instances will be placed over tiles that correspond to impassable barriers (such as fences or mountains). Also, when designing each level, the top 64 pixels of the layout should be reserved for the user interface area, so this area should be filled with a barrier of some sort. After setting up the tilemap, you will also create sprite objects for trees, bushes, and rocks (to which interactivity will be added later).

To begin, add a Tilemap object named World to the Map layer of the layout, using the tileset image adventure-tileset.png. These tiles are 32-by-32 pixels, so no properties need to be changed. Design a level using these tiles. For variety, there are lots of variations of grass tiles. Create a border around the perimeter of the layout. Figure 14-2 shows one such layout, which contains a grassy field with some dirt paths leading to two mountains, one of which contains a cave entrance (which will actually lead the player to a new screen), while the other has a ladder leading up the side to the top (which will be a good location to place the treasure chest, as you will see later). Figure 14-2 is displayed using a 32-by-32 grid to make the tile selection more apparent. When you are finished, click the Tilemap panel, click on the *Select Tool,* and then lock the Map layer.

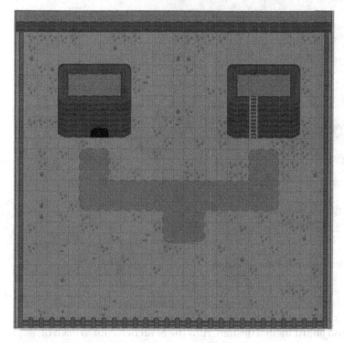

Figure 14-2. *Tilemap for a sample level*

Next, you will create wall objects that specify the solid parts of the level. Make the Walls layer active in the layout, and add a new sprite named Wall. Draw anything you like in the image editor. Close the image editor, set *Opacity* to 50 (to make it easier to position in the layout), and set *Initial visibility* to Invisible. Add the *Solid* behavior. Then, create as many additional instances as necessary, resizing and positioning each one, until the tiles corresponding to solid objects are all covered, such as the fence and mountainside (but not the ladder or cave entrance!) tiles. When you are finished, the wall layout corresponding to Figure 14-2 would look similar to Figure 14-3, for example; a diamond pattern was drawn on the Wall sprites to make them easier to see in the diagram. When you are finished, lock the Walls layer, and uncheck the box next to the layer name so that the objects in this layer are no longer visible (even at 50 percent opacity, they can be distracting).

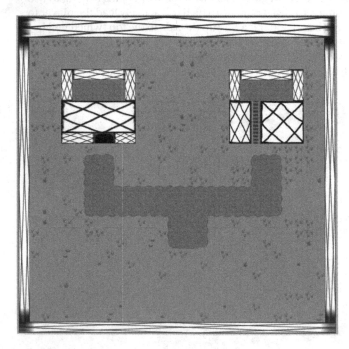

Figure 14-3. *The wall objects added to the layout*

Next, make the Main layer active in the layout. Create three new sprites named Tree, Bush, and Rock, using the images tree.png, bush.png, and rock.png, respectively. Check their collision polygons, and adjust them if desired. Add the *Solid* behavior to each of these objects. Add the *Fade* behavior to the *Bush* object, and change *Fade out time* to 0.25 and *Active at start* to No. Create multiple instances of each of these objects, and position them throughout the level. Change the size of individual tree instances for variety, if desired. When finished, the layout corresponding to Figure 14-2 could look similar to Figure 14-4, for example. Later in this chapter, you will add interactivity to some of these objects: bushes will be able to be destroyed by the hero's sword, and rocks will be able to be destroyed with bombs.

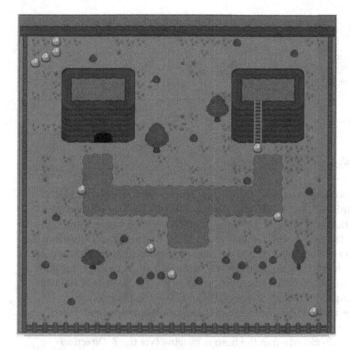

Figure 14-4. *Adding trees, bushes, and rocks to the layout*

Hero Setup

First, you will set up the hero character, just as you did for the Cleanup Challenge and Maze Runman games. Create a new sprite named Hero; in the *Animation frames* window, load the spritesheet general48.png (three horizontal cells and four vertical cells), and set the *Animation* properties *Speed* to 6, *Loop* to Yes, and *Ping-pong* to Yes. Then duplicate this animation three times so that there are four animations total. Next, rename the animations to South, West, East, and North. Select the animation named *South* in the list, and in the "Animation frames" window, click each frame that does *not* correspond to the character walking south (those initially numbered 3 through 11), and press the *Delete* key. Repeat this process for the West, East, and North animations, deleting the frames not required within each of the animations. Next, adjust the sprite's collision polygon to a smaller circular shape (as shown in Figure 14-5), right-click the polygon, and select *Apply to all animations*. Close the image editor, and change the size of the sprite to 32,32. Add the behaviors *Bound to layout*, *Scroll to*, and *8-Direction*; change the *8-Direction* properties *Speed* to 120 and *Set angle* to No.

Figure 14-5. *Collision polygon for the Hero sprite*

Next, you will set up some events to set the correct hero animation, but instead of relying on key press conditions, as you did in previous projects, here you will use the angle of motion to select the correct angle. For convenience, you will convert this value to the nearest multiple of 90 (similar to the calculations in Maze Runman) and store it in an instance variable. Also, as was the case in the Maze Runman game, angles of motion are measured in the range from -180 to 180 (in contrast to the sprite object's *Angle* property, which uses the range from 0 to 360). Therefore, the angles -180, -90, 0, 90, and 180 will correspond to the directions West, North, East, South, and West, respectively.[1]

Select the *Hero* sprite, and add an instance variable named AnimAngle with an initial value of 90. In the event sheet, create a group named Hero Animation. To this group, add a subevent that checks whether the hero is moving (via the *8-Direction* condition), in which case the Hero instance variable *AnimAngle* should be set to round(Hero.8Direction.MovingAngle / 90) * 90, which calculates the nearest multiple of 90. Then add four subevents to this event, each of which will compare the value of the hero's *AnimAngle* variable and, depending on the result, will set the Hero animation accordingly. If *AnimAngle* is equal to 90, for example, the animation name should be set to "South". Similarly, the value 0 corresponds to "East", and -90 corresponds to "North". Since "West" has two corresponding values, set the condition to an "or" block, and check whether *AnimAngle* is equal to 180 or whether *AnimAngle* is equal to -180. Finally, add another subevent to the group (not a subevent of the event currently numbered as 2) with the *System* condition *Else*, in which case the Hero animation should be stopped. Note that this event corresponds to when the *Hero – Is moving condition is false*, and the left edges of these conditions should line up in the event sheet. When you are finished, these events should appear as in Figure 14-6.

---

[1]Note that the direction West has two corresponding angles; because of the cyclic nature of angle measurement, no matter what range of values is used, two different multiples of 90 (the minimum and maximum values in the range) will end up corresponding to a single direction.

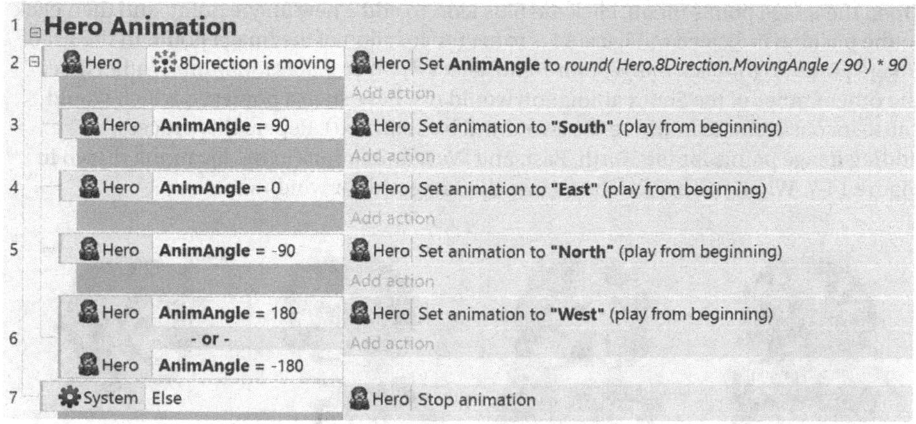

1	Hero Animation			
2	Hero	8Direction is moving	Hero	Set **AnimAngle** to *round(Hero.8Direction.MovingAngle / 90) * 90*
				Add action
3	Hero	**AnimAngle = 90**	Hero	Set animation to **"South"** (play from beginning)
				Add action
4	Hero	**AnimAngle = 0**	Hero	Set animation to **"East"** (play from beginning)
				Add action
5	Hero	**AnimAngle = -90**	Hero	Set animation to **"North"** (play from beginning)
				Add action
6	Hero	**AnimAngle = 180** - or -	Hero	Set animation to **"West"** (play from beginning)
	Hero	**AnimAngle = -180**		Add action
7	System	Else	Hero	Stop animation

Figure 14-6. *Events for setting the Hero animation*

Sword-Fighting Mechanics

A separate sprite will be created for the sword. The goal is that when the player presses the attack key, a sword will be spawned (at the correct position and angle), it will rotate (to give the appearance that the hero is swinging it), and then it will be destroyed. (Presumably, the hero is extremely quick at sheathing and unsheathing his sword.) For simplicity, the hero will not move while swinging the sword.[2]

To begin, add a new sprite named Sword with the image sword.png. In the image editor, set the origin of the sword to the point on the sword handle where it should appear held by the hero, and apply the change to all animations. You may want to consider setting the collision polygon so that it is set to the bounding box of the image to make it easier for the player to hit moving targets. Close the image editor, change the size of the sprite to 32,12, and position it outside the layout. Add the behaviors *Destroy outside layout* and *Rotate*. For this game, the goal is for the sword to swing through 180 degrees in 0.25 seconds; therefore, set the rotation speed to 720 (since one-fourth of 720 is 180). Since the midpoint of the sword's swing should be aligned with the direction the hero is facing, after the sword is spawned, you will have to subtract half the range of the sword swing from the direction the hero is facing, as you will see later.

When spawning a sprite, the default setting is for the origin of the new sprite to be aligned with the origin of the sprite that is spawning it. However, it would be best if the handle of the sword spawned in the location of the hero's hand (we will assume the hero is right-handed in this game). To accomplish this, you will create another image point for each animation, indicating the position of the hero's right hand in each case. Double-click the hero to open the image editor windows, and select the *South* animation.

---

[2]To implement this, you would need to consider adding the *Pin* behavior to keep the sword in the correct position relative to the hero, as well as some events to adjust the anchor point and z-order of the sword in the case that the hero changes direction suddenly.

Open the image points menu, click the plus icon to add a new image point, and then click in the position indicated in Figure 14-7 to set the location of the image point. In the list of image points, right-click *Imagepoint 1* and select *Apply to whole animation* (otherwise, the other frames of the South animation would not have such a point set, which would cause inconsistencies in where the sword will be spawned). Repeat this process, adding image points for the North, East, and West animations in the locations shown in Figure 14-7. When you are finished, close the image editor windows.

Figure 14-7. *Positions for new image points to indicate sword spawn location*

Now you are ready to create the events related to sword-swinging. In the layout, add a *Keyboard* object to the project. In the event sheet, add a new group called Sword Mechanics. To this group, add an event that checks whether the spacebar has been pressed and uses a *System* condition to check whether *Sword.Count* is equal to 0 (which will prevent multiple sword instances from being onscreen at the same time). Create actions for the following set of tasks:

- The hero's movement should stop, and the *8-Direction* behavior should be disabled.

- The hero should spawn a sword on the Main layer, at image point 1.

- The sword's angle should be set to Hero.AnimAngle - 90 degrees.

- Wait for 0.25 seconds (the duration of the sword swing).

- Destroy the sword, and reenable the *8-Direction* behavior.

In addition, since the hero is presumably right-handed, the hero needs to appear above the sword if he is facing north or west, so add an event that checks either whether the hero's North or West animation is playing, in which case the hero should be moved to the top of the layer. Finally, add an event that checks whether the sword has collided with the bush, in which case start the bush fade-out process. When the events in this section are finished, they should appear as shown in Figure 14-8.

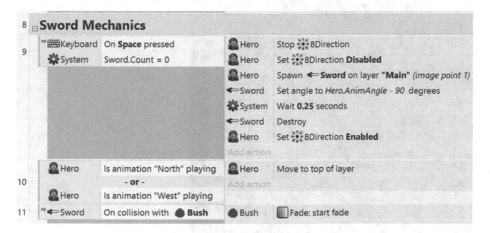

Figure 14-8. Events for swinging the sword and destroying bushes

Multiple Levels

Next, you will set up the ability for the hero to move between multiple screens. To begin, you will set up a second level. In the projects panel, right-click the layout folder and add a new layout, but do not create a new event sheet. Once the layout is created, change the name to Cave, set the size to 480,480 (which is smaller than the field but matches the window size exactly), and set up the layers and grid options just as you did for the Field layout. Click the Cave layout, and in the *Properties* panel, set the layout property's *Event sheet* (which is currently set to *none*) to Game Events. Set the active layer to Map, open the project panel again, and drag World (the tilemap object) onto the layout area. This will create a copy of the preexisting tilemap. Resize this to fit the layout, and draw a simple, empty, cavelike interior, as shown in Figure 14-9, making sure to leave a gap (some dirt tiles) in the bottom area where the hero will be able to exit, and an empty 64-pixel high region across the top, where the user interface will eventually be displayed. Lock the Map layer, and set the active layer to Walls. From the project panel, drag a Wall object onto the layout, positioning it over tiles that should be considered solid. Duplicate this object, and repeat this process until the wall tiles are all covered by Wall objects, just as you did when designing the previous layout. When finished, lock the Map layer, and set the active layer to Main.

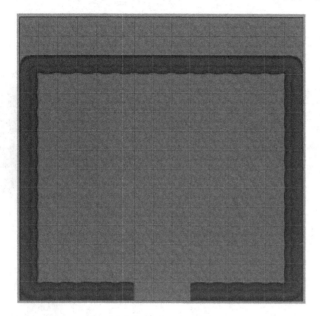

Figure 14-9. *Initial design for the Cave layout*

Next, you will implement the layout-switching mechanic using a pair of sprite objects named Spawn and Portal. When the hero collides with a portal, a new layout will be loaded, and the hero will be positioned at a particular spawn instance, both of whose names are stored in instance variables of the Portal object.

Return to the Field layout. Create a new sprite named Spawn; in the image editor, fill in the area with a solid color and draw a letter *S*. Close the image editor windows, set *Size* to 32,32, and set *Initial visibility* to Invisible. Add an instance variable called Name of type Text with an initial value of Start. Similarly, create another new sprite named Portal, drawing an image of a letter *P* in the image editor and setting it to be initially invisible. (Setting the portal size is not as important here; spawn instances should be the size of the hero, while portal sizes may vary.) Add two instance variables to the Portal object, one named Layout of type Text with an initial value if Field and the other named Spawn of type Text with an initial value of Start. In the Field layout, place the Spawn object at a position where you want the hero to be when the game starts. Place the Portal object over the entrance to the cave, and change its *Layout* variable to Cave and its *Spawn* variable to Entrance.

Next, create another spawn instance, and place it a bit below the entrance to the cave (making sure the two objects do not overlap, which could cause the hero to immediately warp to another layout), and change its *Name* variable to CaveExit. Switch to the Cave layout, and from the project panel, drag an instance of the Portal object and an instance of the Spawn object onto the layout. Position the Spawn instance above the cave exit, and change its *Name* variable to Entrance (to match the Spawn variable of the portal from the previous layout). Position the *Portal* instance along the bottom edge of the cave exit, and change its *Layout* variable to Field and its *Spawn* variable to CaveExit (to match the *Name* variable of the spawn instance by the cave in the previous layout). Figure 14-10 shows the positions of these Portal and Spawn objects.

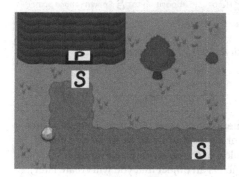 

Figure 14-10. *Placement of the Portal and Spawn instances in the field layout (left) and Cave layout (right)*

Now you will set up the events that control this game mechanic. In the event sheet, add a global variable named SpawnLocation with an initial value of Start. This is necessary to store the name of the spawn instance that the hero should be moved to when switching between layouts. In particular, if you were to create an event with an action that switches the layout, followed by an action that moves the player to the new spawn point, it would not work properly since the new layout isn't loaded until after the event is finished (and thus the spawn point you seek is not yet available).

Next, select the Hero object, and change the *Global* property to Yes. The result of changing this property is that the Hero instance will not be destroyed when switching to the new layout; it will still be present after the next layout loads. This is important because every layout requires an instance of the Hero object, and it is preferable to share the same instance between them so that any instance variables you may set up for the hero will preserve their values when layouts are switched. Finally, in the event sheet, create a new group called Portal and Spawn. Add an event that checks whether the hero has collided with a portal, in which case the global variable *SpawnLocation* should be set to Portal. Spawn, and then the layout should be changed with the action *System - Go to layout (by name)*, entering Portal.Layout. Create a second event with the *System* condition *On start of layout* and with the Spawn condition that checks for the instance whose *Name* variable is equal to the global variable *SpawnLocation*. To this event, add an action that sets the hero to the location of the Spawn object. When you are finished, these events should appear as shown in Figure 14-11.

When testing these new features, make sure the Field layout is displayed when clicking the *Run layout* icon so that the field level is displayed first. If you run the project while the Cave layout is displayed, the cave level will be loaded first instead, and since there is no hero instance available, you will not be able to test any of the features.

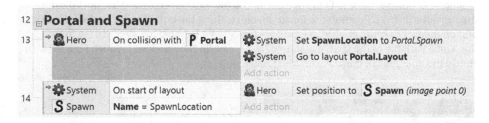

Figure 14-11. Events for switching layouts with the Portal and Spawn objects

User Interface Design

In this section, you will set up the various elements of the user interface. There are three main features that the user interface will support: a display of the hero's status (health remaining, coins collected, and bombs available), win and lose message graphics, and an area that displays the text written on signs (which is an object that you will create later).

To begin, in the Field layout, set the active layer to UI. In the Layers panel, select the *UI* layer, and change the property *Global* to Yes. The effect of this setting is similar to the effect of the *Global* setting of the Hero object; the objects contained in the global layer will not be destroyed when switching to another layout, provided that the layout contains a layer with the same name. (This will be apparent only while the game is running, however.) If you switch to the Cave layout and select its *UI* layer, you will see that its *Global* property has been automatically changed to (Yes, overridden), which indicates that this layer will in fact receive copies of the objects in the Field layout's UI layer. For the *Global* property to work correctly, it is important that the layout containing the *Global* layer is loaded before any other layouts that also contain this layer.

Create two new sprites, one named MessageWin with the image file message-win. png and the other named MessageLose with the image file message-lose.png. Resize both of these sprites so that their width is less than 400 (so they fit within the window), and change their height proportionally. To horizontally center these sprites in the window (which is 480 pixels wide), change their position so that their *X* coordinate is 240. Set their *Initial visibility* to invisible. The events that cause these objects to appear will be added later in the chapter, as they require additional objects to be created.

Status Display

The player will want to be aware of three quantities at all times: the hero's health, the number of coins the hero has collected, and the number of bombs the hero has available to use. Although the coin and bomb objects have not yet been added, you can still set up the corresponding variables and text displays at this time. Select the Hero object, and add three new instance variables: Health, Coins, and Bombs. Each of these will store a number; the initial values should be set to 3, 0, and 0, respectively. Create a new sprite named BackgroundUI, and in the image editor, fill it with a dark gray color. Change the size to 480-by-64 pixels, and position it in the top-left corner of the layout. (This is why you needed to fill the top 64-pixel area of each layout with a solid barrier; this part of the map will always be obscured by the user interface.) Next, create three new Text objects, named TextHealth, TextCoins, and TextBombs; set their font to Arial, bold, size 18; set their font colors to pink, light yellow, and light gray, respectively; and set their initial text properties to "Health: 3", "Coins: 0", and "Bombs: 0", respectively. Resize and position these objects on the BackgroundUI object, equally spaced from each other, as shown in Figure 14-12. In the event sheet, create a new group named User Interface. To this group, add an event with the condition *System - Every tick*, and add actions that set the text of the three text objects TextHealth, TextCoins, and TextBombs to "Health: " & Hero.Health, "Coins: " & Hero.Coins, and "Bombs: " & Hero.Bombs, respectively. Figure 14-13 shows this event.

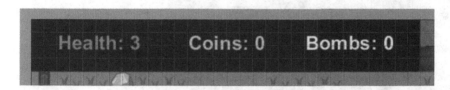

Figure 14-12. Positioning of Text objects in the status display area of the user interface

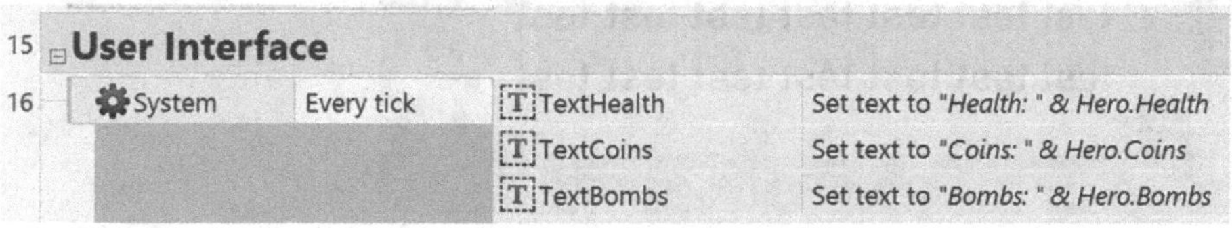

15	▭ **User Interface**			
16	⚙ System	Every tick	[T] TextHealth	Set text to *"Health: "* & Hero.Health
			[T] TextCoins	Set text to *"Coins: "* & Hero.Coins
			[T] TextBombs	Set text to *"Bombs: "* & Hero.Bombs

Figure 14-13. Group and event for updating user interface text

Sign Mechanics

Signs, which have the ability to display text to the player, can serve a variety of purposes and have the potential to greatly improve the overall gameplay experience. Signs can help the player navigate the game world, introduce new game mechanics, provide clues, or remind the player of the control scheme. In this section, you will create a sign object for the game world that the hero can interact with and will create a corresponding display in

209

the user interface that displays the sign message. To keep the player controls as simple as possible, the sign text will be displayed whenever the hero collides with a sign (in contrast to requiring the user to press a button to read the sign), and the sign text display will be hidden once the hero moves a few pixels away from the corresponding sign.

Since the UI layer is currently active, you will add the display objects first. In the Field layout, add a new sprite named BackgroundMessage using the image file background-message.png. Change its size to 400,160, and position it toward the bottom of the user interface area. Next, add a Text object named TextMessage, and change the font to Arial, bold, size 18. Position and resize the Text object so that it nearly fills the same area as the BackgroundMessage object. Then, for the initial text, enter the word test 20 to 30 times; this is simply to give you an idea of how much text this object can display in the given area at the current font size (which can be adjusted as desired). Set the initial visibility of both these objects to Invisible. Figure 14-14 illustrates the position of these new objects, with the other UI components included for reference.

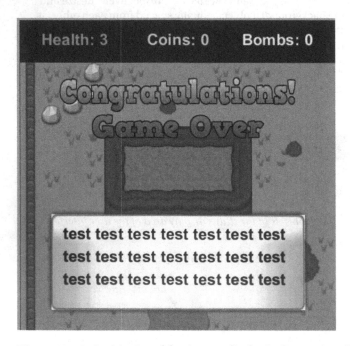

Figure 14-14. *Positioning of the sign text display in the user interface*

Next, you will add the sign with which the hero can interact. In the layout, set the active layer to Main, and create a new sprite named Sign with the image sign.png. Change its size to 32,32, add the behavior *Solid*, and add an instance variable named Message of type Text with the initial value This is a sign.

In the event sheet, you will create two events: one for displaying this message in the user interface and one for hiding the display objects once the hero moves far enough away from the sign. In the *User Interface* group, create a new event that checks whether the hero has collided with a sign, in which case the BackgroundMessage and TextMessage objects should become visible and the TextMessage object should have its text set to Sign.Message. The event to "turn off" the display is a bit more complicated, as it needs to measure the distance between the player and the correct instance of the sign (as many games may contain more than one sign per layout). In particular, when the player is next to the sign, the distance between their center points will be about 32 pixels (the size of most of the game objects); you will hide the display elements once the hero moves an additional 4 pixels away or, in other words, once the distance becomes greater than 36. The distance between two points can be calculated using the function distance, which takes four inputs: the *X* and *Y* coordinates of the two points between which the distance is being measured (similar to the inputs of the angle function). With this in mind, create a new event that checks whether TextMessage is visible. Add a second condition that checks whether the *Sign* instance variable *Message* is equal to *TextMessage. Text* (this selects the correct sign instance in case of multiple signs being present). Add a third condition with the *System* condition *Compare two values*, and check whether *distance (Hero.X, Hero.Y, Sign.X, Sign.Y)* is greater than 36. To this event, add actions that set *BackgroundMessage* and *TextMessage* to be invisible. When you are finished, these events should appear as shown in Figure 14-15.

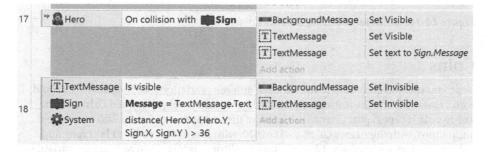

Figure 14-15. *Events for the user interface displays*

Items

In this section, you will create the items referenced by the text displays in the user interface, as well as related objects used to implement the corresponding game mechanics. These objects and their purpose are as follows:

- *Heart*: Restores the hero's health
- *Bomb*: Destroys rocks (and enemies, which will be added later)
- *Explosion* An animated effect that appears after the bomb explodes
- *Bomb bag*: Increases the hero's bomb count

- *Coin*: Used to purchase hearts and bomb bags; there are different types, which have different values

- *Coin door*: The hero may pass if he has enough coins; can be used to implement a shop mechanic

- *Treasure chest*: The ultimate item the hero is trying to collect

Hearts

Hearts are the simplest item to implement. In the layout, make sure the active layer is set to Main, and then create a new sprite named Heart with the image heart.png. In the event sheet, create a new group named Items. Add an event to this group that checks whether the hero has collided with a heart, in which case the hero's instance variable Health should be increased by 1, and the heart instance should be destroyed. Figure 14-16 shows this event.

Figure 14-16. *Event for collecting the Heart object*

Coins

Next, you will add coins. There will be three different variations: copper, silver, and gold, with values 1, 5, and 20, respectively. In the layout, add an object named Coin with the image coin-copper.png. Change the name of the animation to Coin1. Add two more animations, with the names Coin5 and Coin20, with image files coin-silver.png and coin-gold.png, respectively. Close the image editor windows. Add an instance variable named Value of type Number with a default value of 1. In the event sheet Item group, create a new event with the *Every tick* condition that sets the Coin animation name to "Coin" & Coin.Value; this will set the correct image for the coin, depending on its value (provided it is 1, 5, or 20). Create another event that checks whether the hero has collided with a coin, in which case the hero's instance variable Coins should be increased by Coin.Value, and the coin instance should be destroyed.

Coins are "spent" by the hero when he passes through doors, which have an associated cost. Just as there are variations in the coin image and value, there will be variations in the door image and cost. In the layout, add an object named CoinDoor with the image door-05.png. Change the animation name to Door5. Add another animation with the name Door25 and the image door-25.png. Close the image editor windows. Add an instance variable named Cost of type Number with a default value of 5. Also add the behavior Solid. In the event sheet, add an action to the *Every tick* event, and set the *CoinDoor* animation name to "Door" & CoinDoor.Cost. Create a new event with that checks whether the hero has collided with a door and also checks whether the hero's instance variable Coins is greater than or equal to CoinDoor.Cost (to make sure the hero has enough coins). The associated actions are to subtract DoorCoin.Cost from the hero's *Coins* variable and to destroy the door. Figure 14-17 shows these events.

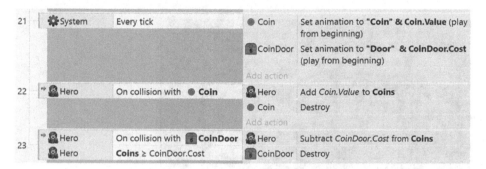

Figure 14-17. Events for Coin and CoinDoor objects

You are now ready set up the Cave layout to function as an item shop. Switch to the Cave layout, unlock the Map and Walls layers (if they were previously locked), and edit the tilemap to add two borders surrounding rectangular areas, each containing a single gap for a CoinDoor object in the front, as shown in Figure 14-18. Add instances of the solid Wall object covering the newly added tiles so that the hero is prevented from simply moving through them. Add *CoinDoor* instances to each of the gaps; change the left door's *Cost* variable to 5 and the right door's *Cost* variable to 25. In the center of the left rectangle, add a heart instance. Later, after creating the BombBag object, you will add it to the center of the right rectangle. Next, you will add a few signs to explain this room to the player. Near the left door, add a sign with its *Message* variable set to Hearts restore one health. Near the right door, add a sign with *Message* set to Bomb bags contain 4 bombs. Use with the B key. In the center of the screen, closer to the door, add a sign with *Message* set to Doors will open if you have enough coins. You may even want to consider placing a sign near the cave entrance on the Field layout, with its *Message* set to Item shop. To simplify testing the shop mechanic, you may want to add a few coin instances close to the hero, with their *Value* variable set to 20.

You will notice that if you open a door and collect an item and then leave and return to the layout, the door and item will have respawned. For item shops (which typically appear to carry an infinite stock of items in most games), this is ideal. However, for items such as coins, this is probably not desirable, because the player could repeatedly exit and reenter a layout and collect the respawned coins, making them trivially easy to acquire (rather than as a well-earned reward for exploration or combat). To remedy this situation, you may want to consider adding the Persist behavior to the Coin object. Among the effects of this behavior are that once an instance is destroyed, it will not be re-created if the layout is reloaded. (In addition, the property values of a persistent object are stored in memory and not reset to their default values when the layout is reloaded.) In theory, you could consider adding this behavior to other objects (such as bushes, rocks, or enemies), but do not add it to any type of item being sold by the shop, or else the player will not be able to purchase the item a second time (at least, not at that location).

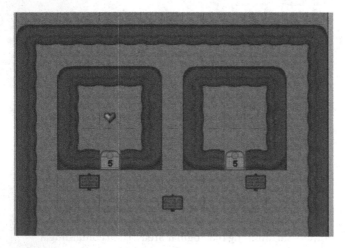

Figure 14-18. *Tilemap design for an item shop mechanic*

Bombs

It is now time to add bombs. In the layout, create a new sprite named BombBag with image bomb-bag.png. Change its size to 32,32. Place an instance of this object in the empty rectangular area in the Cave layout's item shop. In the event sheet Item group, create a new event that checks whether the hero has collided with a bomb bag, in which case the hero's instance variable *Bombs* should be increased by 4, and the bomb bag instance should be destroyed.

Next, in the layout, create a new sprite named Bomb. In the *Animation frames* window, import frames from the sprite sheet bomb-flash.png (which contains eight cells horizontally and six cells vertically), and set the animation speed to 8. Since there are 48 frames altogether, this speed means it will take 6 seconds for the animation to finish. Close the image editor windows, change the size of the sprite to 24,24, and move it to the layout margins. Create another new sprite, named Explosion. In the *Animation frames* window, import frames from the sprite sheet explosion.png (which contains six cells both horizontally and vertically), and set its animation speed to 36. Adjust the collision polygon of one of the frames containing the largest image (such as frame 10) to a circular shape, and apply the change to the whole animation. Close the image editor windows, change the sprite size to 96,96, and move it into the layout margins. Add the *Fade* behavior (and leave the associated properties at their default values).

Finally, you will add the events for the bomb mechanics. In the event sheet, create a new event that checks whether the B key was pressed and also whether the hero's Bombs variable is greater than or equal to 1. When this occurs, you should subtract 1 from the hero's *Bombs* variable, the hero should spawn a bomb on the Main layer at image point 1 (which is also used when swinging the sword), and the hero sprite needs to be moved to the top of the layer (so that the bomb appears underneath the hero). Create another event that checks whether the bomb's animation is finished, and if so, the bomb should spawn an Explosion object on the Main layer, and the bomb should be destroyed. Contact with the Explosion object will be used for damage and destruction purposes; create two new events that check whether the explosion has collided with the bush or the rock, and destroy the corresponding object. Finally, create an event that destroys the Explosion object when its animation is finished. Figure 14-19 shows the events described in this section.

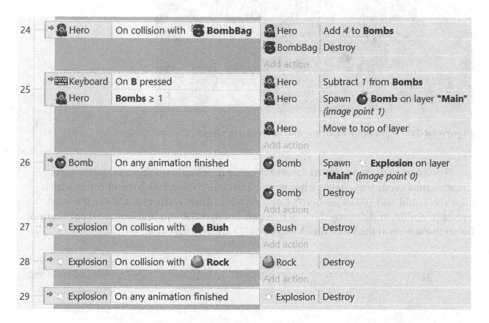

Figure 14-19. Events involving bombs and related objects

The Treasure Chest

The goal in Treasure Quest is, as the title indicates, to obtain the treasure, which you will implement in this section. In the layout, create a new sprite named Chest with the image treasure-chest.png. Choose a strategic location to place the chest in the layout that will present a challenge to the player. For example, Figure 14-20 shows the chest placed on top of a mountain, which will be accessible only after destroying the rock at the base of the ladder, which requires the hero to purchase a bomb bag at the item shop, which in turn requires that coins be collected (and in the next section, you will implement enemies that drop coins when they are defeated).

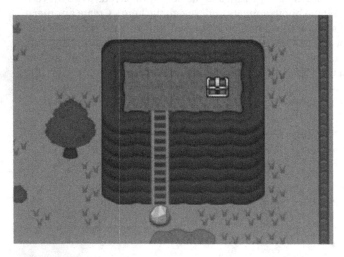

Figure 14-20. *A possible location for the treasure chest*

The event corresponding to the end of game mechanic is fairly straightforward. Create a new event that checks whether the hero has collided with the chest, in which case you could add 500 to the hero's *Coins* variable, destroy the chest, make the win message visible, and destroy the lose message (so that the win and lose messages cannot be on the screen at the same time). Figure 14-21 shows this event.

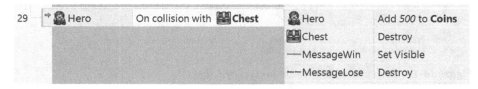

29	Hero	On collision with Chest	Hero	Add *500* to **Coins**
			Chest	Destroy
			MessageWin	Set Visible
			MessageLose	Destroy

Figure 14-21. *The event for collecting the treasure chest and winning the game*

Enemies

At this point, you have a variety of components in place that will enable you to design an intricate level. However, there are no active antagonists in your game yet, and all that the hero's sword does at this point is destroy bushes. If your goal was to create a game called Adventures in Landscaping, then you could stop here. However, it will be assumed that you want to create more interesting opponents for the hero to fight. In this section, you will create three different types of enemies, shown in Figure 14-22.

- Righter, which moves randomly along the ground either north, south, east, or west, changing direction every few seconds

- Flyer, which flies above the ground (and is not affected by solid objects), moves in any direction, and changes direction frequently

- Seeker, which moves randomly along the ground as Righter does, but if it is able to see the hero (provided that no solid objects are blocking the line of view), then it chases the hero

Figure 14-22. *Three types of enemies: Righter, Flyer, and Seeker*

Enemies will do a single point of damage to the hero's health (causing the hero to enter a flashing, invincible state for a few seconds), while enemies themselves can be destroyed by a single sword hit or bomb explosion. To manage the different types of enemies, a single Enemy sprite will be created, and one animation will correspond to each of the types.[3] All the behaviors needed by any type of enemy will need to be added to this one base object and adjusted for each instance, depending on the animation displayed.

To begin, create a new sprite named Enemy. Rename the animation to Righter, and load the image file enemy-righter.png. Create two new animations named Flyer and Seeker, loading animation frames from the sprite sheets enemy-flyer.png and enemy-seeker.png, respectively (each of which contains four cells horizontally and one cell vertically); change the two animations' properties *Speed* to 8 and *Loop* to Yes. Close the image editor windows, and resize the sprite to 32 by 32.

---

[3]There is a much better way to accomplish the same goal using a feature in Construct 2 called *Families*, but it is available only in the paid, licensed version of the software. Since the projects in this book are all designed to be created with the free version of Construct 2, we will use the "single object, multiple animations" approach here.

217

Add the behaviors *Bound to layout, Timer, Bullet, Sine,* and *Line of Sight.* Create two more instances of the Enemy object so that there are a total of three. Among those three, change the *Initial animation* property so that one is Righter, one is Flyer, and one is Seeker. You will next customize the properties of each of these enemies, and if you want to create another enemy of a particular type later, duplicate the instance corresponding to the enemy type you want to add.

First, select the Righter enemy. The *Sine* behavior is used to animate this enemy type with a pulsing effect (but not the others, so this behavior will be disabled for the other enemy types later). Set the *Sine* behavior properties *Movement* to Size, *Period* to 0.5, and *Magnitude* to 4; then set the *Bullet* behavior properties *Speed* to 50, *Bounce off solids* to Yes, and *Set angle* to No.

Next, select the Flyer enemy. Change the *Sine* behavior property *Active at start* to No. Set the *Bullet* behavior properties *Speed* to 80, *Bounce off solids* to No, and *Set angle* to No. Since the bullet behavior is unaffected by solid objects, this will present the illusion of the enemy flying above the world.

Finally, select the Seeker enemy. Change the *Sine* behavior property *Active at start* to No. Set the *Bullet* behavior properties *Speed* to 110, *Bounce off solids* to Yes, and *Set angle* to Yes. This enemy will make use of the *Line of Sight* behavior to check whether the hero can be seen by the enemy. The *Line of Sight* properties define the area in which the enemy can detect (or "see") other objects. Change the property *Range* to 240; this is how far away the enemy can detect other objects. Change the property *Cone of view* to 160; this is the angular range (in degrees, around the direction in which the enemy is facing) where other objects can be detected.

Now you will set up timers for each of the enemy types, which will cause them to change direction periodically. In the event sheet, create a new group called Enemies, and add an event with the condition *On start of layout.* Add three subevents to this event, which check whether the Enemy animation name Righter, Flyer, or Seeker is playing, and in each case start a timer with the Turn tag to repeat regularly, every 3, 1, or 3 seconds, respectively. Create another event in the Enemies group that checks whether the *Enemy timer* tagged as *Turn* has activated, and as before, create three subevents to this event to check for each of the possible Enemy animation names. For the Righter and Seeker enemy types, add the action to set their bullet angles of motion to choose(-90, 0, 90, 180); for the Flyer enemy type, set the bullet angle of motion to random(-180, 180). Finally, the Seeker enemy should select a random direction only if it cannot see the hero, so to the seeker event, add a second condition of *Enemy - Has line of sight to another object (Hero),* and invert it. Then add another event to the *Enemies* group (but not as a subevent to the *On timer* event) that checks whether an enemy is playing the Seeker animation and also whether the enemy has a line of sight to the player, in which case it should set the enemy's bullet angle of motion to the expression angle(Enemy.X, Enemy.Y, Hero.X, Hero.Y); this will cause the Seeker to pursue the hero, until the hero gets hit or runs out of sight behind a solid object. Figure 14-23 shows these events.

30	⊟ **Enemies**			
31	⊟ ➔ ⚙ System	On start of layout	Add action	
32	🐛 Enemy	Is animation "Righter" playing	🐛 Enemy	Start 🕐 Timer *"Turn"* for **3** (Regular)
			Add action	
33	🐛 Enemy	Is animation "Flyer" playing	🐛 Enemy	Start 🕐 Timer *"Turn"* for **1** (Regular)
			Add action	
34	🐛 Enemy	Is animation "Seeker" playing	🐛 Enemy	Start 🕐 Timer *"Turn"* for **3** (Regular)
35	⊟ ➔ 🐛 Enemy	On 🕐 Timer *"Turn"*	Add action	
36	🐛 Enemy	Is animation "Righter" playing	🐛 Enemy	Set 🗡 Bullet angle of motion to *choose(-90, 0, 90, 180)* degrees
			Add action	
37	🐛 Enemy	Is animation "Flyer" playing	🐛 Enemy	Set 🗡 Bullet angle of motion to *random(-180, 180)* degrees
			Add action	
38	🐛 Enemy 🐛 Enemy	Is animation "Seeker" playing ✖ Has •)⟫ LineOfSight to 🧍 Hero	🐛 Enemy	Set 🗡 Bullet angle of motion to *choose(-90, 0, 90, 180)* degrees
			Add action	
39	🐛 Enemy 🐛 Enemy	Is animation "Seeker" playing Has •)⟫ LineOfSight to 🧍 Hero	🐛 Enemy	Set 🗡 Bullet angle of motion to *angle(Enemy.X, Enemy.Y, Hero.X, Hero.Y)* degrees

Figure 14-23. *Events for enemy movement for each of the three enemy types*

Next, you will set up the interaction between the hero and the enemies: enemies colliding with the hero damage the hero, while swords or bomb explosions colliding with an enemy destroy the enemy (which then drops a coin). First, you will add an animated smoke effect that will appear when an enemy is destroyed. Create a new sprite named Smoke; in the *Animation frames* window, load the sprite sheet smoke.png (which has six cells both horizontally and vertically). Set the animation speed property to 72 (so the animation will be finished in 0.5 seconds). Close the image editor, change the sprite size to 48,48, add the *Fade* behavior, and change the fade out time to 0.5 seconds (to match the animation time).

In the event sheet *Enemies* group, create a new event that checks whether the sword or an explosion has collided with an enemy, in which case the enemy should spawn a coin (whose *Value* variable should be set to 1 as a default), the enemy should spawn a smoke object, and the enemy should be destroyed. Occasionally, the enemy should drop a silver or gold coin, so to this event you will add a pair of subevents that generate a random number and, if it falls in a certain range, change the value of the coin object. For the first of these, use the system condition *Compare two values*, and check whether random(0, 100) is less than 20, in which case the coin should have its *Value* set to 5. For the second subevent, check whether random(0, 100) is less than 5, in which case the coin *Value* should be set to 20.

Finally, to damage the player (and implement the temporary invincibility mechanic), add the *Flash* behavior to the Hero object. In the event sheet Enemies group, create a new event that checks whether an enemy has collided with the hero and also checks that the hero is not flashing, in which case the hero should flash for 2 seconds and the hero's *Health* variable should be decreased by 1. Add another event that checks whether the hero's *Health* variable is less than or equal to 0, in which case the hero should be destroyed, the lose message should become visible, and the win message should be destroyed. These events should appear as shown in Figure 14-24.

Figure 14-24. Events for enemy and hero interaction

At this point, you have finished implementing all the features of the Treasure Quest game. Congratulations!

Side Quests

Even though Treasure Quest was one of the largest projects in this book, there are a myriad of features that could still be implemented, many of which have no doubt occurred to you while working through the project. You could redesign the game presented in this chapter or create more layouts and connect them with portals and spawn points. You could develop new items such as arrows that attack enemies from a distance, torches that can be used to burn down wooden barriers, or a portable bridge that can be used to cross small streams. You could add different types of enemies that fire projectiles at you or environmental hazards, such as spikes that damage the hero on contact. You could have alternative goals to win the game, such as clearing out all the enemies from an area or defeating a large boss-type enemy that has many health points of its own. The possibilities are endless, and with the skills you have developed, you are ready to create them on your own!

Summary

In this final project, you applied the skills that you have developed from previous projects to create the complex adventure-style game Treasure Quest, which featured multiple interconnected layouts, various items for the player to use, an in-game "item shop" mechanic, and enemies with greatly different movement patterns. You learned about the behaviors *Line of sight* and *Persist* and about the *Global* property for objects and layers, which preserved them across layouts. Congratulations on reaching this point and having successfully created a great variety of video games! In the next and final chapter of this book, you will read a variety of advice for continuing on in game development.

CHAPTER 15

■ ■ ■

The Journey Continues

In this final chapter, we'll present a variety of steps you could consider as you continue on in game development. Among these, we'll discuss working on additional projects, learning skills in related areas, and bringing your games to a wider audience. Along the way, we'll present lists of resources of all types and general advice for many situations.

Continue Developing

In this section, we'll begin by talking about how you could refine your current projects and start working on new projects, either on your own or as part of a game jam event. We'll provide a list of online resources where you can obtain art assets to help you along the way. Finally, we'll give a healthy dose of advice for overcoming the inevitable obstacles that will arise.

Working on Projects

Ideally, you've been working through all the project examples in this book. Many of the projects presented have concluded with a section titled "On Your Own"; you should try to complete as many of these suggestions as you can; this is vital to your growth as a game developer because *you learn by doing*, especially by figuring things out independently. After each of the projects is functional, you should always experiment, create your own additions, and try your own variations. Make sure you understand the purpose of each event and how they fit together as a unified whole.

After you've extracted as much knowledge and experience from this book as you feel is possible, it's time to strike out on your own and start creating your own games. To start, we recommend you continue creating games inspired by arcade-era classics, since these games usually have simple and straightforward mechanics that will still provide great development experience. Some particular recommendations of games to look into include Space Invaders, Missile Command, Joust, and Bubble Bobble. While these games may appear simplistic at first, each has interesting subtleties that will exercise your game development skills. While doing this, we advise creating a physical list identifying and prioritizing the game-specific features you'll be working on: the particular game mechanics, level design, user interface, and artistic style, in roughly this order. For example, if your main character is a winged archer, don't worry about the color of their belt until after the

© Lee Stemkoski and Evan Leider 2017
L. Stemkoski and E. Leider, *Game Development with Construct 2*,
DOI 10.1007/978-1-4842-2784-8_15

character is able to fly and shoot arrows. (In fact, it is common practice for developers to use simple colored polygon shapes during the game mechanic phase of development.) Don't worry if you're not an artist; there are many web sites with freely available video game graphics, and there are many artists in the community looking for collaborators. Finally, once you're comfortable with your skills and abilities, it's time to develop your own original game concept or join a team working on a game and lend your skills.

Obtaining Art Resources

Although this has not been the focus of this book, every game benefits from quality graphics and audio. We recommend the following web sites for obtaining artistic resources. Most of these web sites have both free and paid options, while others are driven by user donations.

- *Kenney Game Assets*: http://kenney.nl/ Created by Kenney Vleugels, this site features more than 18,000 art assets that can be useful in many genres. In this book, assets from this site were featured in most of the games you created.

- *Game Art Guppy*: www.gameartguppy.com/ Created by Vicki Wenderlich, this site contains a collection of high-quality art crafted especially for independent game developers. In this book, the koala character from the Jumping Jack game was obtained from this site.

- *OpenGameArt*: http://opengameart.org This is a repository for all types of media (2D and 3D graphics, as well as sound effects and music). Contributions are community driven. Licensing details and conditions are determined by the individual creators.

- *The Spriter's Resource*: www.spriters-resource.com/ This features a nearly comprehensive set of game art assets from many game console systems throughout history. Because of copyright restrictions, however, these assets cannot be used in published or commercial games.

- *CoolText*: http://cooltext.com This is a free text art graphics generator that can be useful for creating graphics for title screens as well as text and buttons for user interfaces.

- *Textures*: http://textures.com This site offers images of many types of materials, both natural and constructed.

- *BFXR*: www.bfxr.net/ This resource randomly generates a wide range of retro-style sound effects for use in games.

- *FreeSound*: www.freesound.org/ This is a collaborative database of Creative Commons–licensed sounds, organized into packs and also grouped by tags.

- *Incompetech*: http://incompetech.com/ Created by Kevin Macleod, this web site features a collection of royalty-free original music compositions that can be searched by genre, tempo, feel, or instrumentation. In this book, the background music for the game Starfish Collector (in Chapter 5), called "Master of the Feast," was obtained from this collection.

Participating in Game Jams

One way to gain valuable game development experience is to participate in a *game jam*. A game jam is a gathering of game developers for the challenge of designing and creating a game in a short time span, typically about 48 hours. Participants may be programmers, artists, writers, or others with related skills. Because of the time limit, these events require rapid prototyping and development skills, and they encourage participants to focus on creativity, core mechanics, and bringing a project to completion (or at least a playable state). Individuals often take part in these events for the express purpose of increasing their skills in these areas. In addition, many game jams select a theme that must be incorporated by all games developed at the event. The themes are usually announced at the start of each event to discourage advanced planning and to encourage creativity.

Although some game jams have panels of judges and declare one or more winners, these events are typically informal and friendly, and they give participants the chance to connect with each other and provide a sense of community. Some events may be held at one or more physical locations. Some events may have no central location; developers work in areas of their own choosing (but are still held to the same time and schedule restrictions). The following are some notable long-running game jam events:

- *Global Game Jam*: `http://globalgamejam.org/` This is the largest game jam in the world. It's an international event that takes place once each year, typically at the end of January. This is *not* an online event; on-site participation is required, and for this reason there are typically hundreds of physical locations ("jam sites") around the world where individuals can attend.

- *Ludum Dare*: `http://ludumdare.com/` Major events are held three times a year, and minor ("mini") events are held during the months when there is not a major event. Some participants attend gatherings at various sites, but most developers work from their own locations.

- *One Game A Month*: `www.onegameamonth.com/` As the name suggests, these game jams are held monthly. The rules are particularly relaxed, and each jam takes place over the course of the entire month, so as to provide maximum flexibility to participants. The web site is extremely gamified and awards "experience points" for completing various objectives, which can be a great source of motivation. The organizer is Christer Kaitila, who has also written a book called *The Game Jam Survival Guide*, which discusses these events in great detail and provides a plethora of advice on how to have a successful experience.

Overcoming Difficulties

On your journey as a game developer, you will stumble at times. Everyone does. Perhaps you can't figure out how to start implementing a particular game mechanic. Perhaps your game entities are behaving in strange and unexpected ways. Whatever your difficulty may be, don't give up! Spend some time wrestling with the problem. Try different conditions or actions. Try to implement simpler ideas first, and test your project as often as possible to pinpoint exactly which addition has caused problems. Don't give up; remember that the process of overcoming difficulties helps you grow as a game developer.

However, also remember that balance is key in development (just as it is in games). Yes, it is valuable to learn how to fix your projects, but if any particular problem persists for a long time, take a break before you become overly frustrated or discouraged. Keep things in perspective: it probably wouldn't be worth spending five straight hours trying to figure out why your platformer character gets stuck or glitches through a tilemap, for example. In such a situation, spend some time away from your computer—take a walk, think about something else, and come back to your problem later with a refreshed outlook.

After making a sincere effort to resolve any difficulties yourself, if you are still stuck, don't despair. There is a vibrant and active community of fellow game developers and enthusiasts out there that may be able to be of assistance. The Scirra forums are an excellent place to ask for help. Start by searching these sites to see whether someone has asked the same or a similar question in the "How do I..." FAQ. If not, then you can create a post to ask your question. Make sure you clearly describe what you are trying to do, and include details about what you have tried, what has worked, and what hasn't. Including a .capx file of your attempt can be very helpful in case you are only able to implement part of a feature or to demonstrate what isn't working in your project. Most of all, be polite and patient. The people who frequent these forums usually do so voluntarily and provide general assistance out of a sense of community. It's perfectly normal that a posted question might not generate a response for 48 hours or more. (In the meantime, be active in the community and see whether anyone has posted any questions that *you* might be able to answer; helping others will also help you develop a deeper knowledge of Construct.) Whenever someone responds to your question, be sure to acknowledge them; if they suggest a course of action, write a follow-up post as to whether it worked. And finally, if you turn out to be the person to resolve your own question or decide to proceed in a completely different direction to circumvent the problem altogether, you should post that information as well, to provide future readers a sense of closure.

Broadening Your Horizons

In addition to increasing your depth of knowledge and programming proficiency, you should devote time to developing a breadth of knowledge in game-related areas, which will have a positive impact on the quality of the games you produce. We briefly mention a few ways to work toward this goal in the following text.

Playing Different Games

Most game enthusiasts have a favorite genre. Some people spend most of their time playing first-person shooters, others prefer to devote their time to role-playing games, and so forth. As a game developer, you should consider playing games from as wide a range as you can, including action, adventure, puzzle, strategy, role-playing, sports, simulation, storytelling, and so forth. At the same time, try games from various time periods (from classic to modern) and from different size developers (from large professional companies to smaller studios to independent gamemakers and game jam competitors). Even if you don't find a particular game or genre compelling, you will grow as a developer if you spend some time playing such games, especially when you do so with a developer's mind-set. Try to understand why people like a given game. Examine each game's level progression, gameplay balance, narrative and character development, artistic style, and interface design. Keep an eye out for what makes each game innovative or unique. Try to mentally place yourself in the role of the original game developers who created the game, think about possible reasons why they might have made the decisions they did, and ponder whether you might have done the same or branched out in a different direction.

Increasing Your Skill Set

While you continue to develop games, you should also consider broadening your overall skill set. A solid set of programming skills is highly desirable, but game developers (especially those working independently or in small studios) often need to be a jack-of-all-trades, especially in the areas of graphics and audio. To get started in these areas, we recommend the following software and tutorials:

- *Inkscape*: http://inkscape.org/ This is software for creating vector graphics, freely available. The web site contains a list of high-quality tutorials for all skill levels. Most relevant to our interests, however, is a set of game art tutorials written by Chris Hildenbrand, available at http://2d-game-art-tutorials.zeef.com/chris.hildenbrand.

- *Audacity*: http://audacityteam.org/ This is a multitrack audio editor and recorder, freely available. The Audacity manual contains an extensive list of tutorials that will teach you all sorts of useful recording and editing skills.

Recommended Reading

In addition to broadening your skill set, it is also worthwhile to broaden your knowledge base. There are a variety of books available on topics related to game development that will help you do exactly that. Of course, there are far too many to list here, and no doubt we have omitted a number of high-quality titles. Nonetheless, we have listed a few representative samples from across a range of fields, with a cross section of topics, to give you an indication of what's available out there: game design, literary aspects, history, and social impact.

- *Fundamentals of Game Design, 3rd edition*, by Ernest Adams (New Riders, 2013). This book discusses a variety of topics such as concept development, gameplay design, core mechanics, user interfaces, storytelling, and balancing; exercises, worksheets, and case studies are also included.

- *The Ultimate Guide to Video Game Writing and Design*, by Flint
  Dille and John Zuur Platten (Lone Eagle, 2008). Topics covered
  include integrating story elements into a game, writing a game
  script, creating design documentation, the creative process, team
  dynamics, and business considerations.

- *Vintage Games: An Insider Look at the History of Grand Theft
  Auto, Super Mario, and the Most Influential Games of All Time*,
  by Bill Loguidice and Matt Barton (Focal Press, 2009).
  This book explores the history of some of the most influential
  video games of all time, with a particular focus on their
  development, critical reception, and impact on the industry.

- *Reality Is Broken: Why Games Make Us Better and How They Can
  Change the World*, by Jane McGonigal (Penguin Books, 2011).
  In this book, the author discusses theories from psychology,
  cognitive science, sociology, and philosophy in the context
  of game playing, and explains how games can make us more
  productive and change the world for the better.

It is also useful to stay abreast of current news and developments in the game
industry, as well as to hear the opinions, approaches, struggles, and successes of your
fellow game developers. For these purposes, there is no better alternative to following
blogs. We list some particularly substantial sites, each of which features regular blog
postings (as well as additional useful information and resources).

- *Gamasutra*: `www.gamasutra.com/` This web site is devoted to the
  art and business of making games, which, among other resources,
  contains curated lists of blog postings that touch on all aspects of
  the industry.

- *GameDev.net*: `www.gamedev.net` This is a resource for developers
  of all fields and expertise, containing articles and tutorials on
  technical, creative, and business aspects on game development.

- *Hooby Game Dev*: `www.hobbygamedev.com/` Maintained by Chris
  DeLeon (a professional video game developer, author, and
  instructor), this regularly updated web site contains articles,
  advice, tutorials, case studies, interviews, and more.

Sharing Your Games

Once you have designed and created some games of your own, you should consider
sharing them with others. After all, games are meant to be played! This process will
require you to export your games to a playable format and find an audience of eager game
enthusiasts, both of which we discuss here.

Construct 2 features many ways to share your games. The easiest approach, which is
included with the free version of the software, is to select *Export* from the *File* menu and
convert your game to HTML5 format. The exporter will create a directory containing an

HTML file, store all the images, and convert all the events into JavaScript code for you; the files can be uploaded to a web site (either your own personal web site or web sites such as those listed in the following text) and played online. There are other export formats available (for platforms such as desktop computers and smartphones), but access to these exporter options will require you to purchase a personal license for the software, which may be a good investment by this point!

One of the greatest joys of being a game developer is when others play your games. Even if a project is unfinished, having people playtest your game and provide feedback can help your creations to reach even greater heights and attract an even larger audience. Scirra provides web hosting services specifically for games created with Construct 2 on its site. In addition, there are many other web sites that support independent game developers and provide forums where you can share your work with the community. We list some of these here, and note that some of these web sites (such as Itch.io, IndieDB, and GameJolt) will also provide you with the ability to upload your games onto their servers after you register for an account.

- *Scirra Arcade*: www.scirra.com/arcade/

- *Itch.io*: www.itch.io

- *IndieDB*: www.indiedb.com/

- *GameJolt*: http://gamejolt.com/

- *GameDev.net*: www.gamedev.net/

- *The Independent Games Source (TIGSource)*: www.tigsource.com/

- *Indie Gamer forums*: http://forums.indiegamer.com/

If you post a game to one of these sources, while you're waiting to hear people's opinion on your work, you should strive to be an active participant in their forums. Try a few games and provide feedback to your fellow developers. We all benefit from a vibrant game development community, so be sure to join in and be a part of it!

With that final piece of advice, we come to the end of our journey together through this book. We hope, however, your journey as a game developer will continue. May you have good fortune on all your future endeavors!

APPENDIX A

■ ■ ■

Game Design Documentation

While you will learn many technical and practical aspects of game development as you work through the example projects in this book, it is equally important to have a solid foundation in the theoretical aspects of game design. The first effort to create a framework for these concepts was discussed in a paper published by Robin Hunicke, Marc LeBlanc, and Robert Zubek in 2004.[1] In it, they proposed the Mechanics-Dynamics-Aesthetics (MDA) framework, which provides a useful way to categorize the components of a game.

They defined *Mechanics* as the formal rules of the game, expressed at the level of data structures and algorithms, *Dynamics* as the interaction between the player and the game mechanics while the game is in progress, and *Aesthetics* as the emotional responses experienced by players as they interact with the game. Since then, other frameworks have been proposed, each of which provides a different way of analyzing games. A popular example is Jesse Schell's *Elemental Tetrad*,[2] which consists of Mechanics, Story, Aesthetics, and Technology (where *aesthetics* is defined more broadly than in the original MDA framework). Frameworks such as these are valuable tools to help people consistently and fully analyze games. Players can use frameworks to better understand and express what they enjoy about particular games. Developers can use the formal structure to help them create a more cohesive design and to organize and document the development process; explaining how to write such documentation is the goal of this appendix.

A *game design document* (GDD) serves as the blueprint or master plan for creating a game: it describes the overall vision of a game, as well as the details (often based on a game design framework such as MDA). Practical aspects are also included, such as a schedule that lists when certain features will be completed, a list of team members and responsibilities, and plans for testing and releasing the game. A GDD can provide clarity and focus, while serving as a guide and a reference to the person or people working on the game. To be most effective, the GDD should be as complete as possible before the development process begins. Depending on the flexibility of the developers, a certain amount of modification may be permitted over the course of development, and various adjustments may need to be made after collecting feedback from gameplay testing.

---

[1]Hunicke, LeBlanc, and Zubek. "MDA: A Formal Approach to Game Design and Research." *Proceedings of the Nineteenth National Conference on Artificial Intelligence*, 2004.
[2]Schell. *The Art of Game Design: A Book of Lenses*. CRC Press, 2008.

© Lee Stemkoski and Evan Leider 2017
L. Stemkoski and E. Leider, *Game Development with Construct 2*,
DOI 10.1007/978-1-4842-2784-8

There is no one standard format for game design documents; an Internet search will provide many templates for a variety of development scenarios. GDD templates often contain a bulleted list of topics or questions for your consideration (when applicable). In what follows, we present a similar list of questions for you to ponder as you design your own games; the scope of these questions is particularly good for individual developers or small teams working on projects with game engine software such as Construct 2. By recording detailed responses to the following queries, you will effectively create your own game design document to help guide you through the development process.

1. Overall vision.

    a. Write a short paragraph (three to six sentences) explaining your game. (This is sometimes called the *elevator pitch*: a short summary used to quickly and simply describe an idea or product during a 30-second elevator ride.)

    b. How would you describe the genre(s)? Is it single-player or multiplayer (and if the latter, cooperative or competitive)?

    c. What is the target audience? Include demographics (the age, interests, and game experience of potential players), the game platform (desktop, console, or smartphone), and any special equipment required (such as gamepads).

    d. Why will people want to play this game? What features distinguish this game from similar titles? What is the hook that will get people interested at first, how will the game keep people interested, and what makes it fun?

2. Mechanics: the rules of the game world. (Note that the following questions are phrased in terms of the game's main character, as distinguished from the player, since the player is the focus of the section on dynamics. However, if no such character exists, the player can be considered as the character.)

    a. What are the character's goals? These may be divided into short-term, medium-term, and long-term goals.

    b. What abilities does the character have? This should include any action the character is capable of performing, such as moving, attacking, defending, collecting items, interacting with the environment, and so forth. Describe the abilities or actions in detail; for example, how high can the character jump? Can the character both walk and run?

    c.   What obstacles or difficulties will the character face? Some obstacles are active (such as enemies, projectiles, or traps) and should be described in detail (how they affect the player, their location, their movement patterns, and so forth). Other obstacles are passive (such as doors that need to be unlocked, mazes that need to be navigated, puzzles that need to be solved, or time limits that need to be to beat). How can the character overcome these obstacles (items, weapons, spells, quick reflexes)?

    d.   What items can the character obtain? What are their effects, where are they obtained, and how frequently do they appear?

    e.   What resources must be managed (such as health, money, energy, and experience)? How are these resources obtained and used? Are they limited?

    f.   Describe the game world environment. How large is the world (relative to the screen)? Are there multiple rooms or regions? Is the gameplay linear or open? In other words, is there a strictly linear progression of levels or tasks to complete, or can the character select levels, explore the world, and complete quests at will?

3.   Dynamics: the interaction between the player and the game mechanics.

    a.   What hardware is required by the game (keyboard, mouse, speakers, gamepad, touchscreen)? Which keys/buttons are used, and what are their effects? How is the player informed of the control scheme (a separate manual document, game menus, tutorials, or in-game signs)?

    b.   What type of proficiency will the player need to develop to become proficient at the game? Are there any complex actions that can be created from combinations of basic game mechanics? Do the game mechanics or game world environment directly or indirectly encourage the player to develop or discourage any particular play strategies? Does the player's performance affect the gameplay mechanics (as in feedback loops)?

    c.   What gameplay data is displayed during the game (such as points, health, items collected, time remaining)? Where is this information displayed on the screen? How is the information conveyed (text, icons, charts, status bars)?

d. What menus, screens, or overlays will there be (title screen, help/instructions, credits, game over)? How does the player switch between screens, and which screens can be accessed from each other?

e. How does the player interact with the game at the software level (pause, quit, restart, control volume)?

4. Aesthetics: the visual, audio, narrative, and psychological aspects of the game; these are the elements that most directly affect the player's experience.

a. Describe the style and feel of the game. Does the game take place in a world that is rural, technological, or magical? Does the game world feel cluttered or sparse, ordered or chaotic, geometric or organic? Is the mood lighthearted or serious? Is the pace relaxing or frenetic? All the aesthetic elements discussed should work together and contribute to create a coherent and cohesive theme.

b. Does the game use pixel art, line art, or realistic graphics? Are the colors bright or dark, varied or monochromatic, shiny or dull? Will there be value-based or image-based animations? Are there any special effects? Create a list of graphics you will need.

c. What style of background music or ambient sounds will the game use? What sound effects will be used for character actions or for interactions with enemies, objects, and the environment? Will there be sound effects corresponding to interactions with the user interface? List all the music and sounds you will need.

d. What is the relevant backstory for the game? What is the character's motivation for pursuing their goal? Will there be a plot or storyline that unfolds as the player progresses through the game?

e. What emotional state(s) does the game try to provoke: happiness, excitement, calm, surprise, pride, sadness, tension, fear, frustration?

f. What makes the game "fun"? Some players may enjoy the graphics, music, story, or emotions evoked by the game. Other features players might enjoy include the following:

i. Fantasy (simulating experiences one doesn't have in real life)

ii. Role-playing (identifying with a character)

       iii.   Competition (against other players or against records previously set by oneself)

       iv.   Cooperation (working with others toward a common goal)

       v.   Compassion (providing assistance or rescuing others)

       vi.   Discovery (finding objects or exploring a world)

       vii.   Overcoming challenges (such as defeating enemies or solving puzzles)

       viii.   Collection (including game items or badges/trophies for achievements)

       ix.   Social aspects (both within the game and the communities that form around the game)

5.   Development.

    a.   If working with a group: list the team members, and list their roles (game designer, programmer, illustrator, animator, composer, sound editor, writer, manager, etc.), responsibilities, and skills.

    b.   What equipment will you need for this project? Include both hardware and software that will be needed for content creation (graphics and audio), game development, and playtesting.

    c.   What are the tasks that need to be accomplished to create this game? Estimate the time required for each task, the estimated completion date, and the team member responsible; then estimate the priority of each feature (in case some features need to be eliminated because of time constraints or unexpected circumstances).

    d.   What points in the development process are suitable for playtesting? How will you find people to playtest your game? What specific kinds of feedback are you interested in gathering? (For example, you could ask how clear the goals are, how easy or intuitive the controls are, how balanced the difficulty level is, and which parts of the game were most or least enjoyable.) Finally, how will you collect this information (such as a questionnaire or a brief discussion)?

    e.   What are your plans for dissemination? Do you have plans to promote this game through social media, forum postings, gameplay videos, or advertisements?

Index

© Lee Stemkoski and Evan Leider 2017
L. Stemkoski and E. Leider, *Game Development with Construct 2*,
DOI 10.1007/978-1-4842-2784-8

Get the eBook for only $5!

Why limit yourself?

With most of our titles available in both PDF and ePUB format, you can access your content wherever and however you wish—on your PC, phone, tablet, or reader.

Since you've purchased this print book, we are happy to offer you the eBook for just $5.

To learn more, go to http://www.apress.com/companion or contact support@apress.com.

Apress®

Printed in the United States
By Bookmasters